A HISTORY *of* US

US

CONCISE EDITION

Front Cover

Addie Card, about 12 years old, was a spinner in a cotton mill in 1910.

 Compilation Copyright © 2011 K12 Inc.
Text Copyright © 1993, 1999, 2003, 2005, 2006 by Joy Hakim
Adapted with permission of Oxford University Press, Inc.

ISBN-13: 978-1-60153-183-4

Printed by LSC Communications, Willard, OH, May 2019.

VOLUME **C** 1865 TO 1932

Joy Hakim

A HISTORY *of* US

CONCISE EDITION

K12

Editors of the K^{12} Concise Edition

John Holdren and Patricia O'Connell Pearson

Concise Edition Volume C Staff and Contributors

Allyson Jacob, Connie Moy, Jill Tunick *Text Editors*
Suzanne Montazer *Creative Director, Print and ePublishing*
Stephanie Shaw Williams *Print Visual Designer*
Victory Productions *Interior Design and Composition*
Kim Barcas, Carol Leigh *Cover Designers*
Meredith Condit, Charlotte Fullerton *Picture Editors*
Jean Stringer *Rights Manager*
David Swanson *Cartographer*
Jay White *Contributing Instructional Designer*
Susan Raley *Senior Manager, Editors*
Candee Wilson *Senior Project Manager*

Maria Szalay *Senior Vice President, Product Development*
John Holdren *Senior Vice President, Content and Curriculum*
David Pelizzari *Vice President, Content and Curriculum*
Kim Barcas *Vice President, Creative*
Laura Seuschek *Vice President, Instructional Design and Evaluation & Research*
Aaron Hall *Vice President, Program Management*

Lisa Dimaio Iekel *Senior Production Manager*
John Agnone *Director of Publications*

About K12 Inc.

K12 Inc., a technology-based education company, is the nation's leading provider of proprietary curriculum and online education programs to students in grades K–12. K^{12} provides its curriculum and academic services to online schools, traditional classrooms, blended school programs, and directly to families. K12 Inc. also operates the K^{12} International Academy, an accredited, diploma-granting online private school serving students worldwide. K^{12}'s mission is to provide any child the curriculum and tools to maximize success in life, regardless of geographic, financial, or demographic circumstances. K12 Inc. is accredited by CITA. More information can be found at www.K12.com.

A Note from the Author

This is the third volume of the concise edition of *A History of US*. Working on the abridgment with the folks at K^{12}, I've had fun immersing myself, once again, in this amazing time in America. Americans are on the move. Immigrants, with dreams in their backpacks, are heading for farms and emerging cities. Blacks, finally free, are moving to those same cities. Some are heading West. America's citizens are creating new industries; they're dealing with innovation, war, a Great Depression, and the continuing demand that this nation be what it set out to be: fair to all its people.

—Joy Hakim

Contents

PART 1

AMERICANS ON THE MOVE

PART 2

INDUSTRY AND REFORM

EXPANSION, WAR, BOOM, AND BUST

Part 1

Americans on the Move

Meanwhile, Out West

While the Civil War was being fought, and afterwards too, there was war in the West. It was the new settlers fighting the Indians, the buffalo, and nature for control of the land. The buffalo didn't have a chance. And nature—well, nature is tough, but no match for people. Six-hundred-year-old trees got axed. Big areas—like the Wisconsin Cutover—were left nude and unable to grow anything. A few people were beginning to worry about the environment, but hardly anyone listened to them.

As for the Indians, they were intelligent and resourceful, but they were outnumbered and outgunned. They didn't have much of a chance either. The settlers had been fighting wars with the Indians since the Pequot War, back in Massachusetts in 1631. The wars were all over the same thing: land and who would control it. The Native Americans had been promised—in treaty after treaty—that if they would just move once more, they would be left alone. First they were asked to move across the Appalachians; then west of the Mississippi; now it was off all the good land left in the West.

Well, they wouldn't do it. But they weren't given a choice. At least, it wasn't much of a choice: it was move or fight. And that led to the 30 years of Indian wars in the West. You'll hear more about them—the outcome wasn't good for the Native Americans.

The buffalo, a vital part of many Indians' way of life, didn't have a chance against waves of new settlers moving to the West. Here, passengers shoot at buffalo from a train. By the 1880s there were fewer and fewer herds left to shoot. ▶

▲ Lured by the prospect of cheap land, from the 1860s on, many thousands of families—like the family shown here in Custer County, Nebraska—left their homes in the East to seek new lives in the West.

▲ When there weren't any trees, you burned dry buffalo chips. A Kansas woman brings home a barrowful. What are buffalo chips?

It is hard to blame the people who took their land. They were just ordinary people who had been told there was free land in the West. So they'd come to settle on it. Many had also been told awful, untrue stories about the Native Americans. They thought all Indians were savages and cruel and monsterlike. They were terrified of Indians and wanted them all to disappear. And some Indians were killing innocent people.

Besides, the settlers weren't having an easy time. Part of the problem was an economic depression in the East. It came on suddenly, and thousands of people were out of work. Many of them headed west, across the Mississippi.

But they found farming in the prairie lands different and difficult—much harder than farming in the East. Plains farmers needed to be able to stand up to extremes of heat and cold, and to violent storms. There was something else about this kind of farming that was important—and new to the easterners: a big investment of capital (which means money) was needed for farm equipment and seeds. Many farmers weren't prepared. IN GOD WE TRUSTED, IN KANSAS WE BUSTED, said signs on the covered wagons heading back east. About one-third of the people who came west turned around and went back home.

▲ Cargo ships on Lake Michigan take on their loads from grain elevators in Chicago. By the 1870s, Chicago was the busiest port in the United States.

But, despite the hardships and the roller-coaster economic conditions, mostly there was optimism. The midsection of the nation began to produce so much wheat it was called "the nation's bread basket." Western ranchers were raising cattle and sheep to put steaks and chops on people's dinner plates. Western miners were digging up important minerals. Railroads could take those products to far places.

In the 1870s, no one knew quite where the nation was heading, but it was easy to see it was going in new directions—and fast.

Cities were springing up everywhere: Ohio's cities were among the fastest growing. Chicago was the nation's busiest port. (Chicago a port? In the middle of the country? Look at a map and see how that could be.) Factories spurred the growth in most cities; they produced affordable goods, and jobs, too—especially for the new immigrants. America's citizens were beginning to have comforts and possessions beyond anyone's dreams.

Presidents and congresses couldn't seem to keep up with all the new ideas, opportunities, and problems. But who could?

Before the Civil War the United States had been a midget in world affairs. Now it was in a growth spurt. Before long the nation would be an industrial and agricultural giant.

Nebraska became a state on March 1, 1867; Colorado on August 1, 1876.

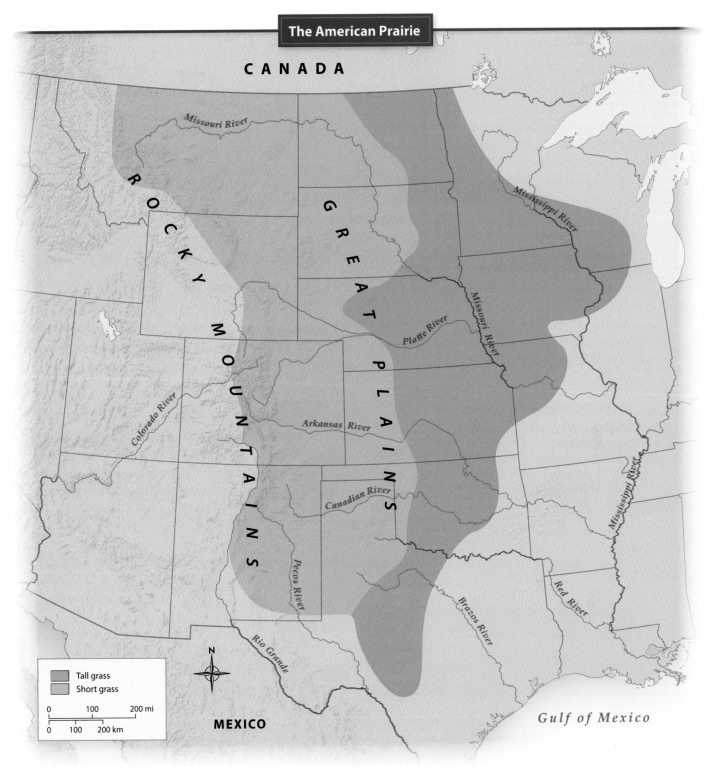

▲ America's prairie, the vast grassland in the center of the United States, was home to millions of bison, wolves, grizzly bears, and other animals, including several billion prairie dogs. During the late 1800s, farmers and ranchers transformed the grasslands into the richest agricultural region in the world.

On the Lone Prairie

The first Europeans in the New World were surprised by America's forests—by their vastness and vigor—but they weren't surprised by forests. Europe was full of trees. It was when the people pushed west, into the continent's heartland, that they found something that was indeed a new world. America's savannas—its grasslands—seemed endless. They were like nothing any of them had seen before. The grass sometimes reached 12 feet, so that the tallest animals and men were hidden in the growth. But if you stood on a rise and looked over the grass, there was nothing to block your view—no mountains, no trees—nothing. Just an enormity of sky that stretched out in every direction and rubbed its belly on the grass.

The unshorn fields, boundless and beautiful,
For which the speech of England has no name—

That was poet William Cullen Bryant's explanation for that French word: *prairie*. It means "big meadow." (There were savannas in Africa—with lions and giraffes and rhinoceros—but the African grasslands were much smaller than the American prairie.)

Our prairie divided itself into three regions. The *tallgrass prairie* began near Lake Michigan, in Illinois, and pushed west. (Almost all of Iowa was filled with tall grass.) The tall grasses thrived where there was plenty of rain; sometimes those grasses—especially big bluestem—grew half an inch a day.

Far to the west, in the shadow of the Rocky Mountains, there were short grasses—just a few inches high. This was the Great Plains region. It was high, flat, dusty-dry grassland—a *steppe*—cold in winter and hot in summer. The grasses that grew best on the Great Plains—buffalo grass and blue grama—were drought-tolerant.

In between the tall and short were—as you might guess—mixed and medium grasses. Altogether it was the greatest grassland on earth, and home to wild flowers, birds, insects, and animals in astonishing balance and abundance. Before the railroads, the homesteaders, and the cattle ranchers pushed west, there were perhaps 60 million bison and 50 million pronghorn, along with millions of wolves, deer, elk, and coyotes—as well as grizzlies, bighorn sheep, cottontails, rattlesnakes, and perhaps 5 billion (yes, billion) prairie dogs. (Prairie dogs aren't dogs at all; they are burrowing members of the squirrel family.) But there were more earthworms and butterflies than prairie dogs. And as for birds and ducks, in migration season they sometimes filled the sky like a dark moving cloud that

◄ As many as 60 million bison grazed on the American prairie before homesteaders, cattle ranchers, and railroads pushed into the region.

Wildfires, a natural occurrence on the dry prairie, posed a constant threat to farms and ranches. ▶

blocked the sun from the earth and stretched as far as anyone could see.

Prairie grass has thick roots that twist and tangle and intertwine with the earth. That root-hard soil made the sod that the settlers cut for their homes. At first it broke the homesteaders' plows—but steel plows mastered the sod. Prairie fires kept the grasslands treeless. The fires started naturally, from sparks of lightning, and they spread—like wildfire. The fires were useful; they cleared out the dead grasses and encouraged new shoots. But animals—or people—were sometimes faced with terrifying walls of flame higher than their heads.

Domestic animals (cattle and sheep) and farmers (who pulled up the grasses and planted food crops) changed the prairie from grassland to market basket. The fertile land where grass grew so vigorously became the richest agricultural region in the world. The vast prairies turned into corn and wheatfields, or cities, or grazing lands, or sometimes forests (when fires were fought). Today, the produce of this region feeds our nation and others, too.

That market basket reminds us the earth is a changing place. The cornfields are just the latest inhabitants of a region rich in environmental history. In the great sweep of time, the grasslands were newcomers. One hundred million years ago, mid-America was a tropical jungle, with lush forests and roaming dinosaurs. Then the climate changed, dinosaurs disappeared (to return on TV screens), and grass took over.

And what of that grassland? Where can you see prairie today—real prairie, like Lewis and Clark saw? Hardly anywhere. Illinois, which once had 37 million acres of tallgrass prairie (and is known as the Prairie State) now has about 3,500 acres of it. There is some tallgrass prairie at Konza Preserve, near Manhattan, Kansas, and the Nature Conservancy has a tallgrass preserve in Oklahoma, 17 miles north of Pawhuska. For midgrass, visit the Willa Cather Prairie near Red Cloud, Nebraska. You can see shortgrass prairie at Coronado National Grassland in Kansas. You'll also find prairie at Blue Mounds State Park in Minnesota and prairie-dog towns in Shirley Basin, Wyoming. To see the prairie, along with an awesome cave, visit Wind Cave National Park in South Dakota.

A pioneer family harnesses the winds that sweep across the plains to power the pump for a deep well. ▶

Riding the Trail

After the Civil War, when soldiers came home to Texas, they found the place swarming with longhorn cattle. Now longhorn, as the name tells you, are cattle with long horns growing out of their heads. They are a tough breed and can walk great distances. And, if there is grass to chew, they can even fatten up on the journey.

The Texas longhorn were descended from cattle brought to America by Columbus and the Spaniards who followed him. The longhorns were running loose on the range. There they bred and multiplied and were soon so numerous that people were killing them for their hides and throwing away the meat. The ex-soldiers knew beef was expensive back East. Now, if they could find a way to get those cattle east—why, there was money to be made.

About this time, Jesse Chisholm—who was half Scot and half Cherokee—drove a herd of cattle north from Texas to Kansas and made a map of his route. That route had plenty of grass for grazing and enough water and it led to Abilene, Kansas. In Abilene, Joseph G. McCoy was paying $40 a head for cattle. Forty dollars was a powerful lot of money in those days, especially since you could get longhorn in

Range is open land for grazing cattle.

Cowboys drove enormous herds of longhorn hundreds of miles along cattle trails. When they reached their destination—a cattle town—the animals were loaded onto railroad cars and sent to Chicago. ▶

Texas for about $5. If you had a herd of 1,000 or more steers and cows and got them to Abilene—well, you can figure out that you'd be rich.

The Kansas Pacific Railroad reached Abilene in 1867, so Joe McCoy could ship the longhorns east in railroad cattle cars and make a lot of money for himself. Which he did. He made a whole lot more money than even he expected. And he became famous. Have you ever heard of "the real McCoy"? Some say that was Joe.

Remember Chicago? The little town where Abe Lincoln campaigned? Well, most of Joe McCoy's cows and steers got shipped to Chicago. That city—some people call it the Windy City—was both a port and a railroad center. It was a distribution hub. When refrigerated railroad cars were developed, Chicago became the meatpacking capital of the country. Most of the bovines that traveled Jesse Chisholm's trail got turned into steaks in Chicago. Thanks to railroads and ships, they were devoured in Norfolk and Scranton and Mobile.

For the next 20 years the Chisholm Trail (that's what they named it) was a ribbon of longhorn. More than a million cattle were driven north on the trail. Who drove the herds? Why, cowboys, of course. What did the cowboys do when they got to Abilene? Get paid, buy fancy new duds, and have a big old time. Did they get rich? Not the cowboys; they were paid about $90—or less—for the two- to three-month journey from the Texas panhandle, across the Red River, through Indian territory, over deserts, rivers, and prairie. It was the cattlemen, who owned the cows and steers, who got rich, but that's another story.

What the cowboys got was a way of life that turned them into legends. Some people call cowboys "knights of the prairie." And they were like knights: they rode with amazing skill, handled danger

▲ A cowboy trails Texas longhorns. Cowboys drove over a million cattle north on the Chisholm Trail.

Some say Elijah McCoy was "the real McCoy." Elijah was the son of a runaway slave. He went to Scotland and became a mechanical engineer. Then he came back to the United States, where he invented a lubricating cup that fed oil into machines as they operated. He invented many other things, too. He held 75 patents.

▲ Elijah McCoy

Cowboys had to be ready for stampedes at any time. ▶

with bravado, and had their own code of honor. It may sound glamorous, but it was not an easy life. There were killers on the Chisholm Trail; here are some of them: *brutal heat, ferocious blizzards, biting hail, angry Indians, rattlesnakes, quicksand, rustlers, thirst*—and, most common of all, *stampedes*.

A herd of cattle will stampede at the drop of a frying pan. Here is how one cowboy described it: "While I was looking at him, this steer leaped into the air, hit the ground with a heavy thud, and gave a grunt that sounded like that of a hog. That was the signal. The whole herd was up and going—and heading right for me. My horse gave a lunge, jerked loose from me, and was away. I barely had time to climb into an oak. The cattle went by like a hurricane, hitting the tree with their horns. It took us all night to round them up."

That cowboy was lucky there was a tree to climb and the cattle didn't knock the tree over. If they had, it would have been goodbye cowboy.

Cowboys were usually up before dawn and were often still hard at work into the night. But there was something about the life that most of them loved. As one cowhand said, "To ride around the big steers at night, all lying down full as a tick, chewing their cuds and blowing, with the moon shining down on their big horns, was a sight to make a man's eyes pop."

Pretty soon it got to be a regular thing—traveling the Chisholm Trail. Herds of two or three thousand cattle became common. Usually a dozen cowboys were hired to handle a herd, with a trail boss and cook. The cook was important. Cowboys got ornery if the coffee wasn't strong and the food decent.

Like other Americans, cowboys were a mixture: some white, some black, some Mexican, some—like Jesse Chisholm—part Indian. Some were women. It was democratic out there on the trail. People were judged by what they could do, not by the color of their skin, the accent in their speech, or their sex.

Elizabeth E. Johnson was a schoolteacher in Texas before she bought some cattle and became a cowgirl. In 1879, she drove her own herd up the Chisholm Trail to market. When she died, 45 years later, she was worth more than $2 million.

Most cowhands wore tight-fitting clothes, leather chaps, floppy vests, fancy boots, and broad-brimmed hats—clothes adapted from those of the cattlemen who had come to the western land from Spain. Much cowboy lingo was Spanish: *chaps*, *lariat*, *rodeo*, *ranch* (and *lingo*, too).

Women often did branding and other ranch work when extra hands were needed or when the men were out on trail drives. ▼

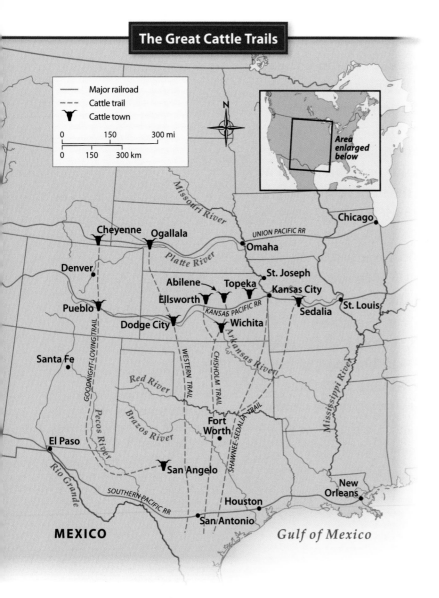

The Great Cattle Trails

Major railroad
Cattle trail
Cattle town

0   150   300 mi
0   150   300 km

N

Area enlarged below

Missouri River

Chicago

Cheyenne   Ogallala

Denver

Platte River

UNION PACIFIC RR

Omaha

St. Joseph

Abilene   Topeka

Ellsworth

Kansas City

KANSAS PACIFIC RR

Pueblo

Dodge City

Wichita

Sedalia

St. Louis

Santa Fe

Red River

Arkansas River

WESTERN TRAIL

CHISHOLM TRAIL

GOODNIGHT-LOVING TRAIL

Pecos River

Brazos River

Fort Worth

SHAWNEE-SEDALIA TRAIL

Mississippi River

El Paso

San Angelo

New Orleans

Rio Grande

SOUTHERN PACIFIC RR

Houston

MEXICO

San Antonio

Gulf of Mexico

▲ The major cattle trails from Texas to railroad towns more than 400 miles north led through thick grass and good water sources for the cattle. A long drive could take three months.

It was a lonely life they led, so they livened it up by singing around the campfire, or telling tall tales. Like the one about the cowboys who ran out of fenceposts in a snowstorm when they had to fence the herd in. So they hammered frozen rattlesnakes into the ground and strung wire on them. It would have worked, except there was a thaw, and the fence just crawled away.

In the Kansas cattle towns there were twice as many saloons as other businesses. On the trail, grub was dished up from the chuck wagon. It had shelves and drawers for coffee and flour, beans and sugar. A swinging leg held up the open box lid and turned it into a tabletop.

And Abilene—what happened to Abilene? It was the first of the Wild West towns—and maybe the wildest of them all—with saloons and pistol-packing cowpunchers raring for a good time. A town like that needed a marshal, and Abilene got the most famous one of all: James Butler ("Wild Bill") Hickok. Hickok had once been a bad hombre himself, a gambling man who had two pearl-handled pistols and was known as the "fastest draw in the West." He could shoot the hat off a man and keep the hat in the air with his bullets and when it finally dropped it would be rimmed with a circle of bullet holes. At least that was the story he told. Hickok was a sharp dresser who wore a coat with satin lapels, parted his long hair in the middle, and slicked it and his mustache with bear grease.

Wild Bill was paid a big salary—$150 a month—for keeping law and order in Abilene. He did a fair job for a while, although most of the time his office was at a gambling table. Then he shot two people; he'd done that before, but it just happened that one was his deputy. That was too much for the good folk of Abilene. They got rid of Hickok and the cattle market, too. Abilene settled down and became respectable. After that the cowboys and their longhorns headed for the new towns of Wichita and Dodge City. About 1875, Dodge City became the main railhead for shipping cattle eastward. Most say it was an even wilder place than Abilene (and its "peace" officers—Bat Masterson and Wyatt Earp—well, you should read about them). But by the end of the century, when railroads crisscrossed the land, and barbed wire fenced it in, the heyday of the wild cow towns was over.

▲ Dodge City, Kansas, was a major railhead for shipping cattle eastward.

Calamity Jane

No one ever knew how many of Calamity Jane's stories were true and how many were tall tales. No one much cared. She was a good storyteller and no ordinary woman—even in those frontier days.

She was Martha Jane Cannary and, at age 13, already an expert rider when her family headed west. It was a five-month trip, and she spent it exploring and hunting. It was a good thing she did. When her parents died—a year and a half later—she could take care of herself. Calamity Jane claimed to have been a gold miner, a nurse, a Pony Express rider, an army scout, an Indian fighter, and a cattle hand.

Now that is what she said. Some people say all of it is true and some say none of it is—including her name. No question, she was a well-known woman of the Wild West, and a friend of Wild Bill Hickok—and a drunk. How did she get her name, Calamity Jane? Well, there are so many stories about that, it isn't worth the bother to tell them. (Do you know what *calamity* means? It describes her.) We do know that at 23 she joined a geological expedition to the Black Hills, and at 24 she was the only woman, among 1,500 men, in an expedition that headed out from Fort Laramie to fight the Sioux.

▲ Martha Jane Cannary, known as Calamity Jane

Rails Across the Country

It was May 10, 1869, and hardly a person in the whole country didn't wish to be at Promontory in Utah. The people who were there listened to speeches, said a prayer, drank toasts (too many, so it was said), yelled, and cheered. Two brass bands blared. All over the country, newspapers held their presses so they could cover the grand event. The newspapers wouldn't tell the whole story—it would take years for the real story to be known—but when Leland Stanford (representing a railroad company that had laid tracks east from Sacramento, California, over the high and dangerous Sierra Nevada mountains and on to northern Utah)—when Leland Stanford shook hands with Thomas Durant (whose railroad company had laid tracks west from Omaha, Nebraska, over land the Indians thought they owned)—why, the whole country got excited. A telegraph operator, on a high pole above the crowd, sent out the message STAND BY, WE HAVE DONE PRAYING. Then Stanford raised a silver hammer, whomped at a solid gold spike—and missed. No matter, the next swipe hit the nail on its head.

Five states had sent gold and silver spikes for this historic event, so the other bigwigs each got a chance to hammer away. When they were done, Chinese workmen quietly removed the fancy spikes and nailed regular ones in place. By that time the news had been sent to America's newspapers and people. TRANSCONTINENTAL RAILROAD COMPLETED. EAST AND WEST LINKED. In Philadelphia the Liberty Bell rang. Chicago held a parade that stretched for seven miles. In New York cannons blasted 100 times. You could now go by train from New York to California.

The building of that railroad had begun, in a way, on July 1, 1862, the day Abraham Lincoln signed the Pacific Railroad Act. There were visionaries—people with clear sight and imagination—who had talked

The joining of the Central Pacific and Union Pacific railroads at Promontory, Utah, made it possible to go from coast to coast by train. ▼

even earlier of a railroad to cross the country. Lincoln's act got it started. But slowly. After all, there was a Civil War being fought. The country learned of the importance of railroads during that war, when armies were moved by train. But a railroad that stretched across the continent—that would have to wait until the war was over.

Two companies built the railroad. The Central Pacific (starting in the West) and the Union Pacific (coming from the East). No one knew exactly where they would meet. It became a race—East against West. It was an important race for those who owned the railroad companies. The government was giving subsidies for each mile of railway track that was laid. So, of course, each side wanted to lay the most track.

A *subsidy* is a grant of money, land, or something of value. The railroads got valuable land grants.

Under the best conditions, laying track isn't easy. Conditions were rarely "best." Remember, this was frontier land they were crossing. The railroads had to bring all their supplies with them. If there was an emergency there was no place to go for help.

You lay tracks by putting heavy metal rails on top of wooden cross pieces—trimmed logs—called "ties." The Union Pacific used 40 railroad cars to haul the 400 tons of rails, timber, fuel, and food needed for each mile of track. The Central Pacific brought its rails, locomotives, and supplies from the East Coast on clipper ships that sailed around Cape Horn at the tip of South America.

▲ Workers laying track on the Union Pacific Railroad

▲ Chinese laborers working for the Central Pacific Railroad often did the most dangerous jobs, such as loading dynamite on high cliffs.

Laying tracks on flat land is not too difficult. But try crossing a mountain. You have a choice: you can go over or through. The railroad men did both of those things—they dug tunnels through some mountains and laid tracks over others. At first the equipment they used was about as fancy as what you might find in a neighbor's garage. Workers attacked rocks with pickaxes; they dug tunnels with shovels and their bare hands. They carried stones and dirt in wheelbarrows. Sometimes they used explosives; sometimes they blew themselves up.

Do you want to build a railroad, 19th-century style? Start with *graders*: men with picks, shovels, wheelbarrows, and wagons—they grade the land, making it as level as possible. Muscular *tracklayers* follow. They lift and place the heavy wooden ties and the heavier metal rails. Next come *gaugers*, *spikers*, and *bolters*—who get it all together and hammer the spikes in place. Each rail takes 10 spikes and each mile 400 rails.

The Central Pacific Railroad sent ships to China and brought 7,000 Chinese workers to California just to build the railroad. They paid them $1 a day. The Chinese worked incredibly hard, for long hours, and, mostly, were treated with contempt.

Coming the other way, on the Union Pacific, most workers were either ex-Confederate soldiers, former slaves, or Irish immigrants. They, too, worked hard. They lived in tent cities put up and taken down as the railroad went west. Those moving towns were tough, violent places where there was too much drinking and too many guns. There was constant fear of Indian raids.

The Indians—by treaty—had been guaranteed land west of the 95th meridian as a permanent home. When the railroad got to Nebraska it was already at the 100th meridian. So Indians, understandably,

A *meridian* is a line of longitude.

The Transcontinental Railroad and Time Zones

Pacific Time Zone

Mountain Time Zone

Central Time Zone

Eastern Time Zone

▲ An 1884 international conference in Washington, D.C., established uniform time zones worldwide. Time zones in the United States have changed slightly since then.

were angered. They hated the thundering locomotives that were destroying the buffalo ranges. Native Americans raided the railroad camps, but not as often as the tales say. Indians didn't kill many trainmen; it was disease, accidents, avalanches, heat, and cold that were the worst killers. Some people deserved medals for what they accomplished—especially the engineers and organizers who arranged for the food and shelter, who planned the route, and who supervised the work. None of that was easy. They did it with incredible speed.

After the railroads met at Promontory, everyone had to wait two days to celebrate. That was because Thomas Durant was late. Union Pacific workmen had chained his fancy parlor-car train to some railroad track. They kept him hostage until he paid them overdue wages.

▲ Members of the board of the Union Pacific Railroad meet in a private railway car.

By that time Durant was rich enough to make King Midas envious. So was Leland Stanford, who made his employees salute when he rode past in his private railroad car. When the transcontinental railroad was finished, Stanford, Durant, and the other railroad tycoons were national heroes. Today, many historians call them crooks.

You see, they had asked for government aid in building the railroad. That was reasonable. It was too big an undertaking for individuals. They demanded more than money from the government; they wanted—and got—enormous and valuable land grants. That was greedy, but it wasn't illegal. Then they sold stock in their companies to the public, and got more money that way. That wasn't illegal either. But when their companies gave out contracts for building the railroads, and those men in charge—Stanford, Durant, and company—took all the contracts for themselves, that was crooked. They didn't even share profits with their stockholders. That was really foul play. Worse than that, they charged the government twice what it actually cost to do the building. As you know, they hardly paid their workers. And, still worse, they allowed poor and unsafe workmanship, because it was cheaper and made their profits higher.

So that side of it was a mess, and when some of the story came out a few years later it created a big scandal. That was when U. S. Grant was president. It almost destroyed his term in office. All the fuss did help get laws passed to regulate business greed.

Still, to be fair, it took great imagination and some risk to finance the railroads. The men who did it had foresight and courage (even if they had no consideration for their employees, stockholders, or fellow citizens).

The good part of the story is that people in the United States could now travel from coast to coast in 10 days. Some people still went west in covered wagons, but it wouldn't be long before the wagons were history. Soon there were several transcontinental railroads. They were hauling things as well as people.

Railroads made the United States into a united country. People from different parts of the nation got to know each other. New immigrants could go west and settle. People on the West Coast could meet relatives back East. And, even if they didn't travel themselves, Americans could now buy goods from other states, or talk to people who had traveled about. The railroad made the country seem smaller.

Fencing the Homestead

Imagine: you are settled on a farm in Kansas. You've worked hard, your crops are thriving, you're pleased with yourself. Then a cowpuncher decides to drive his herd to market and, though you're not right on the Chisholm Trail, you're near enough. The herd stampedes and longhorns trample your land. Wham, bang, squash! You have no crops. Nothing left of a year's work. And maybe no farm, because without a crop to sell, you don't have money to buy more seed and supplies.

That kind of thing happened. It was just one of the things that discouraged farming in the Plains states. The early pioneers and the forty-niners (who headed to California when the gold rush started in 1849) leapfrogged over the plains and mountains and settled in the Far West. They called the plains the "Great American Desert" and believed it was no good for farming. They were wrong. The region would become one of the best agricultural areas the world has ever known. But they were right about one thing. It wasn't an easy place to be a farmer. There were hardly any trees and not enough water. The soil was wonderfully rich—the pioneers found native grasses tall enough to hide a man on horseback—but the weather was either blisteringly hot or frigidly cold, with tornadoes thrown in just to keep people on their toes. Besides that, there were invasions of grasshoppers that ate crops, droughts that dried them up, and a loneliness on the open plains that drove some people mad.

The Plains states stretch from Texas to Canada and from Kansas and Iowa to the Rocky Mountains. The Plains states are Iowa, Kansas, Minnesota, Missouri, Nebraska, North Dakota, South Dakota, and Wyoming.

Farmers on the Great Plains battle a swarm of crop-destroying grasshoppers. ▶

The Homestead Act of 1862 allowed the government to sell millions of acres of public land to men and women who were willing to move west as farmers. ▼

▲ Homesteaders on the Great Plains

None of that seemed to matter. The dream of many Americans was to have a farm. Land in the East was spoken for. Even with problems, those vast plains looked inviting to people who wanted land of their own. Winds blew much of the time, which meant that windmills could be used to pump water from deep wells. That water made irrigation possible.

In 1862 (which was during the Civil War), Congress passed a bill called the Homestead Act. It said that for $10 any citizen, or anyone who had filed papers to become a citizen, could have 160 acres of public land. That included women. As soon as the Civil War was over, a lot of people headed west to get land and become farmers. Some say a quarter of a million widows and single women were among those who became homesteaders.

Many homesteaders were immigrants—right off the boat. Some western settlements became all German, or all Danish, or all Swedish, or all Norwegian. Many immigrants tried to hang on to their original culture. Food was one way to do it. Greek, Polish, German, or Italian food was found in surprising places.

A photographer was on hand to shoot history's greatest land rush: on April 22, 1889, 6 million acres of "unoccupied" Oklahoma land were claimed.

The newcomers didn't have to worry about buffalo herds anymore—the buffalo were practically gone—but they did have the problem of cattle wandering about. They couldn't fence their land because there were no trees to make fenceposts; besides, wooden fences rotted, or got knocked over, or burned. Joseph Glidden solved their problem. He invented barbed wire. He experimented in his backyard with an old coffee mill and a big grindstone that turned. He used them to twist two wires together, and then he coiled sharp barbs around the wires. With barbed wire, farmers could fence in their property.

Pronghorns Abounding

Brewster Higley, a Pennsylvania doctor, packed his bags and headed west to become a homesteader in Kansas. He was so happy in his new home that he wrote a poem about it called "The Western Home." A neighbor set the poem to music and gave it a new name, "Home on the Range." Before long everyone was singing it. When Higley used the words *buffalo* and *antelope* everyone knew what he meant, but the proper names for those animals are *bison* and *pronghorns*.

> *Oh, give me a home,*
> *Where the buffalo roam,*
> *Where the deer and the antelope play,*
> *Where seldom is heard*
> *A discouraging word,*
> *And the skies are not cloudy all day.*
>
> *Home, home on the range,*
> *Where the deer and the antelope play,*
> *Where seldom is heard*
> *A discouraging word,*
> *And the skies are not cloudy all day.*

Now the cowboys had a problem. Those fences got in the way of their herds. Well, cowboys and farmers did some fighting, but before long the farmers and ranchers won. The cattle drives were over and most cowboys turned into ranch hands. By 1890, railroads seemed to be about everywhere, so the cattle drives weren't necessary anyway. Railroads meant farmers and ranchers could send their cattle and grains to faraway markets.

A new kind of agriculture developed on the Plains. The early American farms had been self-sufficient. The farmer took care of most of his own needs. Farm families raised cows, hogs, and chickens, grew wheat and vegetables, killed game, caught fish, built their own homes, and made their own furniture and clothes. They didn't have much use for money; they bartered for the few things they needed.

Self-sufficient farming wasn't suited to the Plains area or to the times. In the 19th century, agriculture became a big business. Many farmers became specialists who grew only one or two crops. It happened quickly. For thousands and thousands of years men and women had used the same methods of sowing and harvesting. Then a few inventions came along and changed everything.

Home on the Grange

In 1867, Oliver Hudson Kelley founded a social and political organization for farmers called the National Grange of the Patrons of Husbandry. (*Husbandry* means "farming," and more specifically, the application of scientific principles to farming, especially animal breeding. And the word *grange* comes from England, where a grange was a farm or a farm building for storing grain, like a barn.) The Grange was a way for farmers to band together and protect their interests. Working people were joining unions; farmers joined the Grange. It grew rapidly, especially in Minnesota, Wisconsin, Illinois, and Iowa. The grangers (that's what members were called) influenced lawmakers and established cooperative stores and mills. They made politicians pay attention to the farmers' concerns.

The Grange was a way for farmers to band together and protect their interests. ▶

Reaping a Harvest

Plains land is fertile—you just learned that—but it is also firm, so firm you can dig it up in blocks, called "sod blocks," and build a house with them. Try plowing that hard land. The old-style wooden plows broke. Iron plows didn't work either; soil stuck to the iron. John Deere designed a steel plow. It was strong and the soil fell away from it. It revolutionized agriculture.

> *Sod* is turf—grass with the soil that it grows on.

But that was nothing compared to what Cyrus McCormick's reaper did. More than anything else, it was that reaper (and the railroads) that brought people west and changed the way they farmed.

A reaper cuts and harvests grain. Old-style farmers cut grain with a scythe (SEYE-TH), which is a hand tool. That was hard, backbreaking work. It took a good worker all day to reap an acre. If he had 40 acres to cut, that meant 40 days. In 40 days a crop would be overripe and rotten. McCormick's machine—pulled by horses or mules—could harvest a huge field in no time at all. The mechanical reaper did to wheat farming what Eli Whitney's cotton gin did to cotton growing. It made big farms practical.

> Railroads brought large-scale commercial farming to the Midwest, and that began the reign of King Wheat. Wheat exports rose from 2 million bushels in 1860 to 90 million bushels in 1890. Today we export over a billion bushels a year, feeding people in many other nations.

▲ Cyrus McCormick's reaping machine, patented in 1831, could cut 10 times more wheat in a day than a farmer could using a scythe.

▲ Cyrus McCormick

A *phenomenon* (fuh-NOM-uh-non) is a fact or event that you can see for yourself (often a remarkable one).

Cyrus Hall McCormick was a Virginia boy, born in the beautiful Shenandoah Valley, of Scotch-Irish Presbyterian parents. As a child, he spent many hours in his father's workshop. He rarely wasted time or played games. It was his father, Robert, who understood the need for a mechanical reaper and attempted to invent one. He mounted scissorlike knives on a long bar pulled at the side of a horse or mule or ox. Cyrus improved the invention.

He sold a few of his reapers in Virginia, but Shenandoah land is hilly and farms are small. When he took a trip to the Middle West—and saw the vast, flat plains—Cyrus McCormick knew his future was there.

Then he met the mayor of Chicago, who was a shrewd businessman; the mayor lent Cyrus money to build a big factory to make reapers. That factory became one of America's greatest business successes.

Before Cyrus McCormick came along, the Industrial Revolution had been mostly a city phenomenon. McCormick brought that revolution to farm life. He was more than just a fine inventor. He was a business and marketing genius, too. He guaranteed his machines: if they broke down he saw that they were repaired—no one had done that before. He trained experts to show farmers how to use them; no one had done that before either.

The machines were expensive, more than most farmers could afford. Cyrus McCormick let farmers take several months to pay for them. It was called "installment buying"—that was another of McCormick's ideas. He added a research department to his factory, and he kept improving the models. That, too, was something new for a businessman to do.

John Deere and Cyrus McCormick had developed the plow and reaper before the Civil War—in the 1830s and '40s. Their inventions were first widely used in the cleared woodland farms of the region to the east of the Mississippi. But after the war, those mechanical tools went west with all the people who were turning the American plains into farmland.

Note this statistic: in the 30 years between 1860 and 1890, more land was turned into farmland in the United States than in all the years from 1607 to 1860. In 1879 the McCormick factory produced 18,760 reapers; two years later it made nearly 49,000 machines.

And it kept growing. Farming was becoming an industry. The new equipment made huge, businesslike farms common. Farm equipment became necessary. Capital—money, often from bank loans—was now an important part of farming.

The farming revolution was hard on some people. Revolutions usually are. The small farmer was often hurt. More and more small farmers began heading for cities to take jobs in manufacturing and industry. Many didn't want to do that. They had no choice. They either became big or failed.

By 1900 the lone, self-sufficient farmer whom Jefferson admired hardly existed. The new farmer was part of a huge system. His wheat, cotton, beef, and wool were sold around the world. He had to worry about markets and prices in London and Chicago instead of in his neighborhood. He was not self-sufficient.

▲ McCormick improved his reaper over time by combining it with other tools. This machine, on a large farm in Oregon, is pulled by a team of horses. Smaller farms needed smaller machines and far fewer animals.

American Horticulturist Luther Burbank developed hundreds of varieties of new fruits, vegetables, grains, cacti, and flowers. ▶

▲ George Washington Carver, an agricultural chemist, developed new products from peanuts, sweet potatoes, and soybeans. He wanted to encourage crop diversity in the American South, where cotton had exhausted the land.

▲ The russet potato is the most commonly grown variety of potato in Idaho, a major potato-growing region.

One hundred million acres is about the size of Ohio, North Carolina, Maryland, and Illinois combined. Some experts say twice that amount of land was seriously eroded.

Because the country seemed so large, American farmers had always farmed wastefully. When land wore out, they just moved on to better land. For a long time there was better land to move to. But, by the end of the 19th century, there wasn't any frontier left. In addition, poor farming methods had destroyed more than 100 million acres of America's land. Prairie grasses and trees had been cut and plowed under, and then there was nothing to hold the soil in place: much good land turned to dust and blew away in the wind. Rain took the topsoil—the fertile part of the land—and washed it into streams. Land that had once supported buffalo and other wildlife became barren.

A few people were alarmed. Congress passed the Morrill Act. It gave the states large land grants to establish agricultural colleges. At those colleges farmers could learn the best and newest methods of farming. The Hatch Act established agricultural experiment stations in each state. Slowly the American farmer began to turn scientific. Mark Alfred Carleton went to Russia and found a variety of wheat that could take the tough weather in the American Middle West. Luther Burbank, on his farm in Santa Rosa, California, experimented and developed hundreds of varieties of new fruits, vegetables, grains, cacti, and flowers. And George Washington Carver, at the Tuskegee Institute in Alabama, developed hundreds of ways to use the peanut, the sweet potato, and the soybean.

The Trail Ends on a Reservation

Indians are not all alike: some have warring traditions, others peaceful ones. Sioux are as different from Pueblo people as Swedes are from Turks.

The new Americans and the Native Americans were sharing the same land, but they didn't really know each other. They had different ways of living. Neither group wanted to change—and why should they?

The problem was that the two ways of life were not *compatible*. That means they couldn't exist together on the same land. And they both wanted that land. The Plains Indians were mostly hunters. The new settlers were mostly farmers and ranchers. Hunters and farmers have a hard time living together. Hunters need land free and uncultivated so herds of buffalo and deer and antelope can move about. Farmers need land cleared of wild animals so their crops won't be trampled, eaten, and destroyed.

Pueblo people of the Southwest ▼

Indians of the Great Plains ▼

In the early 1800s, when Lewis and Clark explored the West, vast herds of buffalo stretched as far as the eye could see. By 1865 there were still about 12 million buffalo. One observer told of a herd, moving at about 15 miles an hour, that was so big it took five days for the whole herd to pass him by. A few years later, the buffalo were just about all gone. They were hunted almost to extinction. Hunters like Buffalo Bill Cody led the charge, leaving herds where they fell. The land stank with the smell of dead buffalo. Then the plains, which had once vibrated with the sound of animal hoofs, became quiet as a desert. (But not for long; cattle soon replaced the buffalo.)

As white hunters exterminated the buffalo, they destroyed the Plains Indians' means of support. "Your people make big talk, and sometimes make war, if an Indian kills a white man's ox to keep his wife and children from starving," said a Cheyenne chief. "What do you think my people ought to say when they see their buffalo killed by your race when you are not hungry?"

The abundance of the land had turned many Americans into wasters. There were so many buffalo, and so many trees, and so much land, it was hard to imagine an end to any of it.

Most Americans are individualists, and proud of it. But what is good for the individual farmer, or lumberman, or cattle rancher may not be good for a whole society. Native Americans knew that.

As white hunters killed millions of buffalo, they destroyed the Plains Indians' way of life. ▶

▲ A Sioux Indian council meets in 1847. The Sioux were one of the Plains Indian peoples.

The Indian cultures were usually centered on the community, not the individual. But what is good for the whole community may be frustrating for some individuals. These are two different ways of organizing people and governments. One way isn't better, or worse, than the other way. Each is just different, and worthy of respect.

The Indians of the Plains didn't get much respect. They depended on buffalo meat for food and buffalo skins for clothing and shelter, and they were horrified to see the buffalo and the land wasted. That left them hungry, angry, and confused. Those Native American men and women, who had once lived freely on the land, now faced machine guns, cannons, army troops, barbed wire, and the diseases the newcomers brought with them. They fought these new enemies with all the energy they had, but they didn't have a chance of winning.

The new Americans held power, so they got their way. All the Indians had was determination and courage. It wasn't long before the settlers had the land they wanted, and most of the Indians were dead or put on unwanted land called "reservations."

Some people have the idea that the Native Americans lived in perfect harmony with the landscape and never did anything to harm it. That isn't so. Some did; some didn't.

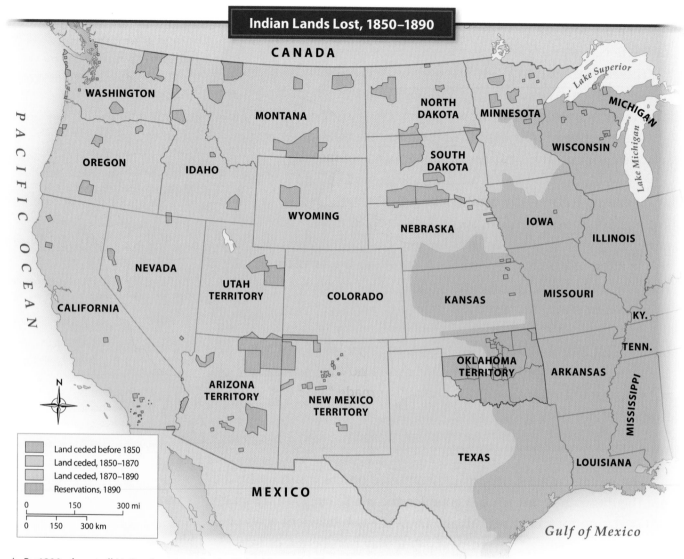

Indian Lands Lost, 1850–1890

CANADA

WASHINGTON
OREGON
IDAHO
MONTANA
NORTH DAKOTA
MINNESOTA
MICHIGAN
Lake Superior
Lake Michigan
WISCONSIN
SOUTH DAKOTA
WYOMING
NEBRASKA
IOWA
ILLINOIS
NEVADA
UTAH TERRITORY
COLORADO
KANSAS
MISSOURI
KY.
CALIFORNIA
ARIZONA TERRITORY
NEW MEXICO TERRITORY
OKLAHOMA TERRITORY
ARKANSAS
TENN.
MISSISSIPPI
TEXAS
LOUISIANA
MEXICO
Gulf of Mexico

PACIFIC OCEAN

Land ceded before 1850
Land ceded, 1850–1870
Land ceded, 1870–1890
Reservations, 1890

0   150   300 mi
0   150   300 km

▲ By 1890, almost all Native Americans in the United States had been forced onto reservations.

In 1876, Indian fighter Lieutenant Colonel George Armstrong Custer (who had won fame during the Civil War) pays no attention to his orders or to his scouts' reports. He leads 266 men against thousands of Cheyenne and Sioux Indians, led by Sitting Bull, who are gathered at the Little Bighorn River in central Montana. It is "Custer's Last Stand," and it is a massacre. The only U.S. Army survivor is a horse named Comanche.

▲ Lieutenant Colonel George Armstrong Custer

To better understand what happened, it helps to realize that after the Civil War there were many former soldiers who had learned, during the war, how to kill people. They were used to doing it, and they didn't know quite what else to do. So they came west and killed Indians. Peaceful settlers who moved west to farm were often innocent victims of angry Indians. All that led to intense hatreds and revenge raids on both sides. The Indians especially hated the iron horses (those roaring locomotives), which thundered across their hunting grounds filled with gun-toting soldiers and settlers.

The Native Americans weren't willing to give up their land and move onto the reservations, which were usually on poor land that was not good for growing crops. Would you be willing?

They fought for their land and their way of life. Army troops—sent west to "control" Indians—slaughtered them instead.

"The only good Indian is a dead Indian," said Philip Sheridan, who had been a Union general during the Civil War. His boss, William Tecumseh Sherman, seemed to agree. Sherman's middle name was that of a great Indian hero, but Sherman didn't brag about that fact. He was sometimes called "Cump," but never *Tecumseh*. He talked about a "final solution" to the Indian problem. By that Sherman meant their destruction.

John Pope (who had been head of the Union forces at the second battle of Bull Run—and lost) announced that he would deal with the Sioux "as maniacs or wild beasts, and by no means as people with whom treaties or compromises can be made." He tried his best to do that.

As far as we know, General Sherman was the first person to use the phrase "final solution" about destroying a whole race of people. In the 20th century the Nazis (an evil political/military party in Germany) used that same phrase in their attempt to kill all the Jewish people in Europe.

The artist Frederic Remington traveled to the West many times as a magazine illustrator. He later turned to painting and sculpting. In *Indian Warfare*, Cheyenne Indians retrieve the body of a fallen warrior. ▼

▲ Buffalo soldiers of the 25th Infantry at Ft. Keogh, Montana

In Colorado, Colonel John M. Chivington, a former minister, slaughtered 150 Cheyenne who had gone to the governor for protection. Most were women and children. Chivington called it "an act of duty to ourselves and civilization."

About one-fourth of the army's western troops were black. The Indians called them Buffalo Soldiers because some had curly hair, like the buffalo. The men liked the name and used a buffalo as their emblem. Blacks were determined to be equal partners with whites in the American way of life. The Indians felt differently. Most had no desire to be partners: they wanted to be left alone to pursue their own way of life. Here are some words from a Minnesota Indian chief:

The whites were always trying to make the Indians give up their life and live like white men—go to farming, work hard and do as they did—and the Indians did not then know how to do that, and did not want to....
If the Indians had tried to make the whites live like them, the whites would have resisted, and it was the same way with many Indians.

From Jamestown to Wounded Knee

1607: First English settlers arrive in Virginia. No one knows the number of Indians on the continent; some estimates are as high as 100 million.

1607–1750: Cooperation and encroachment. Efforts made to convert Indians to Christianity. Many deaths from disease, wars, enslavement.

1787: Northwest Ordinance recognizes existence of Native American property.

1824: Bureau of Indian Affairs formed within War Department.

1830: Indian Removal Act leads to Trail of Tears and other relocations of southeastern tribes.

1840s–'60s: Eastern tribes pushed continually westward; some, like the Sauk and Fox, resist strongly but are eventually overcome.

1871: Congress reverses the Northwest Ordinance. Tribes are no longer independent nations with whom treaties can be made.

1876: Lieutenant Colonel George Armstrong Custer's troops destroyed by Sioux warriors under Sitting Bull at battle of Little Bighorn.

1887: Dawes Act dissolves tribes as legal entities that can own land.

1890: Sitting Bull shot and killed by Indian policemen.

1890: At least 150 Sioux warriors, women, and children massacred at Wounded Knee in the last major armed encounter between Indians and whites in North America.

1924: Indian Citizenship Act.

1934: The Indian Reorganization Act attempts to restore tribal structures.

The Indians wanted to…go where they pleased and when they pleased; hunt game wherever they could find it, sell their furs to the traders, and live as they could.

The chief told how the Indians were herded onto reservations where the land was poor and there was not enough to eat. They had to buy food and supplies from government agents who usually cheated them.

Many of the white men often abused the Indians and treated them unkindly. Perhaps they had excuse, but the Indians did not think so. Many of the whites always seemed to say by their manner when they saw an Indian, "I am much better than you," and the Indians did not like this…the Dakota did not believe there were better men in the world than they.

The Indian wars in the West—the hardest fought of them—lasted from the end of the Civil War (1865) until a final massacre of Indians in 1890 at a place called Wounded Knee. Could the land have been shared? It wouldn't have been easy. Where do you live? Who lived on your land 300 years ago? Would you share your home?

▲ These Sioux children were sent to the Carlisle Indian School in Pennsylvania to be turned into "Americans." The photograph on the right was taken four months later.

The Indian story should have been different. There could have been respect and honesty between the peoples. There could have been strong laws to prevent unfairness and brutality. There could have been more understanding. Even those—like the Christian missionaries—who meant to help the Native Americans usually ended up destroying the tribes because they didn't respect the native cultures. The missionaries were arrogant without realizing it, because they were sure their way of life was better than the Native American way. They thought they were doing right when they tried to force Indians to live as they did. What would you have done?

Pitiful Last Becomes a Winner

When the boy child was born he was given a name that, in the Sioux Indian language, means "Pitiful Last." That was because he was the last of his mother's five children. She died giving birth to him. His father was Many Lightnings, but it was his grandmother who raised him.

Pitiful Last grew strong and quick and bright; when he was still a boy, but close to manhood, he won a fiercely fought lacrosse game. It was then that he received a new name. It was Ohiyesa; it means "The Winner."

But Ohiyesa was not through with names. He was raised as a Plains Indian, but his mother's father was a white man, an army officer and an artist. He was Seth Eastman. So the boy had another name: it was Charles Eastman.

It was well that he had two names, because he lived in two worlds. When he grew up he went to Dartmouth College, and to Boston University, and learned to be a doctor. Then he returned

▲ Seth Eastman painted this picture of Sioux playing lacrosse in 1851, seven years before the birth of his lacrosse-playing grandson Charles/Ohiyesa.

to the Indian world and served his people as a physician. But he wasn't finished learning. He studied law and represented the Sioux nation as an attorney in Washington. Are you amazed that he was both a doctor and a lawyer? Well, that isn't all he was. He is perhaps best known as a writer. One of the books he wrote is about his childhood. It is called *An Indian Boyhood*.

The People of the Pierced Noses

During the 19th century, the West of the traditional Indians, the mountain men, and the buffalo reached its end. A new and different West came into being: a land of farmers, ranchers, miners, city dwellers, and Indians who had to adapt their ways to new realities. But before the change was completed, before the final act in the drama, a great leader attempted to save his people. His name was Chief Joseph, of the people called the Nez Perce (nez-purse).

The Nez Perce Indians were special. Everyone agreed about that. They were honest and honorable, free-spirited and courageous, intelligent and independent, handsome and well built, and, as if all that weren't enough, they lived in a region that was a kind of paradise. Their land—where today Idaho, Washington, and Oregon come together—holds lush valleys, grassy prairies, steep mountains, and canyons that seem to have been cut by a giant's steam shovel.

The Nez Perce shared that land with elk, deer, antelope, rabbits, fowl, and mountain goats (along with some predator enemies: bears, wolves, foxes, and coyotes). Fish, especially the lordly salmon, splashed in their streams.

The Nez Perce were mighty hunters, and known for their strong bows. Most were fashioned of cherrywood or yew, but the best of them were made of the horns of the mountain sheep, which were boiled and bent and backed with layers of sinew. Other tribes traded their most precious goods for those bows.

When horses arrived in this northern region, the Nez Perce quickly became skilled riders, among the best in the land. Horses thrived on the high, abundant pastureland, and the Nez Perce learned to breed the animals for strength and beauty and fleetness.

They lived in a kind of democracy where individuals were respected. But their society wasn't perfect. The Nez Perce had enemies, and, although

It was the French who gave the Nez Perce their strange name. In French it is pronounced "nay pair-SAY," and it means "pierced nose." The French had seen a few Indians with bits of clamshell decorating their noses. It was a fashion of some West Coast tribes but not usually of these people.

In this photo taken around 1910, members of the Nez Perce tribe prepare for a ceremonial dance on a reservation in Washington State. ▼

Representatives of the Nez Perce meet with a railroad commissioner who wants their land. ▶

they loved peace, they fought frequently and captured slaves who then worked for them and had no say in their village affairs.

In late September of 1805, the explorers Lewis and Clark—who had been caught in a snowstorm and were near starving—stumbled into a Nez Perce camp. The Indians fed them and probably saved their lives.

The Nez Perce helped trappers and traders, and befriended those who were beginning to pass through their territory. Then gold was found on their land in 1860. Miners rushed in and settlers followed. It was the beginning of troubles. Some Nez Perce signed treaties to give up some of their land, but others wouldn't sign any treaties.

President Grant tried to set aside a section of land "as a reservation for the roaming Nez Perce Indians." Settlers were not allowed on that land. But that didn't stop the miners and homesteaders. They defied the president. They moved onto the land.

One of the "no-treaty" tribes was led by a man most Americans called Chief Joseph. His real name was *Hin-mah-too-yah-lat-kekht*, which means "Thunder Rolling in the Mountains." Joseph told his people to be patient. He didn't want to fight the white settlers.

In 1876, the U.S. government sent three commissioners to meet with Chief Joseph. They wanted to persuade him to move from his land to another reservation. Joseph was 36 years old. No matter how the government commissioners pleaded, Joseph would not agree to move. "We love the land," he said. "It is our home."

Understand me fully with reference to my affection for the land. I never said the land was mine to do with it as I chose. The one who has the right to dispose of it is the one who has created it. I claim a right to live on my land, and accord you the privilege to live on yours.

—Chief Joseph

But the Nez Perce had no choice; the newcomers had great power. The Indians were to be forced onto a reservation. The commissioners had no patience. The Indians must go, and quickly, they said, even though the weather was bad. One frustrated, angry young Indian, whose father had been murdered by white settlers, killed some of the white men. Now the whites had a reason to call the Indians savages. Now they could attack.

When they were attacked, the Nez Perce fought. The first battle began when Indians, carrying a white flag of truce, approached the soldiers. A shot rang out and the Indians returned the fire. The fight, which was unexpected, was brief: 34 troopers died, and no Indians. The fleeing soldiers dropped their weapons—63 rifles and many pistols. It was a bonanza for the Indians. But they were few in number and they knew that an alarm would go out. Other soldiers would soon be after them.

So they raced for the place where they thought they would be free. They raced for Canada. It turned out to be a thousand-mile journey. First one army, then another, and another, followed and fought them. Now Joseph proved to be strong as thunder. He led his small band brilliantly— although most were children and old people. They fought in their mountains, they fought in their valleys, they fought in their canyons, they fought on their plateaus. Everywhere they were outnumbered and outgunned. Over and over again they outwitted their pursuers. But they were fighting the telegraph as well as an army. Fresh troops were summoned by wire. Finally, just 30 miles from Canada, facing new soldiers, the Nez Perce were surrounded.

Chief Joseph spoke. Here is what he said:

I am tired of fighting. Our chiefs are killed.... The old men are dead.... The little children are freezing to death. My people, some of them, have run away to the hills, and have no blankets, no food; no one knows where they are...my heart is sick and sad. From where the sun now stands I will fight no more forever.

Chief Joseph, who always remembered what his father told him: "Stop your ears whenever you are asked to sign a treaty selling your home." ▼

▲ Chief Joseph

When Chief Joseph surrendered, in 1877, the Indian wars were, for the most part, over. For the next 13 years there were minor skirmishes. Wounded Knee, in 1890, was the very end.

If you want to learn more about the Indians of the West and about the Indian wars (and heroism, too), read about Crazy Horse, Sitting Bull, Black Hawk, and Geronimo.

That day, promises were made to Chief Joseph, but they were never kept. In Washington, the government people did not know the great chief and the brave Nez Perce. Those who wanted Indian land told false stories. The Nez Perce Indians were sent to an empty plain; most sickened and died. Chief Joseph pleaded for justice. Here is some of what he said:

All men were made by the same Great Spirit Chief. They are all brothers. The earth is the mother of all people, and all people should have equal rights upon it. You might as well expect the rivers to run backward as that any man who was born a free man should be contented when penned up and denied liberty to go where he pleases.

Are you reading this quickly? Well, don't do that. These are great words. They are worth rereading. They are worth memorizing.

We only ask an even chance to live as other men live. We ask to be recognized as men. We ask that the same law shall work alike on all men. If the Indian breaks the law, punish him by the law. If the white man breaks the law, punish him also. Let me be a free man— free to travel, free to stop, free to work, free to trade where I choose, free to choose my own teachers, free to follow the religion of my fathers, free to think and talk and act for myself—and I will obey every law, or submit to the penalty.

Here are more of his words:

Whenever the white man treats the Indian as they treat each other, then we will have no more wars. We shall all be alike—brother of one father and one mother, with one sky above us and one country around us, and one government for all.

The time would come, as Chief Joseph wished, when there was one government and equal rights for all men and women of every color and background. Chief Joseph's words would help bring that time. But it would be too late for most of the Nez Perce.

When Chief Joseph died on September 21, 1904, the doctor at the Colville Indian reservation in Washington State listed the cause of death as "a broken heart."

A Villain, a Dreamer, a Cartoonist

Do you ever worry about air pollution or about dishonest politicians? Well, so did people in the 19th century.

Just to reassure you—most politicians are honest and most air is clean. But that is no reason to relax. There are people around who will mess up the world if we let them.

One of the worst, in the years after the Civil War, was a man named William Marcy Tweed. He was called "Boss" Tweed and he ran New York City's political machine. Political machines were unofficial governments that existed alongside the real city governments; each had its own functions. Machines thrived in many 19th-century cities. In New York, Tammany Hall was the most powerful of all the urban political machines. Insiders had their own name for Tammany; it was "the Tiger." That beast did some good—actually quite a bit of good—especially for immigrants who needed help getting started in America—but it was all at a price.

Tammany paid people to vote—sometimes a dozen times each. And bribery? Well, the Tiger bribed the police, the elected officials, anyone who would take money.

New York had problems—big problems—especially problems of air pollution and traffic congestion. Some 700,000 people lived in New York, most of them squeezed into a small area near the tip of Manhattan Island. Much of the city's business took place around a famous street called Broadway. Trying to walk or take a horsedrawn bus down Broadway was a nightmare. There were so many people it sometimes took an hour just to move a few yards. And talk about pollution—whew—hold your nose while I tell you about it.

New York was home to more than 100,000 horses. Now, a healthy horse dumps a whole lot of manure each day. Imagine all that smelly manure spread around by wheels and feet. When the manure dries, it turns into

Artist Thomas Nast's original caption for this Boss Tweed cartoon read, "Well, what are you going to do about it?" ▼

▲ A traffic jam on lower Broadway in New York City, ca. 1895

powder that blows in your face and goes up your nostrils. But that isn't the worst of it. In the 19th century, people and businesses could burn anything they wanted. Mostly that was coal, which puts black fumes in the air. Even worse, Standard Oil had a New York refinery. Oil refineries, without controls, give off terrible, noxious fumes. That oil refinery was a big polluter. Hold on, that's not all. When Boss Tweed controlled New York there wasn't much in the way of sanitary services. So people often dumped their garbage in the streets. Garbage smells—especially in August. Are you choking? Well, I still haven't mentioned the pigs. Pigs ran about eating garbage and leaving their own smells and dumplings. And then there were flies, and disease. But you may have heard enough.

There you are in the middle of Broadway, and you want to get away. You climb on a horsedrawn bus. It sways back and forth so violently that some passengers get seasick. You try walking. But there are no street lights (they haven't been invented yet). Horses, people, buses, and carriages are all pushing and shoving on Broadway. Pedestrians often get killed in traffic accidents. Have you had enough of the good old days? So had a lot of people in the 19th century. The politicians said that soot in the air was a sign of modern progress, but most people were beginning to gasp for fresh air.

Fresh air was the last thing that Boss Tweed cared about. He was a scoundrel—a real bad guy who controlled most of the city's jobs and services. He used his power to get money for himself. He bribed others and forced them to do as he wished. Here is an example of the way he worked. A new city courthouse was to be built; Boss Tweed became the contractor and charged the city three or four times what the building actually cost. He put the difference in his pocket. Then he filled the building with $50 sofas and charged the city $5,000 for each. How did he get away with that? Well, he was charming—in a scoundrelly way—so he fooled people. Many citizens didn't realize he was stealing from them. And because he was so powerful, those who did know were afraid to do anything about it.

Who's the Boss?

William Marcy Tweed was called "Boss" Tweed because that was exactly what he was: the boss. He wasn't elected to run New York, but he did it anyway. He was actually a city alderman. (An alderman is a member of a city legislative body.) He was never mayor. It didn't matter. He controlled the New York State Democratic Party and the Tammany Hall political machine.

Tweed put graft (getting dishonest money) on a businesslike basis. All city contracts were padded by a fixed amount, which went to Tweed and his cronies. At the Tammany clubhouse, he slept in a bed with blue silk sheets. He sometimes entertained on his yacht, the *William M. Tweed*, which had a crew of 12, fancy furniture, and Oriental rugs. When Tweed went to jail, he was asked his occupation. He said, "Statesman."

▲ William M. "Boss" Tweed of Tammany Hall

Beach invented many things, and because of that he understood about patents. If you invent something, and you want to be sure that your idea is not stolen, it is necessary to register your idea with the patent office in Washington. As a patent lawyer, Beach helped many inventors with their patents.

Hydraulic means "water-powered"; *pneumatic* means "air-powered."

Except for a quiet, frail little man named Alfred Ely Beach. Beach was a genius—an inventor, a publisher, and a patent lawyer. He invented one of the world's first typewriters. When he was only 19, Beach took over a small magazine named *Scientific American* and helped make it the fine journal it is today. He became publisher of the *New York Sun* and it became an important newspaper.

But that isn't what this story is about. It is about Ely Beach's fight with Boss Tweed. Beach wanted to do something about the traffic congestion on New York's streets. He thought and thought and finally came up with the idea of putting a railroad train underground. He called it a subway. He knew Boss Tweed wouldn't let him build it—unless he agreed to give Tweed millions of dollars. And Beach was too honest a man to pay off a politician.

He decided to build a subway and not tell Tweed. He built it right under Broadway and hardly anyone knew he was doing it! He invented a hydraulic tunneling machine and a pneumatic subway. He got laborers to work at night and to haul dirt away in wagons with wheels muffled so they wouldn't make noise. It took 58 nights of secret work to get the tunnel done.

In February 1870, a group of New York newspaper reporters were invited to a reception. They were surprised when they were led underground into a beautiful, large waiting room. Paintings hung on bright walls, a pianist played at a grand piano, a fountain splashed, and goldfish swam in a giant tank. Beach had done it! His subway

Alfred Ely Beach's New York pneumatic subway, ca. 1870: the subway's blower sucked air in from a grating on the street. If you were standing near the grating when the fan sucked, your hat came off; if you were there when it blew, the street garbage flew up and hit your ankles. ▶

was ready. The reporters all took a ride in a cylinder-shaped wooden car. The car had handsome upholstered seats, fine woodwork, and gas lamps. It fit tight—like a bullet in a rifle—and moved down tracks inside a round brick underground tube. It went right under Broadway, under all the pollution and traffic.

What made it move? A giant fan blew it 371 feet. There the subway car stopped and tripped a wire; that made the fan reverse itself, and that sucked the subway car back.

Beach saw his subway as a model for a grand subway he had planned. It would carry 20,000 passengers a day and go for five miles—to Central Park, he said—at a speed of a mile a minute. A mile a minute? Nothing had ever gone that fast.

Boss Tweed was outraged! He controlled all the streetcars in the city. This was a threat to his power. He must have pounded his diamond-ringed fingers. He got in touch with the governor—*his* governor (he'd bribed and bought him).

What happened is a long and complicated story, and I can't tell it all here. People flocked to Beach's little subway; they rode back and forth under Broadway. Beach gave the subway's profits to charity. The state legislature passed a bill allowing Beach to build the grand subway. Tweed's governor vetoed it. Beach worked hard, talking to congressmen, and a second subway bill was passed. Governor John T. Hoffman vetoed it again.

Finally, the newspapers began writing editorials telling the truth about Boss Tweed. A cartoonist—named Thomas Nast—drew funny cartoons that showed Tweed as the wicked man that he was. Tweed threatened Nast. "I don't care what the papers write about me—my constituents can't read," said Tweed, "but, damn it, they can see pictures!" When threats didn't work, Boss Tweed offered Thomas Nast half a million dollars to stop drawing his cartoons. Nast kept drawing. Now people were getting angry about Boss Tweed. Most New Yorkers just hadn't known what he'd been doing.

> *Constituents* are the people a politician represents.

Tweed was arrested and charged with fraud. He had lied, stolen, and cheated. He was sent to jail. William Marcy Tweed died in jail at age 55. So much for that bad guy.

> *Fraud* is deception and swindling.

The state legislature finally passed a third Beach transit bill. But by this time Alfred Ely Beach was a tired man. The stock market was in trouble. It was hard to raise money. Beach no longer had the energy,

▲ Thomas Nast's cartoon depicts Boss Tweed's downfall in the New York City and state elections of 1871.

or the money, to build his grand subway. The subway under Broadway was closed and sealed up.

Beach concentrated on publishing and helping others. Inventors loved him. One day Thomas Edison brought a talking box to him. Beach turned a handle on the box. *Good morning, sir,* said the machine. *How are you? How do you like my talking box?*

Beach spent what money he had left on others. He founded an institute in Savannah, Georgia, to give free schooling to former slaves. He taught himself Spanish and founded a scientific magazine in that language. At age 69 he died quietly of pneumonia, loved and respected by those who knew him.

When the city of New York finally built a subway in 1904, workers tunneling under Broadway were startled to come upon a grand reception room and a small, elegant, wood-paneled subway. Today, scientists say a jet-powered subway in a vacuum tube could whoosh people across the country at amazing speeds. They call it a new idea. Alfred Ely Beach had something like that in mind more than 100 years ago.

Honest Graft?

George Washington Plunkitt, a member of Tammany Hall, and a New York state senator, liked to talk about "honest graft." A journalist named William Riordan called Plunkitt "Tammany's philosopher," and took down some of his words:

> Everybody is talkin' these days about Tammany men growin' rich on graft, but no body thinks of drawin' the distinction between honest graft and dishonest graft. There's all the difference in the world between the two…
>
> There's honest graft, and I'm an example of how it works. I might sum up the whole thing by sayin': "I seen my opportunities and I took 'em."
>
> "Just let me explain by examples. My party's in power in the city, and it's goin' to undertake a lot of public improvements. Well, I'm tipped off, say, that they're going to lay out a new park at a certain place.
>
> I see my opportunity and I take it. I go to that place and I buy up all the land I can in the neighborhood. Then the board of this or that makes its plan public, and there is a rush to get my land, which nobody cared particular for before.
>
> Ain't it perfectly honest to charge a good price and make a profit on my investment and foresight? Of course it is. Well, that's honest graft.

Today, Plunkitt's kind of "honest" graft will get you in jail. It's not fair for public officials to take advantage of their knowledge of government business to make a profit.

Phineas Taylor Barnum

Phineas Taylor Barnum was probably the most successful showman America has ever had. He had a knack for fooling people and for taking their money. Barnum called himself "the Prince of Humbug," and a humbug is a hoax or an impostor. Barnum is supposed to have said about the people who fell for his jokes: "There's a sucker born every minute."

P. T. Barnum's American Museum was the biggest tourist attraction in New York. It featured a collection of stuffed animals, a family of trained fleas, and a "real" mermaid.

Since most Americans couldn't get to New York to the American Museum, Barnum took his showmanship and laughter around the country. He built a circus—the Barnum and Bailey Circus. He called it "The Greatest Show on Earth," and it was. At P. T. Barnum's three-ring circus, there was no way to get bored. He built a circus so large that 20,000 people could sit under one big tent. Then he took his circus out to towns across America.

When the circus came it was the biggest event of the year—especially for children. The circus would unload at the railroad tracks and march through town in a big parade of clowns, musicians, and trapeze artists, as well as horses, camels, elephants, lions, and tigers, all decorated with ribbons, sparkles, and banners.

The star of Barnum's circus was an elephant whose name was Mumbo Jumbo—but everyone just called him Jumbo. Jumbo, who was said to be the largest elephant in captivity, was more than 11 feet tall. He also happened to be sweet as a lamb. Jumbo captured the heart of the nation. Then he was hit by a train. Grown people wept. Children wept. Barnum never found another elephant to match Jumbo.

P. T. Barnum got rich and built himself a fantastic home with pagoda-like wings and Gothic turrets. But there was a serious side to Barnum. He became a congressman and was a strong supporter of equal rights and of the 14th Amendment (which, as you know, made the laws equal for everyone of every color).

Barnum lived in a time when some big businessmen—called "robber barons" (after wicked nobles in medieval England who fought each other and plundered everybody else)—acted as if they owned the country, and they practically did. It was also a time when some people—called "reformers"—tried to make the country better. Barnum fit the age in which he lived—he combined its extremes: an obsession with money and a desire to do good. But most people in America after the Civil War needed to laugh. Barnum let them laugh at others and especially at themselves.

▲ Barnum and Bailey advertise a side show as part of the "Greatest Show on Earth."

CHAPTER 9

Huck, Tom, and Friends

Some people say that Mark Twain's book *Adventures of Huckleberry Finn* is the best book ever written in America. And they may be right. No question, it is very good reading. So are *The Adventures of Tom Sawyer, The Prince and the Pauper, Pudd'nhead Wilson,* "The Celebrated Jumping Frog of Calaveras County," and his other books and stories.

Twain was like a storybook character himself. When he was an old man and had bushy white hair and a bushy white mustache, he dressed in a rumpled white suit and went around the country telling stories and jokes. People came from far away just to hear him. He had a wry sense of humor and you never quite knew if he was telling the truth or pulling your leg.

"When I was young," he said, "I remembered everything about my life whether it happened or not." Actually, when he was young he had the kind of adventures that boys had in a Mississippi River town, and later he put most of them into his books.

Mark Twain's real name was Samuel Langhorne Clemens. Sam Clemens grew up in Hannibal, Missouri, a town on the banks of the wide Mississippi River. Back then, Hannibal was a sleepy place until a riverboat appeared. Then the town came to life. All the boys

A scene from Mark Twain's *The Adventures of Tom Sawyer*—here, Tom convinces other boys to whitewash a fence for him. ▼

Samuel Langhorne Clemens, known as Mark Twain ▶

◀ Riverboats at night churn the waters of the Mississippi River. The mighty river plays an important role in Mark Twain's *Huckleberry Finn*.

in Hannibal wanted to be riverboat pilots when they grew up. Sam became one—for a while. Riverboats sometimes got stuck in shallow water. It was important that the pilot know the depth of the water. The call *mark, twain,* meant water two fathoms (12 feet) deep. That was safe water.

In Hannibal, young Sam Clemens was apprenticed to a printer. The printer was his brother. Sam gave his brother a hard time. But he did learn about the printing trade, and he began to write—mostly humorous stories. Then he caught the wandering bug and drifted around the country. Later, he traveled to the Middle East and other faraway places, and wrote about what he saw and heard there. But, before that, he tried to be a prospector and find silver in Nevada, where some people were striking it rich. He never hit a lode of ore, but he did find a subject for his pen—the mining camps—and he turned them into a book called *Roughing It.*

Then he was off for San Francisco, where he got a job as a newspaper reporter; there he wrote a story about a jumping frog, and it helped make him famous.

California was a freewheeling place in those just-after-the-war years. Cattle ranching and fruit growing were replacing mining as a source of income. And Nevada's silver, pouring in from the fabulous

In *Roughing It,* Mark Twain wrote about the mining camps of Nevada. Here, miners push ore carts through the tunnels of the Gould & Curry Mine in Virginia City, Nevada. ▶

Comstock lode, was making San Francisco rich. That city was the literary capital of the West; it was a good place for a young writer to be.

Mark Twain had a way of writing that made people chuckle and then realize that he really had something serious to say. And what he kept saying was that this land of America was pretty terrific, but that its promise—to offer freedom and opportunity to all—was not being met. There was unfairness in the land, like the unfairness of segregation and child labor. Americans were becoming too concerned with making money: the nation was forgetting its ideals.

Mark Twain and his writer friend Charles Dudley Warner named the years after the Civil War the "Gilded Age," a name inspired by a verse from Shakespeare, which says that "to gild refined gold…is wasteful and ridiculous excess."

Twain believed he lived in a time of "ridiculous excess." He was right. In the after-the-Civil-War years, there was a lot of glitter and gaudiness. People were making money and spending it on show-off things.

When Twain wrote *Huckleberry Finn* he created two heroes: a slave, Jim, and a boy, Huck, who were both searching for freedom. It is a funny book and an adventure story, too, but really it is about the wonder of simple things: of friendship, of a great river, and of the wish to be free.

Gilded Age Excess

Cornelius Vanderbilt, a railroad tycoon and one of the world's richest men, died in 1877. Vanderbilt's Fifth Avenue mansion was fancier than most kings' palaces. At Newport, Rhode Island, Cornelius Vanderbilt's grandson William lived in a sumptuous summer "cottage" with 70 rooms. At one of his parties, each guest was given a silver bucket and shovel to dig for rubies and diamonds buried in a sandbox in the middle of the dining-room table.

Huckleberry Finn changed the direction of American literature. Huck Finn's voice is the voice of a real American boy as it might have been heard in a 19th-century Missouri town. Here is how the book begins:

> *You don't know me, without you have read a book by the name of* The Adventures of Tom Sawyer, *but that ain't no matter. That book was made by Mr. Mark Twain and he told the truth, mainly. There was things which he stretched, but mainly he told the truth.*

A great 20th-century Amercan writer, Ernest Hemingway, said, "All modern American literature comes from one book by Mark Twain called *Huckleberry Finn*. There was nothing before. There has been nothing as good since."

Sam Clemens spent his boyhood in the antebellum (before the Civil War) times. After the war people liked to think of those years as uncomplicated and idyllic (which means charmingly simple), which wasn't quite true. If there had been no problems, there would have been no war. But for a boy in a river town it seemed a mighty good time.

That Missouri boy grew to be a famous man and one of the best writers this country has ever produced. Mark Twain's writing made him rich, but he never got fancy ideas or forgot where he came from. He seemed to have the whole country tucked into the pockets of his white suit. Maybe it was because he'd been everywhere, from Hawaii to Connecticut. Or maybe it was his youthful, questioning, homespun vitality that surprised and delighted people. Even when he was an old man—and looked like a polar bear—he could still think like a child, which isn't a bad thing. He wrote of the world honestly, directly, and with a lot of humor. He didn't ignore bad things, not at all; sometimes he could get downright heavy about them; but, mostly, he made us Americans think about who we are and what we want to be.

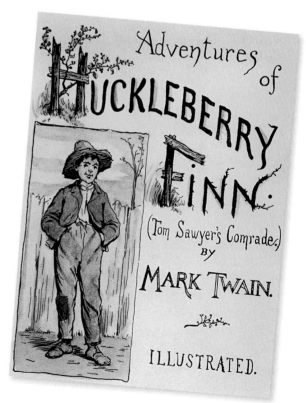

The cover of the original 1885 edition of Mark Twain's *Adventures of Huckleberry Finn* ▶

Some Words from Mark Twain

It's better to keep your mouth shut and appear stupid than to open it and remove all doubt.

Nothing so much needs reforming as other people's habits.

Put all your eggs in one basket and—watch that basket.

Always do right. This will gratify some people and astonish the rest.

Immigrants Speak

Back in 1608—not long after the first settlers arrived in Jamestown—John Smith wrote to his bosses in the London Company and told them the kind of settlers to send to America:

> *When you send again I entreat you rather send but thirty carpenters, husbandmen, gardeners, fishermen, blacksmiths, masons, and diggers up of trees, roots, well provided; than a thousand of such as we have: for except we be able both to lodge them, and feed them, the most will consume with want of necessaries before they can be made good for anything.*

During the 19th century, the kind of people John Smith wanted—working people who could build and farm and invent—came to America in ship after ship after ship. And just in time; with all the new technology there was plenty for them to do. They were needed to work in the new factories, to settle land, and to invent things. Immigrants did all that.

Germans made up the largest single group of 19th-century immigrants. Carl Schurz was one of them, and he went, with remarkable speed, from immigrant to national leader. Here are Schurz's own words telling his story:

German immigrants in Hamburg crowd onto a steamer, bound for New York. ▼

> *It is one of the earliest recollections of my boyhood.... One of our neighboring families was moving far away across a great water, and it was said that they would never again return. And I saw silent tears trickling down weather-beaten cheeks, and the hands of rough peasants firmly pressing each other, and some of the men and women hardly able to speak when they nodded to one another a last farewell. At last the train started into motion, they gave three cheers for America, and then in the first gray dawn of the morning I saw them wending their way over the hill until they disappeared in the shadow of the forest. And I heard many a man say, how happy he would be if he could go with them to that great and free country, where a man could be himself.*

Carl continued:

That was the first time that I heard of America, and my childish imagination took possession of a land covered partly with majestic trees, partly with flowery prairies, immeasurable to the eye, and intersected with large rivers and broad lakes—a land where everybody could do what he thought best, and where nobody need be poor, because everybody was free.

Schurz fought in a freedom movement in Germany (in 1848), but, when the freedom fighters lost, he was in trouble and had to flee to Switzerland. Then, being uncommonly brave, he went back into Germany to help his college professor escape from jail. But he knew if he stayed in Germany, he, too, would be jailed. Schurz was 23, and he set out for the land of freedom.

When Schurz arrived in America, before the Civil War, he found that some people weren't free. He wasn't the kind of person who kept quiet about something he thought was wrong. After all, he'd been a freedom fighter. He hated slavery, and he spoke out and said so. He reminded people that there was no freedom of speech in the slave states. Without free speech, said Schurz, no one is free, neither slave nor master.

In his new country Carl Schurz found the opportunity he had dreamed of in Europe. He studied law, moved to Missouri, and became active in politics. Just 10 years after he arrived in the United States, President Abraham Lincoln named him American minister to Spain. But he soon came home to serve as a general in the Union army. He became a newspaper correspondent, an editor, a U.S. senator from Missouri, and secretary of the interior. He was a public official who talked of conservation of the wilderness and fairness to Indians when hardly anyone else thought of those things.

Like so many other immigrants, Carl Schurz had fallen in love with the ideals of the Declaration of Independence and the guarantees of the Constitution.

▲ Carl Schurz, who emigrated from Germany, became an American army officer, politician, and reformer.

▲ Young immigrant boys who work during the day attend an evening class for all nationalities at the Washington School in Boston, Massachusetts.

Next to the Germans, the Irish were the largest immigrant group. Before the Civil War, one-fourth of the whole population of Ireland came to America. (That was 1.7 million Irish men, women, and children.) They kept coming, during and after the war. The Irish were desperate because in Ireland crops had failed, especially the potato crop. There was a famine. More than 1 million people died of starvation in Ireland. The Irish spoke an ancient language called Gaelic (GAY-lick), although most were bilingual: they could speak English, too.

Many other immigrants didn't know a word of English. But America's free public schools, which developed in the 19th century, soon taught their children to speak the language. People were now coming from countries that had not sent many people to America before: countries such as Russia, Italy, Poland, Denmark, Sweden, and Hungary.

The population of Europe doubled between 1750 and 1850. All those extra people needed food, homes, and jobs—and there just didn't seem to be enough of them in Europe. Many Europeans came to America to find work and to avoid hunger.

Others came for religious freedom. Religious dissenters came from Holland, and Jews (who were often persecuted for their beliefs) came from Germany, Poland, and Russia. Still others came to escape political wars that were leaving parts of Europe in turmoil.

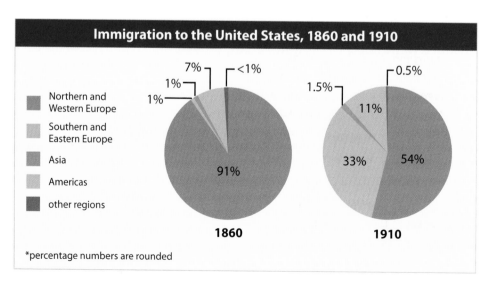

Immigration to the United States, 1860 and 1910

- Northern and Western Europe
- Southern and Eastern Europe
- Asia
- Americas
- other regions

1860: 7%, 1%, 1%, <1%, 91%

1910: 1.5%, 0.5%, 11%, 33%, 54%

*percentage numbers are rounded

In the half century after the Civil War, some 26 million immigrants arrived in the United States. Think about that—26 million is a whole lot of people. Many of the newcomers began life in the cities—in overcrowded apartment buildings called "tenements." Sometimes eight families shared one bathroom. (City codes make that illegal today.)

Mary in the Promised Land

Mary Antin ▶

Mary Antin was born in 1881 in a region of Russia called "the Pale of Settlement." Most Russian Jews were forced to live there. They could not hold public office or open businesses, and they were taxed more heavily than Christians. Mary had a good mind, and she loved to read, but the schools in Russia were closed to most Jews. When her father got sick, and then her mother, the family became very poor and had hardly enough to eat.

Between 1860 and 1890, some 10 million Europeans came to the United States. Mary's family made the journey. None of them had ever seen the ocean, or been beyond the Pale, or heard English spoken. It was a difficult journey on a crowded ship.

Later, Mary wrote about her early experiences in America. She recalled walking along a city street that first night:

So many lamps, and they burned until morning, my father said, and so people did not need to carry lanterns. In America, then, everything was free, as we had heard in Russia. Light was free; the streets were as bright as a synagogue on a holy day....

Education was free. That subject my father had written about repeatedly, as comprising his chief hope for us children, the essence of American opportunity, the treasure that no thief could touch, not even misfortune or poverty. It was the one thing

that he was able to promise us...; surer, safer than bread or shelter. On our second day I was thrilled with the realization of what this freedom of education meant. A little girl from across the alley came and offered to conduct us to school. My father was out, but we five between us had a few words of English by this time. We knew the world "school." We understood. This child, who had never seen us till yesterday, who could not pronounce our names, who was much better dressed than we, was able to offer us the freedom of the schools of Boston!... The doors stood open for every one of us.

Mary Antin became the best student in her elementary school. When she grew up she wrote her autobiography and called it *The Promised Land*. In it she wrote of her adopted nation's priceless heritage—the freedom and opportunity that let even the poorest immigrant, like herself, become rich in learning.

▲ Immigrants arrive in New York City, on their way to be examined at Castle Garden.

Imagine that you are a 19th-century immigrant. (Maybe some of your ancestors were.) You don't know the English language, and everything in this land seems different and strange. At school almost everyone speaks English. How do you like it here?

Most of the immigrants knew very little about America except that it was a land of freedom. But that's what they wanted: freedom and a chance to work.

They came on steamships. If they were poor, they were crowded into belowdecks areas called the "hold" or "steerage." It wasn't pleasant down there, but the trip cost $30 and now took just 10 days. Most of the immigrants came into New York Harbor, to a place called Castle Garden, and after 1892 to Ellis Island (where the early Dutch settlers had picnicked). There they were checked before they could enter the United States. If they had a disease, or if the papers they brought from their former country were not right, they might be sent back where they came from. So they were frightened when they arrived.

Bianca de Carli sailed from Italy. Conditions for poor people in Italy were awful (especially on the island of Sicily). Bianca wrote about how she felt when she arrived at Ellis Island:

A thousand times during the last day or two I put my hands on my passport and papers which I kept wrapped in a handkerchief under the front of my dress. This was just to make sure they were still there.

One of my companions said, "Signora, you are very foolish! When you keep your hand inside your dress…you are telling everyone that your papers and money are there! Maybe a bad person will see. Take your hands away."

Now, years later, I know it was foolish and silly, but we heard so many stories about others who were turned back because their papers were not in order.…

Jacob Riis was a boy who sailed from Denmark. He had read books about America, and he thought he knew something about the country. What he had read in Denmark were cowboy books. He expected to find buffaloes and cowboys in New York.

Later he said he was surprised to find New York "paved, and lighted with electric lights, and quite as civilized as Copenhagen."

Riis was very poor for his first seven years in America. Then he got a job as a newspaper reporter and wrote about the difficulties of life for the poor in America's cities. He learned photography. Most photographers took pictures of beautiful scenery or prosperous people. No one was taking pictures of the poor. Riis did. He showed exactly how some people had to live. His books helped get laws passed that made things better. Jacob Riis and Carl Schurz were reformers (and they knew each other). Some Americans, who had been in this country for a long time, had forgotten the nation's founding ideals. But the immigrants had come here to find freedom and opportunity in a land that said *all men are created equal*. They cherished America's ideals.

"Equality of rights…is the great moral element of true democracy," wrote Carl Schurz, who understood exactly what that means. Do you?

Jacob Riis, an immigrant from Denmark, became a New York reporter who used photography to promote reform by exposing the miserable conditions endured by the city's poor. This photo from 1901 shows children seeking warmth by sleeping on a steam grate from an underground newspaper press room. ▼

Lady Liberty

It was June 1885, and workmen prepared to unload 214 wooden cases. They held the body of Lady Liberty—the Statue of Liberty. She was a gift from the people of France to the people of America. She was 151 feet from tip to toe, weighed 225 tons, had a waist 35 feet thick, and could hold 40 people in her head. She was about to become a *metaphor* (MET-uh-for)—a symbol, something that represents something other than itself. She soon came to represent two things: the spirit of freedom and America's policy of welcome to people from around the world.

Where and how was she conceived? It happened in France, at a dinner party in 1865. Edouard de Laboulaye (luh-boo-LAY), the scholarly host, was talking about liberty and America. His guests talked with pride about the French hero of the American Revolution, the Marquis de Lafayette, and about the long friendship of America and France.

▲ The unveiling of the Statue of Liberty on Liberty Island in New York Harbor in 1886

Laboulaye wanted to create a symbol of liberty for the whole world to admire. Among the guests at his dinner party was a young sculptor named Frédéric Bartholdi. Laboulaye encouraged him to visit the United States. Bartholdi did. He went to Newport, Pittsburgh, Chicago, St. Louis, Denver, Salt Lake City, Sacramento, San Francisco, and Niagara Falls. "Everything is big here," he wrote to Laboulaye, "even the green peas."

When he sailed into New York, Bartholdi was struck by the beauty and openness of its harbor. He saw it as a symbol of the openness of America. In the harbor he found a small island—Bedloe's Island—and he knew almost at once that this was where he wanted his statue to stand. By now he had a great statue in his mind. Bartholdi was not only an artist of amazing imagination but also a great publicist. As he toured America, he sold the idea of his statue to everyone, from President Grant on down.

Bartholdi's huge statue would be an expensive project. The liberty-loving French people pitched in. Ordinary people gave small amounts of money, and so many gave that soon those small amounts added up to a large amount.

To build a huge statue that would stand unprotected in a harbor, an engineering genius was needed. Enter Gustave Eiffel. (He would soon build a famous tower in Paris.) Eiffel designed a skeleton of iron bars. It was flexible enough to bend with the wind, and strong enough to support the giant lady and the people who would climb up inside her body. The lady's skin was to be made of delicate sheets of copper.

When Liberty was finished she needed a place to stand. No pedestal had been built on Bedloe's Island, and there was little money and little interest—or so it seemed—for the project in America. What was needed was another kind of genius, one who could tell the story of Lady Liberty

Emma Lazarus ▼

▲ Joseph Pulitzer

A 10-year-old sent "my pocket-piece—20 cents in silver."

Pulitzer made the statue a patriotic cause. All across America, people began to respond. Some gave things besides money. A group of artists and writers gave their work to be auctioned to raise money for the statue. Mark Twain was one of them. A 34-year-old woman named Emma Lazarus was another.

Her ancestors had come to the United States in the 17th century. They were Jews fleeing religious oppression in Europe. That was many generations before her time. But beginning in 1879, Emma Lazarus heard about the *pogroms* that were sweeping Russia. Pogroms were mob attacks on Jews. Thousands of Jewish men, women, and children were killed; thousands more were coming to America.

All of that made Emma Lazarus think about liberty and religious freedom. So she wrote a poem about what the Statue of Liberty meant to her. She called the poem "The New Colossus." What she didn't know, and never learned during her short life (she died at age 38), was that her words would help give the statue a second meaning. It became not only a statue to celebrate liberty but also a symbol of America's policy of welcome—its "golden door"—its unusual decision to embrace people of all colors, races, and religions.

The last five lines of Lazarus's poem are engraved on the pedestal of the statue. Millions of immigrants sailing into New York Harbor have been welcomed by those words:

Give me your tired, your poor,
Your huddled masses yearning to breathe free,
The wretched refuse of your teeming shore.
Send these, the homeless, tempest-tost to me.
I lift my lamp beside the golden door!

and make people listen. America just happened to have that kind of genius. His name was Joseph Pulitzer.

Pulitzer had come to the United States from Hungary when he was 17. He fought in the Civil War and then settled in St. Louis, Missouri, where he became a reporter for a German-language newspaper. He arrived in America speaking only German and Hungarian, but he soon learned English. He created a great newspaper, the *St. Louis Post-Dispatch,* and then went to New York and bought the *New York World,* which he turned into a reform-minded, crusading newspaper. He accused the wealthy and powerful of being greedy. When he discovered that the wealthy citizens of New York would not give money to build a pedestal for the Statue of Liberty, he wrote: "Let us not wait for the millionaires to give this money. Let us hear from the people."

Pulitzer announced that anyone who donated money—any amount—would have his or her name printed in the paper. A girl named Jane sent 50 cents. "I am only a poor sewing girl," she wrote.

More About Immigrants

The immigrants knew the Declaration of Independence well. It was part of what inspired them to come to America. Most of them knew these words by heart: *We hold these truths to be self-evident: that all men are created equal, that they are endowed by their Creator with certain unalienable rights, that among these are Life, Liberty and the pursuit of Happiness.*

Many Americans whose families had been here longer knew those words, too, and believed them and lived by them. But, people being people, there were some who were selfish, or confused, or ignorant, and they ignored that message of fairness.

Some Americans didn't want newcomers in the country, and—this may surprise you—some of the newcomers, as soon as they got settled, didn't want any other immigrants to come. Usually the newest immigrants were poor, and willing to work hard and for less money than those who had arrived earlier. So some people wanted to stop immigration because they feared competition for jobs.

Immigrant children at the Mott Street Industrial School in New York City stand to salute the flag. ▶

In 1890, Jacob Riis photographed these workers making neckties in a tenement workshop in New York City.

There were other reasons. Because the newcomers were poor and couldn't speak the language, they needed extra help in school. That cost money—tax money. The cities where many newcomers lived were overcrowded and filled with crime, so there was a need for extra police and extra city services. That cost money—tax money. Some people said, "Why should we have to pay for the problems of those poor people?"

They didn't stop to think that the newcomers were often doing jobs no one else wanted to do—washing dishes, or digging ditches, or building railroads. They could not foresee that the sons and daughters of poor immigrants would become some of the most productive citizens any country has ever known. This nation of ours was still young and had a lot of growing up to do. And growing up means making mistakes and learning. Americans made some big mistakes.

There was one mistake that was hateful, hurtful, awful. It was the mistake of prejudice. Some Americans faced discrimination—sometimes vicious discrimination—because they were Catholic, Jewish, black, Irish, or Asian.

One group of prejudiced people actually formed a political party. Officially it was named the American Party, but most people called it the "Know-Nothing Party." The Know-Nothings were anti-Catholic and antiforeign. They even managed to destroy a stone block sent from Rome by the pope. It was intended as part of the Washington Monument.

The Ku Klux Klan began in Pulaski, Tennessee, as a social club for Civil War veterans. It soon changed its focus. The KKK became dedicated to the idea of white supremacy. White-robed Klansmen, riding out at night, used terror tactics to intimidate blacks and whites who believed in Reconstruction.

Another group of haters, the Ku Klux Klan, was anti-black and anti-Semitic (which means they hated Jews). On the West Coast, the Workingmen's Party had as its slogan THE CHINESE MUST GO. Its members hated Asians.

Between 1849 (when gold was discovered in California) and 1882, about 300,000 Chinese emigrated to America. In 1882 there were just over 50 million people in the United States, so 300,000 was a small percentage of the total, but that didn't matter to the haters.

Like many other immigrants, the Chinese were coming to the United States to make money. American workers wanted high wages to work in the fields or build railroads. Some employers discovered that Chinese men were willing to work for one dollar a day. Now that doesn't sound like much, and it wasn't, but in China times were hard. You had to work several days to earn as much as a dollar—when you could find a job. If a Chinese man came to America and saved $500, he could go home and be prosperous. If he saved $1,000 he went home very rich. Some Chinese did just that. But many found life difficult in America. So the Chinese, too, began asking for more than one dollar a day.

Then some employers sent boats to Japan and got Japanese workers to come and work for low wages. When the Japanese started asking for more money, the employers sent boats to India.

Some said that the employers were exploiting the workers—taking advantage of them. But the process worked both ways. When the Asians took their earnings and went home, they were exploiting the land of opportunity. Many immigrants to the East Coast did that, too. They came, worked hard, saved money, and went back to Greece, or Italy, or Poland—where their American earnings made them seem rich.

It was all right. America had opportunities to share. Besides, most took more than money back to their old worlds. They took American ideas with

During the California Gold Rush, many Chinese immigrants came to the United States. ▼

◀ A drawing from the 1880s shows Chinese immigrants working at a salmon cannery in Oregon.

them, too. Ideas of individual dignity, of liberty, and of a government founded to help people pursue happiness. Almost everyone understood those ideals—and they also understood that, although there were haters and bad apples around, most people were good. So people from China kept coming to the land they called the Golden Mountain—as long as they could.

The Chinese come from an ancient, proud civilization. A Chinese philosopher named K'ung-fu-tzu (Confucius), who lived from 551 to 479 B.C.E., taught ideas about honesty, fairness, and loyalty that were similar to the ideas most Americans believed in. He also taught about the need for balance in life: between work and pleasure, between consideration of oneself and consideration of others. This led the Chinese to respect learning (especially the study of the past and its lessons), and to have strong family ties.

Now you might think they would be welcomed when they arrived in California, especially since they came seeking opportunity (which meant jobs). The same reason brought others to California, too.

But in the 1860s and '70s, when times were difficult in China, it happened that they were difficult in the United States, too. There was a depression, and during depressions there usually aren't enough jobs to go around. Since the Chinese were willing to work hard for very low wages, they usually found work. That angered many white workingmen. Mobs attacked and killed Chinese people; hoodlums burned Chinese homes and laundries.

In economic terms, a *depression* is a time when the nation's economy goes into drastic decline and there is much unemployment, low prices, and not much business activity.

Little boys in San Francisco's Chinatown walk in single file, holding each other's pigtails, which in 1900 was the traditional way of wearing hair for Chinese boys and men. ▼

▲ In 1877, workers in San Francisco demonstrate against Chinese workers who were willing to work for lower wages.

The Workingmen's Party demanded a law to end Chinese immigration. Congressmen in the East, needing political support from Californians, helped pass that law. Most Americans on the East Coast didn't know any Chinese. They had heard terrible—and untrue—stories of Asians; many people believed the stories because they didn't know any better.

Most Chinese men braided their hair into a long pigtail. That seemed strange to people who weren't Chinese. Prejudice against those who look different from you is *racism*. Racism is found in almost every nation in the world, and it always leads to evil action. In 1882, American racists got a Chinese Exclusion Act passed. It stopped most Chinese immigration into the United States. It was an especially unfair act considering that it came after Chinese had toiled and died to build railroads and dig mines and labor on farms. Asian immigration was restricted until the 1950s.

One Good Idea, One Bad

Have you ever had two ideas at the same time—one good, one not so good? Well, nations are no different from people. That idea that *all men are created equal* was fighting it out with an idea that some people called *nativism* and others called *racism*. In the 1880s, some people were saying this was a nation where everyone was welcome and would be treated equally. Others, such as nativists in California, were burning Chinese homes and businesses and attacking Chinese people. Actually, racism has a nasty history in nations all around the world.

Going to Court

Around the mid-1880s, San Francisco had 320 laundries. Most of the laundries—240 of them—were owned by citizens of China.

Why were there so many laundries? Why did the Chinese own most of them? Why were the Chinese citizens of China and not of the United States? Here are some answers.

The first had to do with sexism. California had a large male population. It was mostly men who had come to California to dig gold. Traditionally, in Europe and America, women were expected to wash clothes. Most American men would not wash their own clothes! But Chinese men were willing to wash clothes, and it took very little money to open a laundry.

According to the Constitution, anyone born in the United States is a citizen—no matter where he or she comes from. So why didn't the Chinese become citizens of the United States? A law passed back in 1790 said that only white people could become

Even today, many countries do not let people of other ethnic backgrounds become citizens. In the 19th and 20th centuries Americans struggled with the idea of citizenship. What makes a citizen? Were women citizens? The freedom and openness of the United States was unusual. It still is. Most 19th-century people thought that made our country special—but some people didn't like the idea at all.

◀ Chinese immigrants in San Francisco's Chinatown, ca. 1895

A scary scene in Denver, Colorado, in 1880: The Chinese were willing to work for low wages. One employer said, "I find this difference: the Chinaman will stay and work, but the white man, as soon as he gets a few dollars, will leave." ▶

A person born in another country—and who then comes here, takes out citizenship papers, and becomes a citizen—is a *naturalized* citizen.

Ordinance is another word for a law, usually a local law.

naturalized citizens. The law had been aimed at African-born persons. As it turned out, that old law was applied only to Asians.

But that wasn't enough for the racists. They got mean-spirited laws passed to try and put the Chinese launderers out of business. A San Francisco ordinance said that all laundries must be placed in brick buildings. The law seemed to make sense. Laundries used fires to heat water, and a fire could spread rapidly in a city where the houses and stores, mostly built of wood, were crowded together. But then fire was used to heat and cook in almost every building in the city. Of the 320 laundries in San Francisco, 310 were in wooden buildings. The sheriff, a man named Hopkins, arrested almost all the Chinese owners of laundries. He arrested only one of the white laundry owners. (That laundry was owned by a woman. What kind of prejudice was that?!) Sheriff Hopkins did not bother the 79 white men who ran laundries.

The Chinese laundry owners went on trial and were convicted and fined. If they didn't pay the fines they were sent to jail. Their businesses were closed. Was there anything they could do? Remember, they weren't citizens. One of the men Sheriff Hopkins arrested was the owner of the Yick Wo Laundry. The fire wardens had inspected the Yick Wo Laundry and certified that it was "in good condition."

If you decide to be a lawyer, and you go to law school, you will probably study the case of *Yick Wo v. Hopkins.*

Here is something the lawbooks won't tell you. There never was a Yick Wo. Sheriff Hopkins made a mistake. He assumed that the man who owned the Yick Wo Laundry was named Yick Wo. Actually, his name was Lee Yick.

We don't know much about Lee Yick, except that he came to California in 1861 and operated a laundry for 22 years. We also know that he was willing to fight for his rights. But what were his rights? He wasn't a citizen. Did he have the same rights as if he had been an American citizen? No one was sure.

After he was arrested, in 1886, Lee Yick went to the other Chinese launderers. He persuaded them to help him hire a good lawyer. If he could get the verdict in his case changed, it would affect them all. They *appealed* his case. Do you know what that means?

Here is an explanation of what an appeal is and a basic idea of how our judicial system works. It may come in handy; most people go to court at some time in their lives.

To begin, there are two kinds of law cases: *civil* and *criminal.* Suppose you buy an expensive bicycle, take it home, and it isn't what you expected. You feel cheated. The bike dealer doesn't agree. He thinks you got just what you paid for. He won't take the bike back. If you can't settle the argument, you can go to court. You can sue the bike seller. It will be a *civil* case. No criminal laws have been broken. It will probably be a judge who decides who is right—you or the bike dealer.

However, in most cases, civil or criminal, you have a right to a *jury trial.* A *jury* is a group of citizens—ordinary people—who listen to the evidence and decide what happened. They decide if someone is wrong, or guilty of breaking a law. Then, in civil cases, the jury decides on the penalty. In criminal cases, if a person is convicted, the judge usually decides on the proper penalty.

> The jury decides on the facts of the case; the judge decides what law applies to the case.

The *Yick Wo* case was a criminal case; it was about a San Francisco law. The case began in a local—San Francisco—court. (We have local, state, and federal courts.) Lee Yick was the *defendant*—the person on trial. The other side—the San Francisco authorities—were prosecuting the case. They were the *prosecutors.*

The judge and jury heard arguments by lawyers from both sides. They called *witnesses*: people who had information about the case.

▲ This drawing from the 1880s depicts the justices of the United States Supreme Court hearing a case.

Lee Yick's lawyer called the safety inspectors. But the law was clear—and, as you know, the San Francisco jury said that the Chinese launderers had broken the law. Lee Yick had to pay a fine or go to jail.

After a decision is made, a case may be *appealed* to a higher court. Lee Yick's lawyer appealed. The case went to the California Supreme Court.

Appeals courts do not hear witnesses. They do not have juries. They aren't like the courts you see on TV. The job of the appeals court is to review the lawyers' arguments and see if the law has been applied properly in the lower court. The appeals court asks: *Has justice been served?*

The California Supreme Court agreed with the lower court. It said the decision in *Yick Wo v. Hopkins* was correct. The Chinese laundries were in wooden buildings, and wooden laundries were illegal.

You can imagine how Lee Yick and his friends felt. They still thought the city of San Francisco was being unfair. White laundry

In a criminal case, the prosecution may not appeal if it loses. No person may be tried twice for the same crime. That is called *double jeopardy*, and we don't have to worry about it in this country.

owners were running laundries in wooden buildings. Why was the city picking on Chinese laundrymen? Lee Yick decided to take his case to the highest appeals court of all—the U.S. Supreme Court.

The Supreme Court doesn't listen to all the cases that people want it to hear. It couldn't possibly do that. It selects cases carefully. It tries to pick cases that will test important issues, especially constitutional issues.

There were two issues in this case. The first was this: Do the police have the right to enforce a law *arbitrarily*? (ar-bih-TRARE-ih-ly—it means "inconsistently"; not the same way to everybody, every time.)

The second issue had to do with the rights of noncitizens. Should the law treat *aliens* (people who aren't citizens) the same way that it treats American citizens?

This was an important case. Police departments in many states were interested. They didn't want their power limited. They wanted the power to treat aliens (those noncitizens) as they wished. *Briefs*—which are written legal arguments—were presented to the Supreme Court by Nebraska, Iowa, Indiana, Mississippi, New Jersey, Wisconsin, and Florida. They were all in support of Sheriff Hopkins. Can you guess what happened?

The sheriff and the states lost the argument. The Chinese laundrymen beat them. This is what the Supreme Court said:

> *For no legitimate reason this body by its action has declared that it is lawful for 80-odd persons who are not subjects of China to wash clothes for hire in [wood] frame buildings, but unlawful for all subjects of China to do the same thing.*

It was a law applied "with an evil eye and an unequal hand." That, said the justices, was wrong. And, said the court:

> *The 14th Amendment to the Constitution is not confined to the protection of citizens. It says: "Nor shall any state deprive any person of life, liberty, or property, without due process of law; nor deny to any person within its jurisdiction the equal protection of the laws."*

Within its jurisdiction: that means that all persons in the United States, citizens or not, are entitled to the same fair treatment. Lee Yick and his friends had won a momentous victory.

Tea in Wyoming

Everyone knows about the Boston Tea Party, but have you heard of the Wyoming Tea Party? Well, in Wyoming the tea actually got served, along with cakes and cookies—and all was delicious. The day was pleasant, and the conversation lively, when Esther Morris got to the point of the tea party.

Esther Morris always got to the point. Everyone expected it of her. She was gracious, very intelligent, and dependable—her two guests thought highly of her; so did most people in South Pass City. And, with its 3,000 inhabitants (mostly miners), South Pass City was the largest town in the Wyoming territory.

Esther Morris grew up in Oswego, New York, became an orphan at age 13, learned to make hats, and earned a living as a milliner (a ladies' hatmaker). Then, when her husband decided to go west in search of gold, she went with him. Esther was so capable that she was asked to be justice of the peace. She took the job and became—so it is said—the world's first woman justice of the peace.

Now, back to the tea party. Esther's guests were the two candidates for the Wyoming legislature—a Democrat and a Republican. (She wasn't going to take any chances; she wanted to cover both parties.) She asked each of them to promise, if he was elected, to introduce a bill into the legislature giving women the vote in Wyoming. This was in 1869; no women, anywhere, had the right to vote.

But, as I said, the tea was delicious and Esther Morris was persuasive. The candidates both agreed. When Colonel William H. Bright, the Democrat, got elected, he kept his word. He introduced the bill and got it through the Wyoming Senate. Suddenly, people got wind of what was happening. The women's suffrage bill still had to pass in the Wyoming House

Esther Hobart Morris worked for passage of the law that made Wyoming the first territory or state in the United States to grant women equal rights with men. ▶

◀ Women voting at the polls in Cheyenne, Wyoming, in the presidential election of 1888

of Representatives, and then the governor had to sign it. Now there was a lot of debate and hoopla; it didn't go easily—but it happened.

On November 9, 1869, the legislature passed *An Act to Grant to the Women of the Wyoming Territory the Right of Suffrage and to Hold Office.* Now there was another worry. Would the governor veto the bill? He was a Republican and all the other officeholders were Democrats. Some thought he would. But Governor John Campbell had attended a women's suffrage convention back in Salem, Ohio, he'd heard Susan B. Anthony speak, and she made sense to him. He didn't veto the bill. Wyoming's women could vote!

Just what would happen when women went to the polls? No one knew. A newspaper reporter, writing in the *Laramie Boomerang*, quoted a mythical railroad man who said of women's suffrage, "It's a kind of wild train on a single track, and we've got to keep our eyes peeled or we'll get into the ditch.... Female suffrage changes the management of the whole line.... We can't tell when Wyoming Territory may be sidetracked with a lot of female conductors and superintendents and a posse of giddy girls at the brakes." Some eastern newspapers made fun of women and of the West. They drew cartoons of tough, cigar-smoking female cowboys lassoing their males. But when Election Day came, 70-year-old Louisa Ann Swain put a clean apron over her dress, walked to the polls, and became the first woman to cast a ballot in a public election. A voting official wrote, "No rum was sold, women rode to the polls in carriages furnished by the two parties, and every man was straining himself to be a gentleman because there were votes at stake."

Eighteen years later, when Wyoming was about to become a state, some U.S. congressmen objected to its tradition of female suffrage. A group of women was afraid that this objection might keep Wyoming from becoming a state. They telegraphed the Wyoming representative in the nation's capital: DROP US IF YOU MUST. WE CAN TRUST THE MEN OF WYOMING TO ENFRANCHISE US AFTER OUR TERRITORY BECOMES A STATE. But the men of Wyoming wouldn't go along with that idea. They telegraphed the same representative: WE MAY STAY OUT OF THE UNION A HUNDRED YEARS, BUT WE WILL COME IN WITH OUR WOMEN. And they did.

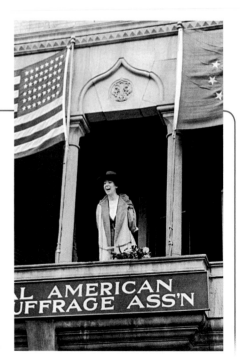

Women in Colorado, Idaho, and Utah all had the vote by 1900. In 1894, Colorado's Clara Cressingham, Carrie C. Holly, and Frances S. Klock became the first women elected to a state legislature. In 1917, Jeannette Rankin, from Montana, was the first woman elected to the U.S. Congress. And, in 1925, Nellie Taylor Ross became the first female governor when she took office in Cheyenne, Wyoming.

Jeannette Rankin ▶

Are You a Citizen If You Can't Vote?

CHAPTER 14

"The best women I know do not want to vote," said Horace Greeley, who was an important newspaperman and politician.

Oh my. The woman he was saying this to was Susan B. Anthony, a tall, rawboned Quaker who had spent much of her life trying to get the vote for women.

Best women, indeed! *Foolish women*, thought Susan Anthony.

So she went to see President Ulysses S. Grant, who had an intelligent wife, named Julia. Grant believed that women could be postmasters, and had named 5,000 women to that job. "Isn't that enough?" he asked Susan Anthony.

No, it wasn't enough. What she wanted was "justice, not favors."

The vote for women was a hot issue. Grant was running for reelection. Suffrage for black men came first, he said. Women would have to wait. Besides, many sensible people thought women's suffrage would be the end of the family. A husband might vote Republican and a wife Democratic. Could a marriage survive that kind of thing?

No one knew for sure, but it sounded ominous.

▲ Susan B. Anthony worked tirelessly for women's suffrage. In our time she has been honored by the Susan B. Anthony dollar, first minted in 1979.

We Don't Want the Vote

Some women were against female suffrage. Mildred Rutherford, who was president of the Georgia United Daughters of the Confederacy, supported the National Association Opposed to Woman Suffrage. This is what she had to say:

The women who are working for this measure are striking at the principle for which their fathers fought during the Civil War. Woman's suffrage comes from the North and the West and from women who do not believe in states' rights and who wish to see negro women using the ballot. I do not believe the state of Georgia has sunk so low that her good men cannot legislate for women. If this time ever comes then it will be time for women to claim the ballot.

Suffragists Susan B. Anthony, Amelia Bloomer, and Elizabeth Cady Stanton believed that *all* citizens should have the right to vote. ▶

▲ Sojourner Truth

But not to people like Susan B. Anthony, Elizabeth Cady Stanton, Lucy Stone, Sojourner Truth, and others who knew that a woman without a vote was not a full citizen.

Those women had worked hard to abolish slavery. They believed that abolition went hand in hand with women's rights. But many male abolitionists—like Horace Greeley—were ignoring women's rights. The women felt betrayed.

The 15th Amendment said:

The right of the citizens of the United States to vote shall not be denied or abridged by the United States or by any state, on account of race, color, or previous condition of servitude.

Anthony and Stanton, who were the nation's leading women's rights leaders, wanted the new amendment to read "race, color, *sex,* or...." But even sympathetic congressmen said that the amendment would be difficult enough to get passed as it was.

The 15th Amendment was ratified in 1869 and became law in 1870. Now the question was: Who was a citizen? Were women citizens?

As you know, it wasn't a question at all in the territory of Wyoming. Of course women were citizens! Few people in the West pretended that women were dependent on men.

But in the East it was hard to break old traditions. Women had never voted. There was something else, too. Many of the women reformers were working for *temperance* as well as the vote for women. (Temperance advocates wanted to put an end to the drinking of liquor.) Some men who might have encouraged women to vote were afraid that voting women would close their bars. They were probably right.

In 1874 the Women's Christian Temperance Union was founded to battle drunkenness. Women went into men-only saloons. Carry Nation went with a hatchet and did some chopping in those places. Carry, like Sojourner Truth, was a powerful, six-foot-tall woman. Men ran when they saw her coming.

But all that was beside the point to Susan Anthony, who believed, as the colonists had in 1775, in "no taxation without representation."

Women could be taxed, but they couldn't vote.

Women could be arrested, but they couldn't serve on a jury.

In 1871, in Washington, D.C., 72 women tried to vote and were turned away at the polls.

That same year three women in Nyack, New York, and one woman in Detroit, Michigan, did vote. The *New York Times* wrote in an editorial, "No evil results followed."

Susan B. Anthony, in Rochester, New York, did a lot of thinking about the 15th Amendment. It said that all citizens could vote.

Anthony visited a friend, lawyer Henry R. Selden. He had been a judge on the New York Supreme Court.

Was she a citizen? Could she vote? she asked. Selden thought the answer to those questions was *yes*.

That was all Susan B. Anthony needed to hear. It was November 1, 1872. She and 15 other women marched to a barbershop in Rochester's Eighth Ward. Three men who sat there were registrars. Their job was to register voters. They were stunned by the women's request. The women wanted to be registered to vote.

The next day the newspaper was full of the story. So were newspapers in other parts of the nation. Mostly the newspapers disapproved. "Lawbreakers" were what the women were called.

But on voting day, November 5, the 16 women were at the polls at 7 a.m. When they voted, that big news went by telegraph from Maine to Florida to California to Washington.

Carry Nation, ax in hand, ready for saloon-smashing, fought for temperance. ▼

◄ This 1874 cartoon shows temperance supporters armored like medieval knights. The picture was captioned "Woman's Holy War."

Twenty-three days later, on Thanksgiving Day, a tall deputy marshal knocked on Susan B. Anthony's door. He looked uncomfortable and stammered a bit. "Miss Anthony," he said, "I have come to arrest you." He had a warrant in his pocket. It said she had broken an act of Congress.

That day the other 15 women voters were also arrested. They were brought to court.

Anthony was asked if she had gone "into this matter for the purpose of testing the question."

"Yes, sir; I had resolved for three years to vote," she answered.

She was ordered to appear before a grand jury. The three men who had registered the women were arrested for registering and accepting ballots unlawfully.

The government decided to prosecute Susan B. Anthony alone—she would represent the 16 women. The three men would all be tried. It was January. The trials were set for June. They had six months to prepare.

The judge may not have realized the kind of woman Anthony was (or perhaps he did and that was why he was afraid to let her vote). She was a fighter and unafraid. She used those six months well. She spoke in all of Rochester's districts. She talked about the Constitution and natural rights. She used Thomas Jefferson's word, *unalienable*.

Law and the Ladies

Myra Colby Bradwell passed the Illinois bar exam. That proved she knew what a lawyer was required to know. But it was 1869 and the Illinois Supreme Court said she could not practice law because she was a woman. Bradwell took her case to the U.S. Supreme Court. That court agreed with Illinois (in 1873), declaring, "The paramount destiny and mission of women are to fulfill the noble and benign offices of wife and mother. This is the law of the Creator."

Belva Ann Lockwood studied law at the National University Law School, but she didn't get a diploma. (It was all right for women to study, but not to hold jobs where they might compete with men.) She wrote a letter to President Ulysses S. Grant: "I wish to say to you that I have been passed through the curriculum of study…and am entitled to, and demand my Diploma." Whew! Belva Lockwood was allowed to practice law. Three years later, Lockwood was told she couldn't argue a case before the Supreme Court. She lobbied Congress, got a bill passed, and became the first woman admitted to practice before the highest Court. Belva Lockwood ran for president as a candidate of the National Equal Rights Party in 1884 and again in 1888.

▲ Belva Lockwood became the first woman admitted to practice before the U.S. Supreme Court.

Rights were not something that governments owned and gave out to people, she explained. They belong to each of us. People are born with rights. Governments are formed to protect those rights.

She called them "God-given rights."

She also talked about the "hateful oligarchy of sex." By which she meant the rule of men over women. Half the people were ruled by the other half, she said.

"*We the people* does not mean *We the male citizens*," she said. And, she added, it was "downright mockery to talk to women of their enjoyment of the blessings of liberty."

The Rochester judge did not agree. But he was smart enough to know that most people in Rochester were being swayed by Susan Anthony's speeches. So he had the trial moved to a little town 28 miles away. Twenty-eight miles was a good distance in horse-and-buggy days.

When the day came, the courtroom was packed. A former president, Millard Fillmore, was one of the spectators. Newspaper reporters sat with their pencils sharpened.

Judge Ward Hunt was a foe of women's rights. He wouldn't let Susan Anthony speak for herself. He judged her "incompetent."

Anthony's friend, lawyer Henry Selden, said, "Every citizen has a right to take part upon equal terms with every other citizen." And, he said, "Political bondage equals slavery."

Judge Hunt turned to the jurors. "Under the 15th Amendment... Miss Anthony was not protected in a right to vote.... Therefore I direct that you find a verdict of guilty."

Now that was something no judge has the right to do. Judges can tell a jury about the law. They can't tell juries how to vote.

The clerk of the court said to the jury, "You say you find the defendant guilty, so say you all?"

No juror said a word.

Judge Hunt said, "Gentlemen of the jury [of course, there were no women], you are dismissed."

The judge ruled Susan B. Anthony guilty. Not a juror had spoken. Most were outraged.

Now the issue was no longer the vote for women. It was an issue of a free trial in a free society. This trial had been a joke.

Anthony's lawyer reminded the court of Matthew Lyon, who had been imprisoned and fined for saying bad things about President

Susan B. Anthony wrote about her trial for years afterward. ▶

John Adams. (That was during the time of the Alien and Sedition acts, when free speech had been in trouble. Later, the court apologized, and Matthew Lyon's fine was paid back, with interest, to his heirs.) That didn't matter to the judge. Susan B. Anthony and the three men were fined and sentenced to jail.

The *New York Sun* wrote of a "jury of twelve wooden [figures] moved by a string pulled by the hand of a judge." A Utica, New York, paper said Judge Hunt had "outraged the rights of Susan B. Anthony" (even though the paper's editor didn't think that women should vote). Another newspaper said, "The right to a trial by jury includes the right to a free and impartial verdict."

Susan B. Anthony refused to pay her fine, and Judge Hunt, perhaps knowing he had gone too far, never demanded it. She did not go to jail. No appeal was ever heard by a higher court.

The three male registrars spent five days in jail. They didn't mind it a bit. While they were there they ate fancy meals sent by the 16 women they had registered. Then President Ulysses S. Grant pardoned them. At the next election, Rochester's male voters reelected them by a large vote. But Susan Anthony, and America's women, lost out. If she had won that court case, in 1873, women all over the nation would have been able to vote. The word *citizen* in the 15th Amendment could have been interpreted to mean "men and women citizens."

Judge Hunt decided things otherwise. At the time, many men, and women, too, believed he was right. It would take much work—by Susan B. Anthony and others—to change their thinking. It would take another amendment (the 19th) before women had the rights of full citizens.

Some Remarkable Women

Anna J. Cooper ▶

▲ Clara Barton

Helen Keller ▶

Clara Barton established the American Red Cross.

Alice Hamilton was the first woman professor at Harvard Medical School.

Anna J. Cooper, born in North Carolina to a former slave, earned a master's degree at Oberlin College and a doctorate at the Sorbonne in France. She became principal of Dunbar High School in Washington, D.C., and made it one of the finest schools in the nation.

Otelia Cromwell, another descendant of slaves, earned her Ph.D. at Yale after attending Smith College and Columbia University. She became a teacher and writer.

Charlotte Perkins Gilman wrote books that made women question many of their old ideas.

Helen Keller proved there are no handicaps to a person of determination and intelligence. Helen, who was born in 1880 in Tuscumbia, Alabama, lost both her hearing and her sight at 19 months after a fever left her unconscious. Most people thought she was beyond hope, but 60 years earlier another blind deaf girl, Laura Bridgman, had been taught to read with raised letter books (called Braille), so Helen's parents decided to look for a teacher for Helen. When they found Annie Sullivan they gave their daughter someone who would transform her life. At first Keller, who was seven, tried all her bad-girl tricks on Sullivan. But Annie Sullivan was patient, and Helen was very bright. She learned to read Braille, and she also learned to write using standard letters.

Helen Keller attended Radcliffe, a very demanding woman's college. Annie Sullivan went with her, finger spelling the professors' words into Helen's hand. Together they studied English literature, history, math, French, Latin, and Greek. Helen Keller went on to write books, give speeches, and travel widely. Everywhere she went she inspired others. One admirer said she showed "the almost indomitable power of the human will."

One Hundred Candles

Our nation's founders knew they were doing something never done before. They were making a nation based on self-government. They called it the "consent of the governed." Back then—at our birth in 1776, when the delegates to the Second Continental Congress signed the Declaration of Independence—people had little time to celebrate. They had to figure out how to fight Great Britain and win that independence.

But now it is 1876 and things are different. The experiment seems to be working. The nation has fought a terrible civil war—and become stronger for it. Americans are proud of themselves. The country is thriving. So everyone is excited by plans for a national birthday party; it will last for six months and be called the Centennial Exposition. This exposition is being held in a big park near Philadelphia; 200 buildings are needed to hold all the displays and activities.

A *centennial* is a 100th anniversary. An *exposition* is an exhibition, often a big, public one.

Let's climb into a time capsule and join the party. In 1776 Philadelphia was tense; now it is mighty excited. America has never seen anything like this exposition. Philadelphia is all decked out in red, white, and blue. WELCOME TO THE CENTENNIAL, says a huge banner.

Eighteen-seventy-six is a big year. Out West the Sioux Indians win a victory at the battle of the Little Bighorn. It will turn out to be their last big win. For the American Indians the battle is almost over. They have lost control of most of their land.

The most popular building at the 1876 Centennial Exposition was Machinery Hall. It showcased state-of-the-art industrial technology of the time. ▼

Ten million people will come to the Centennial before it closes. An article in the *Chicago Tribune* says: "Come at all events, if you have to live for six months on bread and water to make up for the expense." People come from all 38 states and from foreign countries, too. Most are astounded by what they see.

Machinery Hall, the most popular building, is 13 acres big. And that is small compared to the main exhibition hall—said to be the world's largest building—which covers 35 acres. The Woman's Building

is almost as large as a football field. The very idea of a building showing women's accomplishments is an indication of changes that may be ahead. Philadelphia's Mrs. E. D. Gillespie—who happens to be Benjamin Franklin's great-granddaughter—has been one of the most effective workers in promoting this Centennial. She has spoken before Congress and personally raised more money, through women's organizations, than any state (except New York and Pennsylvania). "The women of the whole country," says Mrs. Gillespie, "were working not only from patriotic motives, but with the hope that through this Exhibition their own abilities would be recognized and their works carried beyond needles and threads."

The Woman's Building is filled with women's inventions and artistry (and some needle- and threadwork). One woman demonstrates a woman-designed darning machine; another shows a life-preserving mattress. A newspaper, the *New Century for Women*, is printed while visitors watch. But the most popular exhibit in the Woman's Building is a sculpture of a beautiful girl done in butter.

For a nickel you can ride around the Centennial grounds on a small railroad. What do you see? George Washington's coat, vest, and pants. A tropical garden under the glass roof of Horticulture Hall. The 40-foot-long arm and torch of the Statue of Liberty perched on top of a souvenir stand (this was before Lady Liberty took her place in New York's harbor). Real-looking artificial teeth. A gorgeous white hearse. Fancy coaches. Locomotives. Ben Franklin's printing press. A liberty bell made from tobacco. And the Capitol dome built of apples.

Iowa has sent samples of its soil as well as its farm produce. From Norway there are magnificent furs; from Egypt, saddles and mummies; and from Germany, the biggest and deadliest steel guns ever built.

> On the Fourth of July in 1876, America's leading women reformers, Elizabeth Cady Stanton and Susan B. Anthony, read the Declaration of the Rights of Women at the Centennial. Many people—some women as well as men—laughed at them.

One exhibit at the 1876 Centennial Exposition featured the arm and torch that would later become part of the Statue of Liberty. ▶

Henry Corliss's huge steam engine, the world's largest, highlighted the technological achievements of the day. A noted author, William Dean Howells, marveled at "its vast and silent grandeur." ▶

The Centennial buildings have towers, domes, statues, banners, and flags. Some glass buildings seem just like crystal palaces. A fountain holds a marble sculpture of an Indian girl named Minnehaha, bronze dolphins, a lion's head, and marble basins to catch the splashing water. It is beautiful.

Are you hungry? You can eat a fancy meal or fill up on hot dogs, lemonade, hot roast potatoes, corn on the cob, popcorn, and ice cream. But don't eat too much—you might fall asleep, and you won't want to miss the carnival rides, or the toy displays, or the inventions.

People line up to see the new inventions. There are typewriters, hundreds of sewing machines, a newspaper press that prints and folds 15,000 news sheets in an hour, wallpaper printing machines, washing machines, and even machines to make machines. The technology is so amazing that some people say there is nothing left to invent.

The biggest hit of all is George Henry Corliss's colossal steam engine—the world's largest machine. It looms 40 feet high in Machinery Hall. Steam from the Corliss engine turns wheels; those wheels pull belts strung overhead; and the belts make 8,000 smaller machines work. President Grant sets the big steam engine going.

Just about everyone who enters Machinery Hall lines up to try a new gadget called a *telephone*. They say you can talk into the telephone and actually be heard in another room. When the emperor of Brazil visits the Centennial he puts his ear to it and cries out, "My God, it speaks." The *New York Tribune* calls it a "curious device," and asks, "Of what use is such an invention?" The newspaper answers its own question, "Some lover might wish to pop the question into the ear of a lady and hear for himself her reply, though miles away; it is not for us to guess how courtships will be carried on in the 20th century."

Shall we tell these people what telephones will soon do? Better not. Let them find out for themselves.

The telephone is Alexander Graham Bell's invention. Bell, a Scottish immigrant, now a professor at Boston University, was working with the hard of hearing and the deaf when he built a device that let people see speech

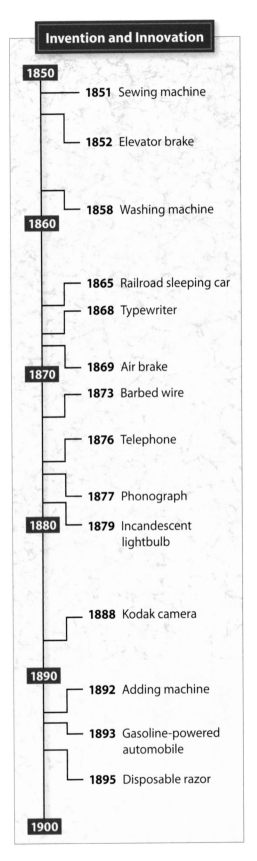

Invention and Innovation

1850
— **1851** Sewing machine
— **1852** Elevator brake
— **1858** Washing machine
1860
— **1865** Railroad sleeping car
— **1868** Typewriter
— **1869** Air brake
1870
— **1873** Barbed wire
— **1876** Telephone
— **1877** Phonograph
— **1879** Incandescent lightbulb
1880
— **1888** Kodak camera
1890
— **1892** Adding machine
— **1893** Gasoline-powered automobile
— **1895** Disposable razor
1900

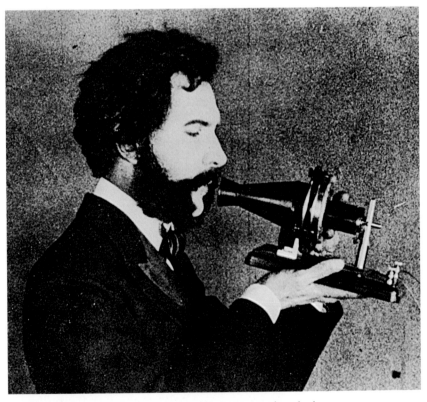

▲ Alexander Graham Bell demonstrated his invention, the telephone, to the public for the first time at the Centennial Exposition.

in the form of sound-wave vibrations. That made Bell believe that sound waves could be turned into electrical current and then back again into sound waves. He was right. But he had to study electricity and conduct experiments to make it happen. He tried many experiments. Finally—just two months before this Centennial opened—he did it. He made the sound waves of his voice travel over a wire.

America is producing practical scientists: inventors who can turn ideas into products that make the world easier to manage. We are patenting inventions at an amazing rate.

Soon there will be electric lights, record players, moving pictures, cameras, automobiles, airplanes, and more—much more.

How Were Things in 1876?

During the Centennial, everyone enjoyed the party, but how about the serious questions? What had the United States accomplished in its first 100 years? How were things going?

Pretty well, thank you.

We were a free country with a constitution all the world envied. We had survived a terrible civil war and ended the horror of slavery. We had grown from 2.5 million citizens in 1776 to 46 million in 1876. Our exports (goods sent out of the nation) were greater than our imports (goods brought from other lands). That was a big change from the days when most manufactured things came from England. We were becoming a world industrial power. Still, our nation had problems, large problems, especially with that idea of fairness for everyone. The gap is growing between rich and poor. While some people starve, others have so much money they do nothing much but show off.

Even though some Americans feel the country belongs to the rich and powerful, most are optimistic and confident. The middle class—those people not rich or poor—is growing large in America and living better than any middle class in all of history. They believe in progress. They feel their problems can be solved. And they are eager to do what Thomas Jefferson suggested: pursue happiness.

Two women in their homes illustrate the widening gap between the rich and the poor in the late 1800s. ▶

The Wizard of Electricity

Sometimes disadvantages can be turned into advantages. Thomas Alva Edison had two big disadvantages: he had almost no schooling, and an accident made him deaf about the time of his 12th birthday.

Edison spent only a few months in school. His schoolteacher mother taught him some at home, but mostly he went to the library, got books, and taught himself. That ability to do things for himself helped him become the most successful inventor the world has ever known. Being deaf—or almost deaf—may have helped, too. It allowed him to concentrate without being distracted by conversation or sounds.

Thomas Edison was a lonely boy. He had a favorite science book and a chemistry set, and he tried experiments over and over. In addition, he was a tinkerer: he liked to see how things worked. He would take something apart and then put it back together. Usually when he put it back together he made it work better.

He was fascinated by the new telegraph machines. When he was 11 he made one of his own. He intended to send messages back and forth between his house and another. But he needed to find a source of power, and he needed money for equipment and experiments; his parents had none to give him. So Edison went to work on a train, selling candy and newspapers. Since he had extra time on the long ride, the train people let him put his chemistry set in the baggage car. That baggage car was his first laboratory.

One warm summer day Tom Edison was standing on the train platform while his train took on water and fuel; he noticed a small child toddling across the tracks. Then he saw a freight train coming down those tracks. Edison jumped from the platform, dashed in front of the train, and rescued the child.

A young Thomas Edison in his workshop—he was world famous by the time he was in his thirties. ▼

That action changed his life. The baby's father was a telegraph operator. He wanted to reward the brave 15-year-old candy seller. What could he do for him? "Teach me to be a telegraph operator," said Edison.

He soon learned Morse code and to send it rapidly. It was a useful skill. A good telegraph operator could work almost anywhere in the country. Edison got a job in Michigan; then he went to Boston, and then to New York. But he was soon bored just sending messages. His tinkering mind was at work; he thought he could improve the telegraph. So he invented a writing telegraph—a machine that wrote words, not just dots and dashes. He had other ideas, too. Western Union—the company that owned the telegraph system—asked him to sell his ideas. Edison figured they were worth about $3,000, but he told Western Union to set a price. When they offered $30,000, he was astounded! From that time on, Edison was a full-time inventor.

In 1876—that centennial year—he set up a laboratory in Menlo Park, New Jersey, with a team of gifted assistants. It was the world's first modern research laboratory. He called it an "invention factory." For the next five years he patented a new invention almost every month. He invented a motion-picture camera, and a projector; he built the first motion-picture studio (which was the beginning of the modern film industry). He invented a mimeograph (a type of copying machine), the storage battery, an electric locomotive, waxed paper, and composition brick. He discovered the movement of electrons in a vacuum—and that led others to radio and modern electronics. Edison patented more than 1,000 inventions before he died.

Edison's motion-picture camera and projector helped launch the modern film industry in the United States. ▼

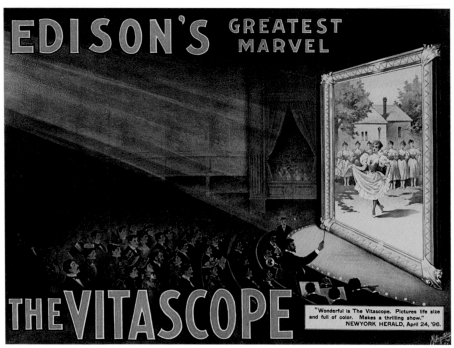

An early recording session with the Edison phonograph

One day Edison left a drawing on the bench of one of his assistants. At the bottom of the paper was a note. "Make this," it said. "What will it do?" asked the assistant. "It will talk back," said Edison. It did. The phonograph came from that drawing. (And that led to the tape and CD players that you listen to.) Edison's first phonograph machine had to be cranked by hand, and the first record was of a song that Edison sang himself: it was "Mary Had a Little Lamb."

The most famous of all Edison's inventions was the electric lightbulb. He didn't actually invent electric light. Others had been working on the problem. In 1859, Moses Farmer, in Salem, Massachusetts, had made two lamps with platinum filaments. Platinum is more expensive than gold. There was no way most people could afford light from that kind of bulb.

Edison announced he would take six weeks to develop a lightbulb that could be made inexpensively. Well, he was wrong. It took him a little more than a year.

Edison and his team at Menlo Park switch on their new electric lightbulb. ▼

The filament glows brightly in this replica of Edison's lightbulb. ▶

He knew that oxygen helps things burn, and he wanted his light to glow, not burn. The air would have to be pumped out of the bulb. And the glass should be clear, so the light would shine through. Edison hired a skilled glassblower to perfect a pear-shaped vacuum bulb.

Now he had to find a way for a *filament*—some kind of fiber, or something—to carry electricity, give off light, and last. He tried metals, papers, cork, and lemon peel. He plucked a hair from a friend's beard. He tested 6,000 vegetable fibers. Most of them fizzled or collapsed.

Finally he used a simple cotton thread made stiff with carbon. On October 21, 1879, Edison took some of that thread, put it in a glass bulb, pumped out the air, and turned on the current. The bulb "glowed like the setting sun in the dusk of early autumn," wrote one of his assistants. Edison and his staff sat down to wait. How long would the bulb glow?

They waited. And waited. Night came. In the morning the lamp was still glowing. The next night came. The bulb was burning as brightly as ever. That light shone for 45 hours. Edison had found what he sought; improving the bulb would be easy.

Edison was a practical genius. He had devised a lamp that would not only provide light but could be used by everyone. "We will make the lightbulb so cheap," he said, "only the rich will be able to burn candles." But lightbulbs are no good without sockets to plug them into, and light switches, and safety devices, and meters, and electric wiring, and dynamos to provide power. Edison invented some of those things and improved others. He turned the switch on the modern world of electricity.

Thomas Edison helped develop a long-lasting electric lightbulb that could be used by everyone. ▼

Edison wanted to electrify New York City. That meant laying wires under the ground. It meant building huge generators. It was an untried idea. It would be very expensive. Edison needed help. He needed money— a lot of money.

Grosvenor Porter Lowrey, a Wall Street lawyer who was fascinated by science, convinced bankers and wealthy individuals to finance Edison's schemes. Lowrey also helped to convince politicians to arrange for city rights—after all, Edison needed permission to dig up city streets and lay wires in order to take electricity from house to house.

On September 4, 1882, Thomas Edison stood in the offices of J. P. Morgan's New York banking firm. He pulled a switch. A few blocks away, six giant dynamos began to hum. Minutes later electric lights lit the bankers' offices and other parts of New York City.

Edison's inventive mind was soon hard at work on other projects. "Genius," said Thomas Alva Edison, "is 99 percent perspiration and one percent inspiration." Edison must have done a lot of perspiring. He slept only a few hours a day and expected those in his laboratory to keep up with him.

Edison was our most gifted and famous inventor—but, at the end of the 19th century, America seemed a land of inventors. In 1815, the U.S. Patent Office gave patents to 173 inventions. Between 1860 and 1890, the number was 440,400.

Tesla and the Battle of the Currents

In 1884 the brilliant Serbian-American inventor Nikolai Tesla came to the United States to work in Thomas Edison's New Jersey labs. It wasn't a happy collaboration; the colleagues soon became competitors. Tesla went head to head with Edison in what became known as the "battle of the currents."

When Edison set up his power distribution system to deliver electricity to part of New York City, he used direct current (DC). Direct current works in batteries but it's not easily transmitted over long distances. Tesla developed a system of motors and generators to transmit electricity in the form of alternating current (AC), which can travel over wires for hundreds of miles.

▲ Nikolai Tesla sits calmly in his laboratory as an apparatus generates a spectacular display of artificial lightning.

A wealthy industrialist named George Westinghouse bought Tesla's patents and proceeded to develop an AC power system using generators devised by Tesla. AC won the "battle of the currents"—today, when factory motors turn, or when you switch on a light, it's AC at work.

Tesla liked to give public lectures about the wonders of electricity. He would wow audiences by putting on dazzling electrical displays with sparks flying from his fingertips. While he became famous as a showman, he was in fact a serious inventor whose work helped make possible the readily available electrical power we now take for granted.

Jim Crow—What a Fool!

Jim Crow wasn't real. He was the name of a character in a song—a song about a black man who sang and danced and never gave anyone any trouble.

> *Wheel about, turn about, dance jest so—*
> *Every time I wheel about I shout Jim Crow.*

The Jim Crow character was well-known on the stages of the North. Later, offstage, his name came to stand for an evil policy—the policy of separation of the races, also known as segregation.

Before the Civil War, the North had something the South didn't have. It had segregation. In the North, the races were separated—not by law, but by habit. Usually blacks (and Indians and Asians) were not welcome in white hotels, restaurants, schools, or theaters. They could not get good jobs. The name for that policy of segregation became *Jim Crow*. Jim—that old fool dancer—sang and danced and acted as if he was content with things as they were, but he was crying on the inside.

In the antebellum South there was slavery but not segregation. Whites were the masters, but whites and blacks often lived and worked together. (This is a little tricky; be sure you understand it.) In the South blacks and whites often had close ties. Although it may seem strange to us now, some slaves and slave owners liked each other.

No Forty Acres, and No Mule

The former slaves expected to be given free land with their freedom. There was a rumor, and it was widely believed, that they would each get "forty acres and a mule." After all, African Americans had worked for nothing for generations. Thaddeus Stevens and the Radical Republicans tried to see that black people got land. But it didn't happen. Blacks got freedom—and poverty.

Former slaves got hard work but not land. ▶

◀ During Reconstruction, many black families struggled in poverty.

After the Civil War, things stayed much the same in the North. Segregation by habit continued. In the South nothing was the same. Remember, Reconstruction was a time of confusion, change, and experiment.

Here's a quick review of what happened to the newly freed men and women during Reconstruction. At first the Southern states passed terrible *black codes* that practically made black people slaves again. Then Congress sent army troops south; some Northern abolitionists went with them. Years of congressional Reconstruction followed: many blacks got a chance to go to school, to vote, and to hold public office.

A one-room school house for African American students ▼

Some white Southerners didn't seem to want a fair interracial society. Some did. Most were confused. For blacks, Reconstruction began as a time of hope. But conditions were terrible in the South. The war had left almost everyone poor.

▲ The words "Equal Justice Under Law" are carved on the U.S. Supreme Court building, but during Reconstruction the Supreme Court upheld certain Jim Crow laws that denied equal justice to African Americans.

In 1877, when the army troops left, congressional Reconstruction was finished; the South was on its own. White Southerners turned to backward-looking leaders. Those leaders blamed blacks and Northern carpetbaggers for all the troubles of the South.

The Redeemers (those who wanted to end Reconstruction) began by counting votes incorrectly. That's called "voter fraud." They paid some poor blacks for their votes. Eventually they took the *franchise*—the vote—from blacks and poor whites by passing poll taxes and other laws meant to keep blacks from voting.

Without the vote, blacks were powerless.

Jim Crow began dancing across the Southern land. Lawmakers passed laws that made it a crime for the races to be together. Soon blacks and whites had to ride in separate railroad cars, go to separate schools, eat in separate eating places, pray in separate churches, and get buried in separate cemeteries.

There was nothing blacks could do about it. Remember, they were no longer able to vote.

The poll tax (later found to be unconstitutional) meant you had to pay a tax to vote. Other laws made people pass a written test in order to vote. Sometimes different tests were given to blacks and whites.

By the time the new century arrived, black citizens, who had high hopes after the Civil War, were now sometimes worse off than before. Hundreds of blacks were lynched—hanged—by white mobs, and police did nothing about it. The 14th Amendment says:

No State shall make or enforce any law which shall abridge the privileges or immunities of citizens of the United States; nor shall any State deprive any person of life, liberty, or property, without due process of law; nor deny to any person within its jurisdiction the equal protection of the laws.

The 15th Amendment says:

The right of citizens of the United States to vote shall not be denied or abridged by the United States or by any State on account of race, color, or previous condition of servitude.

Were the Jim Crow laws constitutional or unconstitutional? What do you think? Were the Southern states defying the Constitution when they passed laws that treated blacks and whites differently?

Of course they were. In 1896 some Louisiana citizens went to the Supreme Court to see what they could do about it. Six years earlier, the Louisiana General Assembly had passed a bill that said railroad companies must "provide separate but equal accommodations for the white and colored races" on passenger trains.

Homer Plessy's great-grandmother was African. Everyone else in his family had a European background. Plessy's skin was white. But, according to the racists, anyone with any African blood at all was black. So Homer Plessy was considered a black. His friends in New Orleans wanted to show the ridiculousness of the whole idea of racial categories. That's why they chose white-skinned Homer Plessy for a test case.

They got Plessy to sit in the white section of a railroad car. When the conductor was told that he was black, Plessy was arrested, charged

Whites confront an African American in a "whites only" railroad car. ▶

with breaking the law, and put in jail. Plessy and his attorneys said that the "separate but equal" law was unconstitutional. New Orleans's Judge John H. Ferguson said they were wrong.

Plessy's case made it all the way to the Supreme Court. The case of *Plessy v. Ferguson* is famous for being one of the worst decisions the Supreme Court ever made. It changed the lives of millions of people—and not for the better.

The court agreed with Judge Ferguson! After that, Jim Crow really went wild. He danced and sang like fury. Separate-but-equal became the way of the South. Before the *Plessy* case there were many examples of integration in the Southern states. Twenty years later there were almost none.

One Supreme Court justice, John Marshall Harlan, disagreed with the other justices. He said so in strong language. He wrote a dissenting opinion in *Plessy v. Ferguson.* Justice Harlan said:

> *In view of the Constitution, in the eye of the law, there is in this country no superior, dominant ruling class of citizens.... Our Constitution is colorblind, and neither knows nor tolerates classes among citizens.*

Justice Harlan's words are worth remembering. Every lawyer knows them. Every American should. It would take time, but, finally, the Supreme Court agreed with Harlan. Separate is not equal. In 1954, the Supreme Court changed its mind. *Plessy v. Ferguson* was reversed. Segregation was found to be unconstitutional. Jim Crow was kicked off the stage.

Frederick Douglass, speaking at the World's Fair in Chicago in 1893, said, "Men talk of the Negro problem, there is no Negro problem. The problem is whether American people have loyalty enough, honor enough, patriotism enough, to live up to their own Constitution.... We Negroes love our country. We fought for it. We ask only that we be treated as well as those who fought against it."

Frederick Douglass ▶

Ida B. Wells

Some people were murdering other people (yes, it was murder), and nearly everyone—and that means the president, Congress, state leaders, and most ordinary people—was looking the other way. They didn't want to face what was happening.

But Ida B. Wells was a newspaperwoman and she had no intention of looking aside. So she wrote about the murders, which were lynchings. What happened to Wells? Her newspaper's printing press was smashed. People said they would kill her, and they meant it. She moved, bought a gun, and kept writing.

Not many people wanted to read what she had to say. Many were embarrassed by the murders. Maybe they thought they would go away. Maybe they thought Ida Wells would go away.

For a while, she did. She went to England, where she gave speeches about the lynchings. People there listened. They were shocked. Stories and articles and editorials were written about her in important English newspapers. Lords and ladies and some of Parliament's leaders met Ida B. Wells. Meetings were held to protest the murders. A few people in the United States were upset by the fuss in England. But most people just didn't seem to know what to do, so the lynchings continued.

But I need to let Ida B. Wells tell you her own story:

I was born in Holly Springs, Mississippi, before the close of the Civil War. My parents, who had been slaves and married as such, were married again after freedom came. My father had been taught the carpenter's trade, and my mother was a famous cook.... My father [called Jim] was the son of his master...and one of his slave women, Peggy.... He was never whipped or put on the auction block, and he knew little of the cruelties of slavery.... My mother... was born in Virginia and was one of ten children. She and two sisters were sold to slave traders when young, and were taken to Mississippi and sold again.... Her father was half Indian.... She often wrote back to somewhere in Virginia trying to get track of her people, but she was never successful.

Holly Springs was a small town with the kind of people—black and white—who, after the war, attempted to live together in harmony.

The Freedmen's Association was run by O. O. Howard. Howard University in Washington, D.C., was named for him.

Our job was to go to school and learn all we could. The Freedmen's Aid had established one of its schools in our town.... My father was one of the trustees and my mother went along to school with us until she learned to read the Bible. After that she visited school regularly to see how we were getting along.

Ida's parents were community leaders. Blacks and whites in Holly Springs rode streetcars and trains together. It was Reconstruction and, mostly, there was racial harmony.

But when voting time came, Ida's father, Jim Wells, was told to vote for the Democratic candidates. Wells voted Republican. His boss wouldn't let him back in the carpenter's shop where he worked. Ida's dad didn't hesitate. He bought some tools, rented a shop across the street, and went into business for himself. It was a lesson Ida would remember.

When black people voted, white people often pressured them to vote for certain candidates. ▼

Ida was the oldest of seven children, and a good student. She planned to go to college. One summer, when she was in high school, she went to visit her grandparents on their farm. Yellow fever was raging through the South. The epidemic was said to have started when a ship docked in Norfolk, Virginia, with some sick people. It traveled like a summer tornado. The germs had no prejudice. They killed men, women, and children of every size and color.

The epidemic was worst in the cities, so people fled from cities to small towns. Some of those people came to Holly Springs. They brought their germs with them. Soon people in that town were sick. Jim and Lizzie Wells helped some of the sick people. And they prayed with them.

One day three horsemen rode up to the farmhouse gate and handed Ida a letter. This is what it said:

Jim and Lizzie Wells have both died of the fever. They died within twenty-four hours of each other. The children are all at home and the Howard Association has put a woman there to take charge of them. Send word to Ida.

Ida Wells was 16, and her parents were dead.

If she went home she was sure to get the fever. Everyone told her to stay with her grandparents. Besides, there were no passenger trains running. No one was traveling while the fever raged. She went anyway. She went on a freight train. It was draped with black cloth to honor two conductors who had died of the fever. The engineer told her to stay away from Holly Springs. She asked him why he was driving the train; after all, he could get the fever, too. He said, "Someone has to do it."

"That's exactly why I am going home," said Ida. "I am the oldest of seven living children. There's nobody but me to look after them now. Don't you think I should do my duty, too?"

Ida Wells always put duty ahead of fear or personal safety. She always spoke up, which is what she did when she got home. But the first thing she learned made her weep some more: her baby brother was dead. Now there were six children. Friends had made plans for them. The youngest children were to be split up between different families. A handicapped sister was to be put in an institution. Ida was thought old enough to take care of herself.

▲ Ida B. Wells

When all this had been arranged…I, who had said nothing before and had not even been consulted, calmly announced that they were not going to put any of the children anywhere; I said that it would make my father and mother turn over in their graves to know their children had been scattered like that and that we owned the house and…I would take care of them.

I took the examination for a country school-teacher and had my dresses lengthened, and I got a school six miles out in the country. I was to be paid the munificent sum of twenty-five dollars a month.

She rode a mule the six miles to school. For Ida Wells, childhood was over.

But I began this chapter by talking about murder and trips to England. How did Wells get from Holly Springs, Mississippi, to London, England?

With her pen. Ida B. Wells became a famous journalist. She began by sending letters to some black newspapers.

As you probably gathered, Wells was a no-nonsense person who said exactly what she thought. Her letters made sense. She told the truth. The letters became popular. Several newspapers wanted to carry them. Soon she had a regular newspaper column.

But writing did not pay enough to allow Wells to quit teaching. One day she boarded a train to Memphis. She was going to teach there. Ida sat in the ladies' coach, as she had always done. But the South was changing. The conductor wouldn't take her ticket. He said blacks had to sit in the smoking car. Ida Wells wouldn't budge.

As I was in the ladies' car I proposed to stay. He tried to drag me out of the seat, but the moment he caught hold of my arm I fastened my teeth in the back of his hand.

I had braced my feet against the seat in front and was holding on to the back, and as he had already been badly bitten he didn't try it again by himself.

The conductor got two men to help him. They tore her dress and dragged her from the train.

Wells hired a lawyer and sued the railroad. The judge said she was right and awarded her $500. But the Chesapeake and Ohio Railroad appealed the case to the Tennessee Supreme Court. That court reversed the lower court's decision. Ida B. Wells had to pay a fine.

Wells had many friends in Memphis, but Thomas Moss and his wife were special friends. Moss was a postman who saved his money and, along with two partners, opened a grocery store. Their store was across the street from a white-owned grocery. The white grocer didn't like having competition. He threatened the new grocers. Then he and his friends marched on the store—with guns. Moss and his friends had guns, too. Three white men were wounded.

The three black grocers were taken to jail. But they weren't safe there. A mob invaded the prison, took the three men, and filled their bodies with bullets. It was a *lynching*. It was murder by a mob.

Between 1882 and 1930, 4,761 people were lynched in the United States. It happened in the North and West as well as the South. Only the New England states were without lynchings. Whites and Asians were lynched. But most lynchings were in the South, and most victims were black. In Mississippi, 545 people were murdered; in Texas, 492; in Louisiana, 388; Montana had 93 lynchings (only two of those victims were black).

In the West it was called "vigilante" (vih-juh-LAN-tee) justice, but it was never just, because in our nation real justice must come through the legal process. If people take the law into their own hands—and decide who is guilty and who is not, without a fair trial— there is no point to laws and government. Then you have *anarchy*, or rule by no one. What you don't have is fairness. Most people thought the lynch mobs were poor and uneducated people. But in every section of the country, the mob murderers—the lynchers—had the consent and often active participation of community leaders.

Wells knew Tom Moss was a fine citizen. Ida Wells decided to find out more. She found out that some of those who had been lynched were innocent victims. She found out that some women and children had been lynched, and that some of the dead were victims of mistaken identity. Wells wrote about what she found in the *Free Speech*. She was fired from her teaching job.

When the city of Memphis refused to even try to find Tom Moss's murderer, she told her readers, "There is only one thing we can

Ida B. Wells urged her readers to boycott the streetcars, like those in this Southern city. ▶

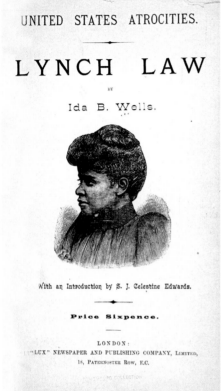

UNITED STATES ATROCITIES.

LYNCH LAW

BY

Ida B. Wells.

With an Introduction by S. J. Celestine Edwards.

Price Sixpence.

LONDON:
"LUX" NEWSPAPER AND PUBLISHING COMPANY, LIMITED,
18, PATERNOSTER ROW, E.C.

▲ In several publications, Ida B. Wells documented the shocking extent of lynching in the United States.

Antilynching laws were finally passed in the mid-20th century.

do—leave a town which will neither protect our lives and property, nor give us a fair trial." Within two months, 6,000 black people had left Memphis. Then she organized a boycott: she told her readers to stop riding the streetcars. When blacks stopped riding the streetcars, white businesses began to suffer.

Ida Wells was soon in danger herself. The *Free Speech* was attacked and its presses ruined. It happened while Ida Wells was on her way to New York. Some people in Memphis were talking about lynching Ida B. Wells. It was 30 years before she could go south again.

Of course, she didn't stop fighting for justice. Ida Wells moved to Chicago, married lawyer Ferdinand Barnett, raised a family, gave speeches, went to England, founded a community center, worked for women's suffrage—and kept writing. Finally, when others were ready to do something about lynching, they could turn to Ida B. Wells's articles and find well-researched data and truths that were hard to face.

A Man and His Times

I was born a slave on a plantation in Franklin County, Virginia. I am not quite sure of the exact place or exact date of my birth, but at any rate I suspect I must have been born somewhere and at some time.

So begins the autobiography of Booker T. Washington, who was born five years before the Civil War began. By the end of the 19th century, he was one of the best-known men—black or white—in America. Here is more of the autobiography:

My life had its beginning in the midst of the most miserable, desolate, and discouraging surroundings. This was so, however, not because my owners were especially cruel, for they were not, as compared with many others. I was born in a typical log cabin, about fourteen by sixteen feet square. In this cabin I lived with my mother and a brother and sister till after the Civil War, when we were all declared free.

The little cabin where Booker lived was also the plantation kitchen. His mother was the plantation cook. Cooking was done in an open fireplace. The family slept on the dirt floor, on bundles of rags.

I was asked not long ago to tell something about the sports and pastimes that I engaged in during my youth. Until that question was asked it had never occurred to me that there was no period of my life that was devoted to play. From the time that I can remember anything, almost every day of my life has been occupied in some kind of labor; though I think I would now be a more useful man if I had had time for sports.

Booker T. Washington became a useful man anyway. He was 10 when the Civil War ended and his mother moved her small family to West Virginia. Booker went to work in a salt furnace. But his mother was determined that he get an education. He wanted to go to school, too.

Booker T. Washington—educator, author, orator, and political leader ▼

Students at the Hampton Institute learn mechanical drawing. ▶

I had no schooling whatever while I was a slave, though I remember on several occasions I went as far as the schoolhouse door with one of my young mistresses to carry her books. The picture of several dozen boys and girls in a schoolroom engaged in study made a deep impression upon me, and I had the feeling that to get into a schoolhouse and study in this way would be about the same as getting into paradise.

Getting into paradise wasn't easy. Booker's family needed the money he earned. He watched other black children going to school, and he ached to go, too. Finally he found a way. He got up early, worked until school began, went to school, and then went back to work.

Then someone told Booker Washington about a Negro college in Hampton, Virginia. He decided that was where he wanted to go. He didn't know anyone there, or if they would accept him; he just headed east until he got to Hampton. It was 500 miles. He arrived without any money and got a job as a janitor to pay for his studies.

Hampton Institute provided vocational training for blacks. That means it taught students to be farmers, carpenters, teachers, brick makers, or to do other useful jobs. Students learned skills and to take pride in their work.

After the Civil War, in the South, few people wanted to work hard. Many blacks thought hard work was slaves' work—and they didn't want to be reminded of slavery. Whites didn't want to work hard either—they had always had slaves to do that. So no one valued hard work.

The teachers at the institute (who were mostly Northern whites) understood that people who work hard get things done and feel good about their accomplishments. At Hampton, teachers worked right along with students. Booker T. Washington was one of the best of those students.

So when the president of Hampton Institute was asked to recommend someone to head a new training institute for blacks at Tuskegee, Alabama, he suggested Booker T. Washington for the job.

Aside from that recommendation, the people at Tuskegee didn't know much about him. They were expecting a white man to head the school. Washington was expecting a "building and all the necessary apparatus ready for me to begin teaching." They were both surprised.

What Washington found at Tuskegee, in June of 1881, was one building and an old church. This is how he described the schoolhouse:

> *This building was in such poor repair that, whenever it rained, one of the older students would very kindly leave his lessons and hold an umbrella over me while I heard the recitations of the others.*

▲ A lab at the Tuskegee Institute in Alabama

Agricultural Revolutionary

George Washington Carver was one of America's great scientists. Carver sparked an agricultural revolution in the American South, urging farmers to change from soil-exhausting crops like cotton and tobacco to those such as peanuts and sweet potatoes, which fed people and the soil, too. He couldn't bear to waste things, and that led him to develop more than 400 synthetic materials from common crops and agricultural leftovers (cheese, dyes, even synthetic marble). When Booker T. Washington invited him to Tuskegee, Carver found a home, adding prestige to that university.

▲ George Washington Carver discovered hundreds of uses for peanuts.

Booker T. Washington is honored with a statue at Tuskegee Institute titled *Lifting the Veil of Ignorance.* He said, "A race, like an individual, lifts itself up by lifting others up." ▶

▲ Washington urged blacks to work hard and not agitate for civil rights.

Washington rolled up his sleeves and went to work. He and his students cut down trees, cleared land, dug wells, and built buildings. By 1900, Tuskegee had 40 buildings and some fine teachers. Booker T. Washington was renowned as the voice of the black people.

He was quite a speaker. He spoke so well that he often left audiences cheering. Contributions poured into Tuskegee Institute. The school's graduates went out and trained others. Booker T. Washington was a wonderful speaker, but in his speeches he urged blacks to work hard and not agitate for civil rights. He said that blacks must first gain economic freedom by learning working skills and getting good jobs; then they could battle for other kinds of freedom. Washington became a national hero.

But some blacks weren't happy with just economic freedom. They were American citizens. They wanted to vote, to ride on buses with everyone else, and to go to the same schools. They wanted to send lynchers to jail and kill Jim Crow. One man began to criticize Booker T. Washington's style of leadership, and that shocked a lot of people.

A Man Ahead of His Time

History is full of surprises. When you're living through it, there is no predicting how it will turn out.

Consider those two leaders—Booker T. Washington and W. E. B. DuBois (do-BOYS). By the end of the century, everyone had heard of Booker T. Washington. He was said to be the best-known Southern man since Jefferson Davis. He was much loved by both races. When Booker Washington spoke, people listened. President Theodore Roosevelt invited him to dinner. Wealthy men like Andrew Carnegie and John D. Rockefeller gave money to the causes he supported.

Now the average person—black or white—had never even heard of W. E. B. DuBois. Those who had knew that he was brilliant, that he was an African American thinker and writer, and that he had earned a Ph.D. from Harvard. They also knew that his ideas often got him in trouble. They knew that he had been fired from some jobs and that he had money problems. But what seemed shocking was that he often disagreed with the great Booker T. Washington, and said so in writing.

How could anyone disagree with Booker Washington? All the newspapers agreed with him; so did most college professors. Why, even the *president* believed his ideas were right and sound.

Well, as I said, history is full of surprises. Today historians say that Booker T. Washington was a man of his times who, without meaning it, may have held his people back. DuBois, they say, was a man who had important things to say to whites as well as blacks—even though, at the time, few people seemed to be listening.

Why do some historians think Booker T. Washington may have held his people back? What did he do wrong?

He compromised. Sometimes compromise is the best thing to do. Booker T. Washington thought he was doing right, and maybe he was. What do you think?

Remember, he lived in the days of Jim Crow. He lived in the days when two or three blacks were lynched—murdered—each week. What did he do about that? Almost nothing.

Washington compromised with the whites who were in power. He told the white leaders that blacks wanted jobs, that all they wanted was a chance to earn money. He believed that if blacks had economic

▲ W. E. B. DuBois was a founder of the National Association for the Advancement of Colored People, which seeks to end racial injustice.

Night—grand and wonderful. I am glad I am living.... I wonder what the world is—I wonder if life is worth the striving. I do not know—perhaps I never shall know—but this I do know: be the Truth what it may I shall seek it on the pure assumption that it is worth seeking—and Heaven nor Hell, God nor Devil shall turn me from my purpose, till I die.

—W. E. B. Dubois, written on his 25th birthday when he was a student in Berlin

W. E. B. DuBois, the first African American to earn a Ph.D. at Harvard, wrote, "We refuse to surrender…leadership…to cowards and trucklers. We are men; we will be treated as men." ▶

opportunities, other opportunities would follow. So he headed a school that trained blacks in working skills. Now that was fine. He taught the value of hard work, and that was important. But he also told white audiences that if blacks could have jobs and economic opportunities they wouldn't demand social equality. They would live with Jim Crow. That made him very popular with some whites. He didn't try to change things. He didn't fuss. Many people are afraid of fuss and change.

During the years that Washington was the leading American black, Jim Crow grew mightier and mightier. He also grew sillier and sillier. In Mississippi, Jim Crow segregated soda machines, and in Oklahoma he segregated phone booths!

But W. E. B. DuBois wouldn't compromise with anyone. He wanted full equality. Nothing less would do.

Besides, DuBois understood that in a democracy all citizens must be treated fairly. Prejudice is not democratic. He wasn't the only one who felt that way. It was the theme of America's Declaration of Independence. Carl Schurz said, "If you want to be free, there is but one way, it is to guarantee an equally full measure of liberty to all your neighbors." By denying full freedom to blacks—and women and Asians—America was weakening its democratic government. W. E. B. DuBois understood that.

He worked to bring the vote to women, he spoke out against anti-Semitism (which is prejudice against Jews), he worked to get fair treatment for immigrant groups, he tried to stamp out Jim Crow. He couldn't do it, but his words and ideas helped those who would do it after him. Some people say he was the father of the civil rights movement of the 20th century.

▲ In 1905, DuBois (second from right, middle row) and other black Americans met at Niagara Falls to discuss civil rights.

William Edward Burghardt DuBois was born in Great Barrington, Massachusetts. His family had lived there for a long time. One ancestor fought in the Revolutionary War. The DuBois family was respected.

Each spring, in Great Barrington, all the townspeople gathered for a town meeting where they decided how to run the schools and how to spend the town's money. While he was still a boy, DuBois went to the town meetings and learned that democracy was "listening to the other man's opinion and then voting your own, honestly and intelligently."

But it was during a visit to his proud grandfather—who would never agree to any form of segregation—that he learned about his African heritage. He met other young African Americans and admired their physical beauty, their enthusiasm, and their good minds. He wondered, could he be both American and black? Or must he choose? Here is his answer to that question:

We are Americans, not only by birth and by citizenship, but by our political ideals.

DuBois understood that each American has a double inheritance that includes:

- the responsibilities and rights that go with American citizenship
- and the personal richness of his or her own ethnic roots.

DuBois believed that our diverse backgrounds enrich us all. No people originated on this continent, not even the Native Americans. It is the collection of heritages that make America special.

▲ A bronze plaque at Hampton University in Virginia honors W. E. B. DuBois (center) and (to his right) Booker T. Washington, surrounded by a Native American and two African Americans.

W. E. B. DuBois's ideas would help lead blacks—and all people—to pride in their achievements. His own accomplishments were intellectual. DuBois wrote many books and edited several magazines. He was one of the founders of the NAACP—the National Association for the Advancement of Colored People—an organization of blacks and whites formed to fight racial injustice. "The problem of the 20th century is the problem of the color line," said DuBois. He didn't think color should be a problem.

DuBois had good ideas, but he didn't have much talent for people. He didn't know how to work well with others. So most people didn't pay attention to him.

Booker T. Washington's talent was in healing differences; in helping people get along. Washington said there was a time when he hated whites, but he quit when he realized that "hating the white man did him no harm and…was narrowing up my soul and making me a good bit less of a human being." Think about those words. Are you sometimes tempted to hate others? What does that do for you?

As it turned out, the ideas and example of both Booker T. Washington and W. E. B. DuBois are important to all Americans. Each wanted to make our country do what it was always meant to do—be fair to all people. As DuBois said:

We are Americans, not only by birth and by citizenship, but by our political ideals….And the greatest of those ideals is that ALL MEN ARE CREATED EQUAL.

Since its founding in 1909, the NAACP has pursued its mission "to eliminate race-based discrimination." In this photograph, a diverse crowd poses in front of the NAACP headquarters in New York City in 1929. ▼

PART 2

INDUSTRY
AND REFORM

An Age of Extremes

It was a confident time in the United States as the 19th century became the 20th. For most people life was good and would get even better. But Mark Twain said there was too much attention to money and gold and glitter. He called this turn of the century a "Gilded Age."

Some historians say it was an "age of extremes." Why? Well, in America, it was a time of

- great riches,
- awful poverty,
- much hope,
- vast immigration,
- new factory jobs, and
- new, BIG businesses called "corporations."

▲ The beginning of the 20th century was a time of stark contrast between extremes of poverty and wealth, as shown by these two scenes. Above, a photograph by Jacob Riis shows desperately poor boys sleeping on the porch of a New York City tenement building. At right, wealthy upper class New Yorkers enjoy a formal dinner.

At the turn of the 19th century to the 20th, railroads were big business. Railroad owners were some of the wealthiest and most powerful men of the time.

It was a time when

- railroads controlled much of America's wealth,
- lumbermen cut down enormous forests,
- the Indian wars ended (badly for the Indians),
- the cattle drives were finished,
- some cowboys became circus stars,
- evil Jim Crow settled across all of the South,
- business tycoons acted like emperors, and
- people filled the land until there was no more frontier.

It was also the time when these things were invented or developed:

- electric lights
- telephones
- moving pictures
- record players
- bicycles
- horseless carriages
- flying machines
- skyscrapers
- baseball and football leagues
- typewriters

More Leisure Time

The Gilded Age brought change not only for the rich and poor but also for middle class people. One thing the middle class got more of was time to enjoy themselves. City folk who had Sundays off could buy a train or trolley ticket and go to the country or to the beach. For the first time, vacations became part of the lives of ordinary people.

▲ Around 1900, many thousands of children worked long hours in American factories. Sadie Pfeifer worked in a cotton mill in Lancaster, South Carolina. She was photographed by Lewis Hine, who, like Jacob Riis, used photography to encourage social reform.

And more, too.

It was a time when most Americans still lived on farms, although cities were booming. It was a time when some women and people of color demanded to be treated as full citizens—and hardly anyone paid attention. When thousands of children worked from sunup to sundown—and a few people began to pay attention.

It was a time when "progressives" and "populists" and "reformers" and "business tycoons" and "working people" all had strong opinions about how to make life better in America.

It was a time when a lot of people enjoyed themselves. They had more leisure than ever before. Some threw grand parties. Some played those new games, baseball and football. Some joined unions. Some joined social or church groups. Some got involved in politics.

It was a time of prosperity and poverty; of corruption and idealism; and, for almost everyone, a time of faith in the future. In other words, it was a very interesting time.

Robber Barons

Big businesses and corporations thrived in late 19th-century America. Before, American business was found mostly in small workshops and foundries, but railroads helped change things. A big factory or a big farm makes sense only if your products can reach far markets. With railroads, they can.

Some of the men who built the railroads became immensely wealthy. Cornelius Vanderbilt, who died in 1877, was the richest of them all. He got things done, but he didn't care about playing by the rules. Every time he could, he put his competition out of business. The *New York Times* called him a "robber baron." He earned most of his money by getting favors from the government. The taxpayers ended up making Vanderbilt very rich.

▲ Cornelius Vanderbilt

Not all of the 19th century's wealthy business people were robber barons. Some were more like one of our Founding Fathers, Benjamin Franklin, a successful businessman who was also a responsible citizen. You'll meet some of them later in this book.

Andrew Carnegie

Andrew Carnegie was born in a stone cottage in Dunfermline, Scotland, in 1835. His father was a weaver who worked at a hand loom. But when the Industrial Revolution came to Scotland, Andrew's father could find no work. Power looms produced cloth faster and cheaper than artisans (handworkers) could. Many weavers lost their jobs. They were angry at the government and the business leaders. But there was nothing they could do about it. Poor workers weren't even allowed to vote.

In the little town of Dunfermline workers were determined to gain the right to vote and to strike. Andrew Carnegie's dad was one of those who spoke out for workers' rights. You might call him an *idealist*. He wanted to make the world better.

Andrew's mother was a *realist*. She was the practical one. She worried about putting food on the table for her family. When there was no money she stitched shoes and sold groceries. She was the one who sold the family's few belongings and decided that they should "flit" out of Scotland and head for America.

Andrew Carnegie had those two sides to him: his mother's side made him sensible and willing to work hard; his father's side made him want to improve the world. There was another important influence on Carnegie. It was his uncle George. George Lauder loved poetry, and he read the words of Robert Burns and William Shakespeare to his nephew. When Carnegie got to be rich—very, very rich—he could still recite Shakespeare. He had great writers and thinkers as friends, and Carnegie could talk with them in ways his fellow millionaires would never have understood.

But while he was getting rich he didn't seem to worry much about the working people who were laboring for him. He forgot his father's troubles. What he did do was work hard himself, use his imagination and intelligence, and take every chance that came his way.

His first job, in Allegheny, Pennsylvania, was as a bobbin boy in a textile factory. He worked from six in the morning until six at night and was paid $1.20 a day. He was 12 years old. A year later he heard that a messenger boy was needed at the new telegraph office

A young Andrew Carnegie ▼

in Pittsburgh. He got the job and set out to be the best messenger boy in town. Soon he knew all the streets and buildings by heart. He watched the telegraph operators and taught himself Morse code. Then he learned to decipher the code from the clicking sound of the telegraph, without needing the tape printer. No one else in Pittsburgh could do that!

One day Andy found a check for $500 on the street. He turned it over to those who could find the owner. A newspaper, the *Pittsburgh Gazette*, wrote a story about him; it called him "an honest little fellow."

And that impressed Thomas A. Scott, who was soon to become a leading railroad man. He hired Carnegie as an assistant—at $35 a month. Andy was now 17 and in a place where opportunity would find him. When it did, he was ready to grab it. He learned about *capital*—which is money—and how to use it to get businesses started. He learned to put money to work. He invested in railroads, railroad sleeping cars, bridges, and oil derricks; by the time he was 33, he was rich.

Then he wrote himself a note. So far it was his mother's side he had followed. At 33 he remembered his father's idealism. He wrote that he would work for money for two more years; then he would work to help others. "No idol is more debasing than the worship of money," wrote Carnegie.

From a very young age, Andrew Carnegie knew what it was like to work hard. At the age of 12, Andrew, like the boy in this picture, worked as a bobbin boy in a textile factory. ▼

Two years later he must have forgotten that note—or maybe the lure of money was too strong. He kept working hard and getting richer and richer. He entered the iron business, but soon realized that steel was the metal of the future. Carnegie became king of America's steel industry and soon American steel dominated the world. The Carnegie steel company was very profitable: it used the best, most efficient machinery and kept wages very low. Carnegie's workers—men who were like his dad and uncle—earned very little. Life for their families was awful. The writer Hamlin Garland visited a steel town and wrote this:

▲ Andrew Carnegie's steel factories dominated world steel production.

The streets were horrible; the buildings poor; the sidewalks sunken and full of holes.... Everywhere the yellow mud of the streets lay kneaded into sticky masses through which groups of pale, lean men slouched in faded garments.

When salaries were cut at Carnegie's Homestead steel mill, in Pennsylvania, the workers went on strike. Carnegie's manager, Henry Clay Frick, refused to talk to the strikers; instead he sent in Pinkerton detectives. (Pinkerton was the name of a company that supplied armed guards. They were called detectives, but they were just men with guns.) Twenty strikers were killed. So were four detectives. Andrew Carnegie was vacationing in Scotland. Had he forgotten his origins?

If you saw the way he lived you would say so. He owned a castle in Scotland and houses in America that seemed like palaces. He lived like a prince while many who worked for him lived like paupers.

▲ Andrew Carnegie spent the last two decades of his life giving away his fortune.

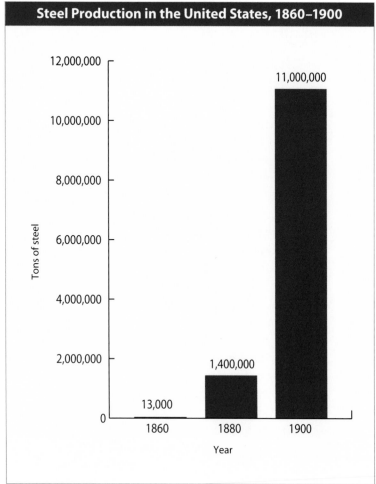

Steel Production in the United States, 1860–1900

Tons of steel / Year

- 1860: 13,000
- 1880: 1,400,000
- 1900: 11,000,000

Andrew Carnegie provided the money for one of the world's finest concert halls: Carnegie Hall in New York. Here is an old joke about it,

A young woman stops an older man on a New York street and says, "Excuse me, sir, how do I get to Carnegie Hall?"

He replies, "Practice, practice, practice!"

Then the most successful banker in America, J. Pierpont Morgan, offered to buy Carnegie out. It was 1901, nine years after the Homestead strike, and Carnegie was 66. It was an opportunity that might never come again. The sale would make him one of the richest men in the world.

At first he hesitated. Perhaps he didn't know what he would do with himself if he was no longer running a business empire. Then he may have remembered the note he wrote when he was 33. Or maybe he remembered his father's ideals. He sold his business interests and began a new career. It was the business of giving away his money. When you're as rich as Andrew Carnegie, that is a big job. Especially if you want to do it well, which he did.

He wrote that "the man who dies thus rich, dies disgraced." He said that millionaires had a duty to distribute their wealth while they were still alive. He didn't want to die disgraced, and he didn't. He began by building libraries in towns all across the country—3,000 of them, costing nearly $60 million. He gave money to colleges and schools and artists and writers and to an institute to promote peace and to another to improve teaching and to another that was to attempt to make the world better. He gave away almost all of his riches.

Not long before he died he turned to his private secretary and asked, "How much did you say I have given away, Poynton?" "Three hundred and twenty-four million, six hundred and fifty-seven thousand, three hundred and ninety-nine dollars," came the answer. "Good heavens!" said Carnegie, "Where did I ever get all that money?"

How Do You Make Steel?

Iron is strong but heavy. It breaks under pressure. Moisture makes it rust.

Pure iron is an *element*. But the common metal we call iron is an *alloy*. An alloy is a mixture. Iron is a mixture of two or more elements: iron, carbon, and others, such as manganese and sulfur.

Steel is also an alloy. It is iron with a very small amount of carbon (the amount varies). Steel is strong, stronger than iron. It resists rust, and it bends rather than breaks. It is lighter than iron.

When the railroad age began in the 1830s, the railroad builders wanted to use steel for rails and engines. But it was very expensive to make steel. You had to take the unwanted elements out of the iron. That meant a slow process of heating and separating. You began with a huge quantity of iron and were left with a small bit of steel.

Near Louisville, Kentucky, William Kelly, the son of Irish immigrants, owned a small business that made iron kettles. Like everyone else in the iron business, he thought about steel. If only he could find a way to make it inexpensively.

By accident, Kelly discovered that blowing cool air on molten iron actually heated the iron and removed the carbon, producing steel. (Cool air heating something? Yes—because of the oxygen in the air.)

In the meantime, Henry Bessemer, in England, was working on a similar idea. He took out an American patent. When Kelly heard of Bessemer's patent he claimed he had been first, and, finally, the U.S. Patent Office agreed with him. Today the method is usually called the "Bessemer process," although William Kelly probably developed it five years before Bessemer.

That new method meant that steel could be made at reasonable cost. Steel rails soon replaced rigid iron ones. Builders had a new tool: a strong, versatile metal. Steel became the foundation for America's astounding industrial growth.

◄ At Carnegie's Bessemer-process steelworks in Pittsburgh, the molten iron in the egg-shaped converters is white hot. Compressed air is blown up through the converter until the impurities are oxidized (combined with oxygen) to form waste, called "slag," which is light and easily separated. The slag is piled up outside in hills that grow into mountains, called "slag heaps."

A Bookkeeper Named Rockefeller

In 1858, oil was discovered near Titusville, Pennsylvania. When the news got out, people raced for the hills and gullies of western Pennsylvania. Before long that state was something like California in the gold rush a decade earlier. Trees came down and derricks went up. Oil wells caught fire and black, smelly fumes filled the air. Railroads pushed in, towns sprouted like dandelions—and disappeared just as fast.

One day a quiet, unflappable young bookkeeper was sent to this disorganized area to see what was going on. "Is the oil business worth investing in?" His employers had sent him to find out. "No," he told them, and then went on to invest in it himself and to become one of the most successful businessmen the world has ever known. His name was John Davison Rockefeller.

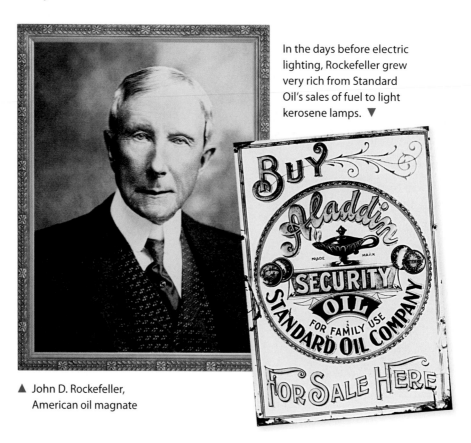

In the days before electric lighting, Rockefeller grew very rich from Standard Oil's sales of fuel to light kerosene lamps. ▼

▲ John D. Rockefeller, American oil magnate

Rockefeller's Scottish Baptist mother encouraged her sons to work. John raised turkeys and saved $50. When a neighbor asked to borrow the $50 he lent the money—and charged $3.50 interest. It was a lesson he never forgot: money could be made to earn money. That is what capitalism is all about. Some say John D. Rockefeller was the greatest capitalist who ever lived. Others say he almost destroyed capitalism for everyone else in America.

One thing is certain. He soon brought order to that disorderly oil business. He saw that the money to be made was in oil refining. In 1863—he was 24—he and a partner bought a small refinery. With his efficient methods, it quickly grew large. Rockefeller began buying his competitors.

If you have oil to sell, there are two costs that are important: the cost of the oil and the cost of transportation (you need to get the oil to buyers). Because there were competing railroads, and because he had quite a bit of oil to ship, Rockefeller made the railroads give him special prices to ship his oil. Actually, what he did was to pay the full price like everyone else. Then he got the railroads to give him back half of what he had paid. He did that secretly. It was called a "rebate," or "kickback," and it wasn't fair. It meant he could charge less for oil than his competitors did. Soon he put most of them out of business. Within 10 years he controlled the nation's oil industry.

The oil business was very lucrative, which means there were big profits to be made. Rockefeller's company, Standard Oil, became spectacularly rich. What seems amazing to us today is that all of this happened *before* the internal combustion engine, which powers automobiles and the other machines that made oil so important in the 20th century. The oil that brought hundreds of millions of

The Spindletop oil gusher in Jefferson County, Texas, was discovered in 1901 and was the largest of its kind in the world. ▼

Spindletop

Everyone knew there was oil in Texas. By the 1880s and '90s, Texans had tapped many small oil wells and brought in drilling machinery, storage tanks, and pipelines.

Patillo Higgins and Anthony F. Lucas drilled a test well at a place called Spindletop, near Beaumont. Early in the morning of January 10, 1901, they heard a roaring sound. The drill pipe lifted straight out of the earth, like a rocket. Then came the oil, surging up 160 feet high. It took 10 days just to get the stuff under control. The oil men were soon filling as many as 100,000 barrels a day at Spindletop. The Texas oil boom had begun.

dollars to Rockefeller was used mostly to light kerosene lamps (in those days before electric light).

The more you read about John D. Rockefeller, or history in general, the more you will see how hard it is to make judgments—good and bad have a way of getting mixed together. You can decide for yourself what to think of him.

In the 19th century, many people thought Rockefeller was one of the great villains of all time. His bookkeeper's mind seemed interested only in money and profits, not in people. When he put others out of business it didn't bother him at all, as long as it made profits for Standard Oil. That company was called "the greatest, wisest, and meanest monopoly known to history." Rockefeller soon had vast interests in many businesses, not just oil, and the less he paid his workers the more efficient the businesses seemed. When some miners tried to form unions, he shut the mines and actually let workers starve rather than pay fair wages. His strikebreaking troops shot and killed workers and their families in mining towns in Colorado. Rockefeller claimed he didn't know what was going on—but he did. After the turn of the century, laws were passed that helped prevent unfair business practices, but, until that happened, tycoons like Rockefeller sometimes behaved as if they were kings. John D. Rockefeller had a quiet, dignified manner, but his company acted like a big, tough bully—beating up anyone who tried to fight it.

A group of people examine the ruins of the Ludlow colony in Colorado where, in April 1914, militiamen and company detectives shot and burned to death 18 people, including 11 children, the youngest of whom was only three months old. ▶

But, as I said, making judgments is difficult. Because it was so well organized and managed, Standard Oil helped make American business grow into world leadership. And it made life better for most people by bringing products to the market at a low price.

Like Carnegie, Rockefeller gave away vast sums of money to help others. He didn't have to do that. Many of the business barons of his day kept all they earned for themselves. Rockefeller lived until 1937; he was 98 when he died. For the last 40 years of his life he spent much of his time giving away his money. While Carnegie gave away 90 percent of his fortune, Rockefeller, always orderly and precise, gave away exactly half of his. Still, it was an immense half, and it created the University of Chicago, the Rockefeller Institute for Medical Research, and a foundation just to give money to worthwhile causes.

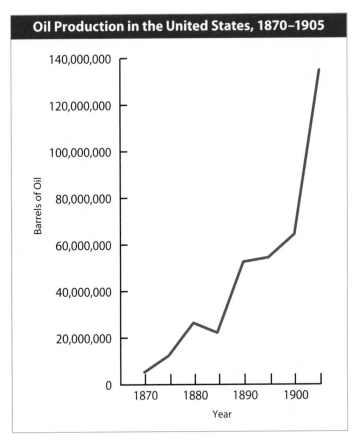

Oil Production in the United States, 1870–1905

▲ Rockefeller and other business magnates sometimes used armed troops against their own workers, like these National Guard members called in to put down a strike by Colorado miners.

Powerful Pierpont

There are so many myths about John Pierpont Morgan that we need to get a few things straight. He was not the richest man in America. (People just thought he was.) Rockefeller and Carnegie were richer. And he was not the most powerful man in America. There were two or three men who were equally powerful.

But he was very rich and very powerful, and vain and arrogant, too. Which means he was very sure of himself.

He was a bit like a regal lion who lords over the whole jungle. The jungle where he was king was the world of business and finance. Morgan was a banker—a money man—and he had the ability to take a confused situation and make it orderly. In the years after the Civil War, the American world of business was very disorderly. J. Pierpont Morgan helped make it efficient.

Once, when the U.S. Treasury seemed on the edge of collapse—it didn't have enough gold in reserve to meet its bills—J. P. Morgan loaned the nation $62 million.

Another time, the country was facing a financial crisis that might have led to a depression. People were pulling their money out of the banks and the stock market. A leading trust company was about to collapse. If that happened, people would panic. Morgan called the country's leading financiers to a meeting in his own marble library building. He asked them to lend money to save the trust. Then he locked the library's doors. He sat and played solitaire while the bankers paced and argued.

▲ Morgan's eyes reminded the photographer Edward Steichen of the headlights of an express train. A young financial reporter, Lincoln Steffens, said, "His eyes glared, his great red nose seemed to flash and darken.

Panicked investors, who have lost confidence in their banks, jam Wall Street in 1907. Morgan raised millions in loans to save the situation. ▶

At five in the morning, when the financiers agreed to do as he wished, Morgan unlocked the doors and let them out. The country was saved from financial disaster.

Few people dared disagree with J. P. Morgan. He was dignified and very imposing. Besides that, he had integrity. Everyone knew that if Morgan gave his word, you could rely on it.

He did not start as a poor boy and work his way to riches. He started at the top. His father was an international banker.

Young Pierpont usually got his way. He was smart, with a talent for mathematics and languages. His mind was very orderly. He got a weekly allowance and he kept a record of every penny he spent. When he grew up he did the same thing.

He was sent to schools in the United States and Switzerland and Germany and became a well-educated man, interested in art and music. He lived in enormous homes—he had seven of them—and he also owned a yacht and his own railroad cars. He was an imposing man, vain about his clothes and his looks. His huge, bulb-like nose, often red as a strawberry, was bad enough to be considered a medical problem—though he never had a doctor fix it.

By the beginning years of the new century, the House of Morgan (the name of J. P.'s bank) could be found in almost every important field of American business. It controlled railroads, shipping, the manufacture of agricultural tools, telephones, telegraphs, electrical power, insurance, and city transportation. Remember, it was J. Pierpont Morgan who bought Andrew Carnegie's steel company; then he bought huge metal ore reserves from John D. Rockefeller and founded the U.S. Steel Corporation. It was the nation's first billion-dollar corporation.

▲ John Pierpont Morgan, on the right, ca. 1900

A typical view of Morgan as an all-powerful banker. People thought him the Rockefeller of the financial world. ▶

When the trustees of Harvard Medical School needed money to expand their school, they went to several rich men. Rockefeller, with his careful, methodical mind, told them it would take him six months to study their plans. Morgan listened to the Harvard representatives, looked at his watch—he was busy that day—pointed to their plans, and said, "I will build that, and that, and that. Good morning, gentlemen." And he led them to the door.

Monopoly—
Not Always a Game

The Civil War made some people very rich. Military supplies—guns, food, clothing, railroads—were needed, and quickly. Suddenly, there were new needs, new industries, and new fortunes. After the war, American inventiveness led to more new ideas and industries that continued to create riches.

Some of those industries grew very big. They became *monopolies*. That means the whole industry was owned by one company. Some business men, like Morgan and Rockefeller, formed business arrangements called *trusts*. The trusts were a form of monopoly. The public suffered.

To understand what a business monopoly is, imagine you are selling soft drinks at a school fair. The day is very hot and everyone is thirsty. You expect to make a lot of money. You plan to sell soda for $1 a glass. Your cost is 25 cents a glass.

What you don't expect is to have competition. But, just as you're getting started, you notice another soft-drink stand. Your competitor is charging 75 cents a glass. Of course you have to lower your price or no one will buy from you.

Then, when sales are going well, another competitor appears. She is selling drinks for 50 cents each. You're annoyed, but there is nothing you can do but lower your price. You still make a fine profit, and people get drinks at a fair price.

Competition makes capitalism work well for the consumer. When there is competition it is called "free enterprise" or a "market economy." The people who are thirsty are much better off if businesses are competing. You, the business person, would like less competition. So you make plans to gain a monopoly in the field. You go to the two other soft-drink sellers and buy their stands. If they sell out, you can charge the public anything you want.

Suppose you start with three soft-drink stands and then buy a soft-drink bottling company and then another, and another, until you own the whole industry. Then suppose you buy up the trucking companies that ship your beverages, and then all the sugar producers and the

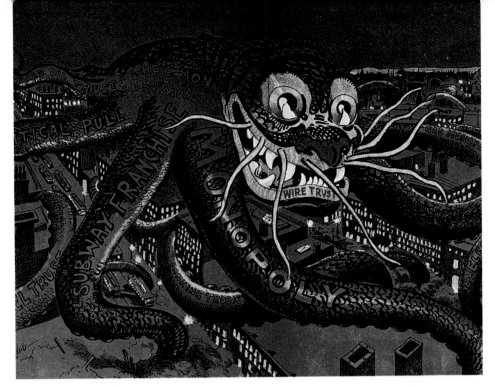

◄ This famous cartoon portrayed the monopoly octopus and its stranglehold on the cities through control of oil, steel, subways, telephone wires, electricity, gas, coal—and political influence.

companies that make all the other ingredients needed in soft drinks. You have become king of the soft-drink world. What power you now wield! You can charge people *five* dollars a glass —or anything you want—and everyone has to pay: you have no competition.

That kind of thing happened in the 19th century. Rockefeller's Standard Oil trust was a huge monopoly. It owned more than 90 percent of America's oil industry, as well as pipelines, tankers, and related industries.

There are some benefits in a monopoly. If it is well run, a monopoly can be very efficient. But usually it is the consumer who suffers when there is no competition.

Americans decided they didn't want monopolies or trusts. A trust is a legal arrangement that allows many different companies to be owned and run by the same people. It is a form of monopoly. The big 19th-century trusts put all their competitors out of business. They were organized in a way that put them mostly beyond government control.

Now you may be saying, "No one *has* to sell out to a monopoly." But that isn't quite true. The monopolies grew so large that they could use unfair business methods. Suppose you are running your soft-drink stand and a big, rich competitor comes and sells drinks for 15 cents. Remember, the drinks cost you 25 cents. You can't stay in business long with that kind of competition. The big monopolies did that kind of thing to put competitors out of business. They could afford to lose money for a while because they were so wealthy.

Economix

Why is it that everyone's eyes begin to close when you say *economics* and open wide when you say *money*? I haven't figured that out, but—stay awake—here are some economic terms that will help you understand how nations earn money. Economists say that there are three basic ways that a nation can organize its system of doing business. These are: as a *market* economy, as a *command* economy, or as a *traditional* economy.

In a market economy the customer (*consumer*) determines what will be produced when he or she spends money. If people in the *marketplace* (stores, offices, catalogues, etc.) ask for green shoes and purple surfboards, someone will soon be making them. The United States is said to have a market economy.

A command economy is organized by the government. The government decides what will be produced and who will do the producing. The state owns production. *Communism* and *socialism* are command systems. There is a big difference

between them, however. Most communist countries (like the former Soviet Union) have been dictatorships where you can't vote out a bad ruler. You can in socialist countries, which are usually democracies (like Sweden).

In a traditional economy people usually do the same work their parents did. If your dad is a government leader, you will be trained for a leadership role. If he is a shoemaker, that's probably what you'll do. In most traditional economies, women work at home. Many Asian and African nations have traditional economic systems.

Now that I've described these systems, I have to tell you that no country is simply market, command, or traditional. There's a fourth system—it is called *hybrid*, which means a mixture. That's what most economies actually are—a little of this and that. It's just that some are more of one than another. France is an example of a true hybrid: its economy is both socialistic and market driven. See what you can find out about our economic system. How much of a hybrid are we?

In 1887, former president Rutherford B. Hayes asked, "Shall the will of monopolies take the place of government by the people?" The answer the American people gave was *no.*

Americans care about individual rights. That has given us strong anti-monopoly feelings; it also makes us want as few laws as possible.

So regulating business in a capitalist country is not easy. Most businesspeople want as little regulation as possible. But the public needs to be protected from unfair business practices. In the 19th century, big business in America got out of control. Politicians were often corrupted by business influences. (What does that mean? How might they be corrupted?)

It was clear that rules and regulations were needed. The American people demanded reforms. In 1890, Congress passed the Sherman Antitrust Act. Senator John Sherman, who sponsored the law, was

Let's Talk Business

WHAT IS A PARTNERSHIP?

Suppose you are a shoemaker, and you make shoes in a small shop by yourself. Then you join with another shoemaker. Now you have a *partnership*. You share the work, the ideas, the profits, and the problems. There are some advantages. It's an easy way to go into business. If you are sick or you want to take a vacation, your partner can keep the business going. But the arrangement does have a problem. Suppose your partner is a bum. He drives the business into debt. Now creditors arrive wanting to be paid back for those debts, but your partner has skipped town. You are stuck with all his debts because you were partners (even though you had nothing to do with those debts).

WHAT IS A CORPORATION?

A *corporation* is a form of business that evolved from the *stock companies* of the past. The London Company, which sent John Smith and others to Jamestown, was a stock company. In the 19th century, corporations became big and sophisticated.

You are a shoemaker, and you want to open a factory with the latest machinery to make thousands of pairs of shoes each week. But renting factory space, buying machinery, and paying salaries will cost a lot of money. So you decide to form a corporation. Now you can sell stock to *stockholders*. Each stockholder then owns a share in your shoe

◀ A woman operates a belt-driven sewing machine at a shoe factory in Lynn, Massachusetts.

factory; but the modern corporation gives them a big advantage over a regular partnership or an old-fashioned stock company. It gives them *limited liability*. That means the stockholders are not responsible (liable) for the debts of the corporation. The corporation holds a business charter (from the government) that recognizes it as a separate being with its own rights and responsibilities—apart from its owners or members. Legally, the corporation is almost like a person itself.

WHAT IS A TARIFF?

A *tariff* is a tax on foreign goods brought into a country. That tax makes the foreign goods more expensive. That means that goods made at home have a better chance of selling. So tariffs help local industry and hurt foreign ones. What do tariffs do to prices? How do they affect the consumer? In the Gilded Age, the Republican Party supported high tariffs, the Democrats low ones.

a brother of General William Tecumseh Sherman. The Sherman Antitrust Act was intended to make business responsible to the public. It said that trusts and monopolies that restrained free competition were illegal. At first no one—not the president, Congress, or the courts—would enforce the law. Nobody wanted to offend the powerful businessmen. But that changed. The presidents, congresses, and courts made the law effective.

Builders and Dreamers

Nineteenth-century Americans thought they lived in the most splendid era in all of history. You can understand why: all those new cities and inventions were mighty exciting. Even the traffic jams in Chicago and New York didn't seem too bad when you considered the things you could do and see in those great cities. Americans seemed to be doing things bigger and better than had ever been done before. Some men and women started thinking about building buildings taller than any built before.

But there was no point in building a really tall building, because people were only willing to walk up four or maybe five flights of stairs. So that was as high as most buildings went until a Vermonter, Elisha Graves Otis, designed a safe elevator. Then, as they say, the sky was the limit. You could build tall buildings and people could ride up inside as high as the building went.

In 1880, if you lived in the elegant Dakota apartment house in New York City, you could drive home in your carriage, back into the elevator, unhitch the horses, and you and your carriage would be lifted to your apartment door.

Central Park

When most people think of architecture, they think of buildings. But land can be transformed by a designer as a sculptor transforms clay or an architect steel and stone. Frederick Law Olmsted, a great landscape architect, did just that when he designed beautiful new Central Park in New York City, America's first great city park. He had lakes dug and hills built. He made formal areas with fountains, playgrounds, and concert shells. He created rugged and wild areas. Notice that word *created*. If you visit Central Park today you may think nature made those rugged areas. Nature had a lot of help from Frederick Olmsted.

Olmsted loved democracy and believed that democratic cities should have large parks for recreation and for quiet walking, open to all people. He thought a public park should be as handsome as a king's park. It took 20 years and 3,800 men to build Central Park, but when it was finished, New York had a park for the people that was lovelier than any king's park.

▲ A view of Central Park, by the popular printmakers Currier and Ives

And now that there were elevators, tall buildings seemed just the thing for America's new cities. But, if you think about it, you will realize there is a problem in building something very tall. The higher a building goes, the more it weighs.

So, if you wanted to build a tall building, you had to build its walls with stone or brick or something very strong to hold the weight. Since America was becoming the world's leading steel producer, maybe it isn't surprising that some American architects came up with the idea of using steel as a *frame* for a building. A steel frame could hold all the weight of a tall building. The walls didn't have to hold any weight at all. So, thick walls weren't needed to support the building. Walls became just a covering, like skin.

The architect was free to use almost anything—even decorated metal, or glass—as the skin of a building. Luckily, when this new idea came on the scene, America produced an architect who was a genius. He was able to take that technology and combine it with artistry. His name was Louis Sullivan.

Louis Sullivan has been called the inventor of the skyscraper. That is not quite true. Sullivan didn't invent tall buildings; what he did was build them beautifully. Sullivan loved nature and poetry. Like Frederick Olmsted, he, too, was imbued with democratic ideas.

Sullivan tried to express his ideas in his architecture. He believed that the individual—each of us—is very important. It was an idea he got from reading the words of people like Thomas Jefferson, Ralph Waldo Emerson, and Henry David Thoreau. Louis Sullivan built tall buildings that are comfortable and human in scale. They are American buildings, not copies of European palaces.

One day, a young Wisconsin-born architect named Frank Lloyd Wright came to work for Louis Sullivan. Frank Lloyd Wright became even more famous than his teacher.

To *imbue* (im-BEW) means to "penetrate to the core," usually with a feeling or an idea.

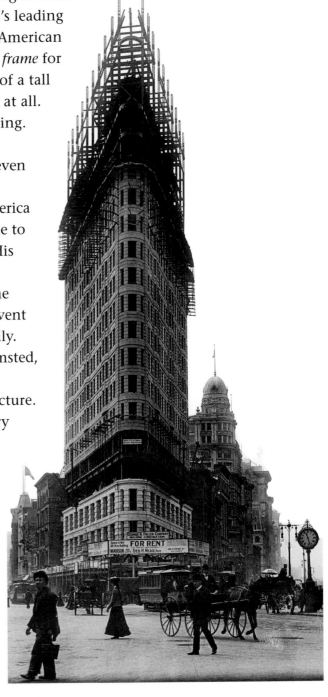

An early skyscraper, New York City's steel-framed Flatiron Building, under construction in 1902 ▶

Many people consider Wright one of the world's greatest architects. Like his mentor, Wright was concerned with that American idea of individual worth. His buildings were meant to make life more enjoyable for all who used them. They often seem a part of the landscape; that's because the architect thought a lot about the natural environment and the ways that people have always lived. One of Wright's homes is built over a brook; another was inspired by an Indian pueblo.

Other things, besides buildings, needed to be built in America. Rivers needed to be crossed.

A German immigrant, John Augustus Roebling, came up with one of the best new ideas. He knew that steel is not only strong, it is flexible. He twisted thin steel wires together and made strong steel cable. That opened up all kinds of new ways to build things. Roebling decided that a bridge could be *suspended*—which means "hung"—from steel cable attached to concrete and stone towers. Roebling designed the world's first modern suspension bridges. Actually, his bridges were similar in idea to the rope footbridges the Indians built in Central America 1,000 years ago. Except that Roebling built bridges strong enough to support railroad trains and cross mighty rivers. But when he suggested a bridge across New York's East River between Brooklyn and Manhattan, most people thought he had lost his mind.

It would be the longest and highest bridge ever built anywhere in the world. It would have to withstand powerful winds and ocean tides. Experts said it was impossible. The stone towers needed to anchor the steel rope could not be placed on land; the distance from shore to shore was too great. The towers would have to be built in the river. No one was quite sure how that could be done. New construction methods would have to be developed.

Steel cables stretch from stone towers during the construction of the Brooklyn Bridge. ▼

▲ The Brooklyn Bridge in about 1900—the bridge spans the East River in New York City, connecting Manhattan Island to Brooklyn.

▲ Workmen cut and tie tension cables during the construction of the Brooklyn Bridge.

Well, it was done. It was called the Brooklyn Bridge, and it took 14 years to build. It demanded courage: from financiers who believed in the idea and raised the money (some were corrupt and made scandalous profits); from workmen who risked their lives; and from John Roebling, who lost his life after his toes were crushed in a construction accident and gangrene set in.

His son, 32-year-old Washington Roebling, took over. He was a Civil War hero and an engineer. It was he who figured out that to build the gigantic stone towers, workers would have to go underwater, into special chambers filled with compressed air. Roebling went right along with the laborers; then he was stricken with an illness that afflicts deep-sea divers. It is called the "bends," and it left him partially paralyzed. He was unable to move about and had to supervise from his bed, using binoculars to watch the workmen. His wife, Emily Roebling, went back and forth to the bridge with his daily instructions. When it was finally done, the bridge was called a "wonder of the world." Its towers were bigger than any other man-made structure except for the Egyptian pyramids. The bridge was so high that tall ships could glide easily beneath it. Horse-drawn carriages, railroad trains, pedestrians, and an electric tram each had a special roadway on the Brooklyn Bridge.

It was the first bridge lit by electricity. People came from all over just to see it. It towered over the buildings on both shores and linked the separate cities of Brooklyn and Manhattan into a united New York. Americans felt that if they could build a wondrous bridge like this one, they could do anything.

A few people wondered if the big bridge was really safe—but after circus man P. T. Barnum led a herd of elephants across it, there were no more doubters.

In 1883, New York City had its biggest party ever. Fireworks filled the sky. President Chester A. Arthur cut the ribbon that officially opened the bridge. Then the president went to Washington Roebling's bedside to thank him on behalf of the nation.

▲ In 1883, on the opening night of the Brooklyn Bridge, fireworks filled the sky to celebrate this "wonder of the world."

Presidents Again

People will tell you the presidents after Lincoln were weak and that Congress wasn't so strong either. In fact, some people say that after the Civil War it was the new, rich businessmen who ran the country. Now there is something to that—but it's not the whole story. So when you read of the nine men who sat in the White House after the Civil War, keep an open mind. Some of these presidents were stronger than they may seem.

But not **Andrew Johnson (1865–1869)**. It probably would have been better for the country if someone else had been vice president when Lincoln was shot. You may already know that. In case you have forgotten the details, here is a review.

After the Civil War, the United States needed a president who could tell leaders from both the North and the South to behave. But Johnson couldn't get Congress to respect or even listen to him. The country needed to solve its racial problems since slavery was abolished. Most people believed that President Lincoln would have attempted to solve them. President Johnson didn't even try. Partly because of that failed opportunity, racial hatreds continued to haunt the nation in the 19th and 20th centuries.

Andrew Johnson let the same men who had seceded from the Union and started the Civil War take power in the South. He seemed to approve of Jim Crow, the spirit behind segregation and white people's hatred of blacks. He vetoed a civil rights bill aimed at helping the freed slaves. (It was passed over his veto.) He opposed the 14th Amendment to the Constitution. He was a backward-looking president at a time when the nation needed to go forward. He was so unpopular that some congressmen accused him of crimes and tried to throw him out of office. He was impeached but saved from conviction by one vote.

Andrew Johnson, 17th president of the United States ▶

▲ Ulysses S. Grant, 18th president of the United States

The country needed a strong, capable president. Unfortunately, the next president was another failure.

He was the great Civil War general **Ulysses S. Grant (1869–1877)**. Being a general isn't at all like being president. In fact, the very things that made him a good general worked against him as president. Like Johnson, he was stubborn—not a bad trait for a general who has to keep fighting, but it doesn't help a president who needs to be flexible enough to compromise.

Grant trusted men who weren't trustworthy; they got rich stealing from the government. There was much corruption and dishonesty when Grant was president, and he didn't realize it until too late.

During the Johnson and Grant presidencies, Congress sent troops south to see that elections were open to everyone. Male former slaves were able to vote. Black men were elected to state office and to Congress.

Some white Southern leaders didn't like that. So when the next presidential election came along they decided to take charge. They wanted to take the vote away from black men, and they began to do it. President **Rutherford B. Hayes (1877–1881)** didn't do anything to stop them.

Hayes's election was one of the closest in our history. More people voted for his opponent than for him. He won in the Electoral College by one vote, and that made him president. His supporters made a deal to pull the government troops out of the South in return for that vote.

An electoral commission, created in 1877 to resolve the 20 disputed electoral votes in the 1876 presidential election, decided in favor of Republican Rutherford B. Hayes over Democrat Samuel Tilden. ▶

That was the end of congressional Reconstruction, and of most attempts to be fair to black people in the South.

Hayes, an honest man, ended the corruption of the Grant years. His wife was a supporter of the growing *temperance* movement. Temperance supporters wanted to prohibit (ban) the drinking of alcohol.

James A. Garfield (1881), our 20th president, was born in a log cabin in Ohio. He might have been a good president, but a man with mental problems shot and killed President Garfield soon after he was elected.

Chester A. Arthur took over as 21st president ***(1881–1885)***. He was a reformer: he wanted to make the government as efficient as possible. He did that by making the Civil Service Commission powerful. Civil-service jobs are government jobs. Politicians had been giving government jobs to their friends, usually as payoffs for favors. That was a terrible practice. It meant that the jobs often went to the wrong people. The Civil Service Commission made people take examinations for government jobs. Arthur's reforms angered some congressmen, and he was not nominated for a second term.

Grover Cleveland, the next president, was a big man with common sense, courage, and integrity. Cleveland was 49 and a bachelor when he was elected. He soon married young Frances Folsom. When they started having children—they had five in all—they really livened up the White House. Cleveland was another reformer. The reforms he had in mind had to do with money and organization and honesty. He didn't concern himself with social justice or fairness. He didn't understand the new problems faced by industrial workers or the old problems of racial injustice.

During Cleveland's presidency, in the southwest, the Apache chief Geronimo surrendered to army forces. That was the end of the Indians' freedom to live as they wished. At the time, hardly anyone—except the Native Americans—seemed to care.

When Cleveland ran for a second term he lost to ***Benjamin Harrison (1889–1893)***.

Grover Cleveland served two terms, but not in a row—he was our 22nd and 24th president. ▼

◄ Benjamin Harrison, 23rd president of the United States

During Harrison's administration the Sherman Antitrust Act was passed. It outlawed the monopolies that suppressed competition. Six new states were admitted to the Union while he was president. (See if you can find out which ones.)

The next president, **Grover Cleveland**, was our 22nd *(1885–1889)* and 24th president *(1893–1897)*. Cleveland came into office at the start of a big, five-year-long depression, one of the nation's worst ever. The stock market went way down, lots of people lost their jobs, and the times were awful for many Americans. Cleveland and his government didn't do much to reverse the depression, but governments then weren't expected to do that.

The next president, **William McKinley (1897–1901)**, was chief executive at the turn of the century. He was a lawyer, and smart, with good manners and a kindly way. He liked people and they liked him.

The United States fought a war with Spain while McKinley was president. Spain's time as a world power was ending; the United States' time was beginning. After the war—which lasted for 100 days—the United States controlled the Philippine Islands, Guam, the Samoan Islands, and Puerto Rico. During the war we annexed Hawaii. There were native leaders in each of those places who wanted independence, not U.S. control. (More on all this later.)

President William McKinley takes the oath of office as he becomes our 25th president. ▶

◄ Crowds fill a plaza at the Pan-American Exposition, a world's fair held in Buffalo, New York, in 1901. President William McKinley would be fatally shot there on September 6, 1901.

McKinley was elected to a second term. Six months after the election he was at a world's fair in Buffalo, New York, shaking hands with citizens who wanted to meet their president. A young man stepped up; one of his hands was wrapped in what looked like a bandage. No one realized it, but the man was an anarchist. He believed all governments were bad. Besides that, he may have been insane. The anarchist pressed the "bandage" against the president's stomach. Inside was a revolver. He fired twice.

McKinley fell to the floor. The assassin was caught and beaten. "Let no man hurt him," cried McKinley. Eight days later the president was dead.

When McKinley's vice president, Theodore Roosevelt, took office, the time of weak presidents was over. You'll read more about him later—the American people had a good time with Roosevelt as president.

The People's Party

The place is Georgia; the time, 1892. A small, redheaded man—his name is Tom Watson—is standing on a wooden platform under tall pines. A crowd of men tries to hear what Watson has to say—he is a fine orator—but they are having a hard time of it. Watson, a congressman, is running for reelection. He is a member of a new political party, the People's Party, also called the Populist Party. The Democrats have sent a brass band to his rally. They are playing loudly—very loudly. They are doing it on purpose.

There is something unusual about this southern crowd. It is both black and white. The people are mostly poor whites and poor blacks. Watson believes they have something in common: their poverty. If they stand together perhaps they can do something about it.

His listeners know that on Election Day, they will be under much pressure to vote for Democratic candidates. Voting is not private. The Democrats have become the only party with power in the South. They have been known to stuff ballot boxes with false votes to ensure their victories. They have paid voters for their votes. Those who

When a man picked a ballot, everyone knew if it was a Democratic ballot, a Republican ballot, or another party's. Some employers fired workers who voted the wrong way. Bribery was common.

This cartoon—which was supposed to show what the Supreme Court would look like if the Populists ran it—sneered at them as a bunch of old fogeys and hayseeds. ▼

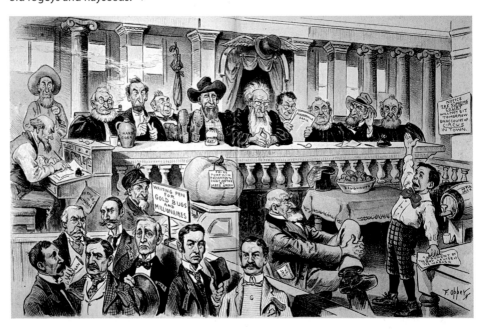

attempt to vote for any other party risk losing their jobs, or worse. Watson wants to change things. The People's Party is campaigning for secret ballots.

Watson and his Populists see themselves as the party of the common man. They believe the government is working for the rich and powerful and taking advantage of the poor and weak. They believe that the people—ordinary people—must take control of the government. They are considered radicals. They want to change the system.

Tom Watson was no common man. He was a skilled lawyer, and the largest landowner in all of Georgia. But he could identify with people in need. He helped guide a third party that flashed across the nation like a brilliant comet. That party—the People's Party— elected five senators, 10 representatives, and three governors. It championed ideas that were laughed at—at first—but later became law. And though the Populists faded away, their ideas keep reappearing, in cycles, as most comets do.

Those reformers spoke for ordinary Americans who didn't want to be left out of the good times that were being enjoyed by others. They demanded rights. Some people called them "communists"; some people called them "hayseeds." But they weren't either thing. They were just people who wanted to take part in the governing process; they wanted their ideas heard. And it wasn't long before there were secret ballots and woman's suffrage and many of the other things the Populists supported. They demanded that government be strong and active and help people—which was, and still is, a controversial path, but one the American government soon took.

What were some of their other ideas? The Populists wanted a graduated income tax. That means they wanted people to be taxed according to how much money they made. Wealthy people would pay more than poor people. They wanted senators directly elected by citizens—instead of by state legislatures, as the Constitution then directed. They wanted the government to lend money to farmers. They wanted the government to protect the consumer from unsafe goods and unfair practices.

All of those, and some other Populist ideas, would be adopted by the other political parties and eventually become law. "The land," said a Populist declaration, "including all the natural resources

▲ Tom Watson got Congress to pass the first ever resolution to have rural mail delivered free. Until then, farmers paid the mailman themselves.

During the Civil War both sides taxed citizens' income, but, aside from that time of crisis, Americans had never paid an income tax. That changed in 1914 when a constitutional amendment made the tax legal. Only 1 percent of Americans were rich enough to pay the income tax, and the average bill that year was $41.

of wealth, is the heritage of all the people and should not be monopolized for speculative purposes." That was a conservation idea before most people thought about conserving land and resources.

But let's get back to Tom Watson. Remember, he is standing on a wooden platform talking to farmers; they are angry. Farm prices are low. In 1865, cotton sold for a dollar a pound. It is 1892 and cotton is 7 cents a pound. It costs more than 7 cents to grow a pound of cotton! In the Midwest, wheat prices have tumbled from $2.50 a bushel in the 1860s to 50 cents a bushel in the 1890s. Farmers can't pay their bills.

When the farmers read the newspapers they learn how good life is for America's millionaires. Some people are calling this time "the Gay Nineties." William Vanderbilt has just thrown a big party for his friends in ritzy Newport, Rhode Island. They sat on red damask chairs and dug with silver shovels in a play sandbox filled with rubies and diamonds. The society columns are full of that story. It is enough to make anyone angry. The farmers can't understand what is happening. They are working hard and helping to feed and clothe the world. Yet while some people are getting very rich, they are losing their farms.

The Populist leaders tell the farmers that there is a conspiracy. They say the eastern bankers, the railroad magnates, and the grain-elevator owners are plotting against them. They are keeping the farmers poor so they can get richer.

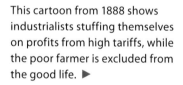

This cartoon from 1888 shows industrialists stuffing themselves on profits from high tariffs, while the poor farmer is excluded from the good life. ▶

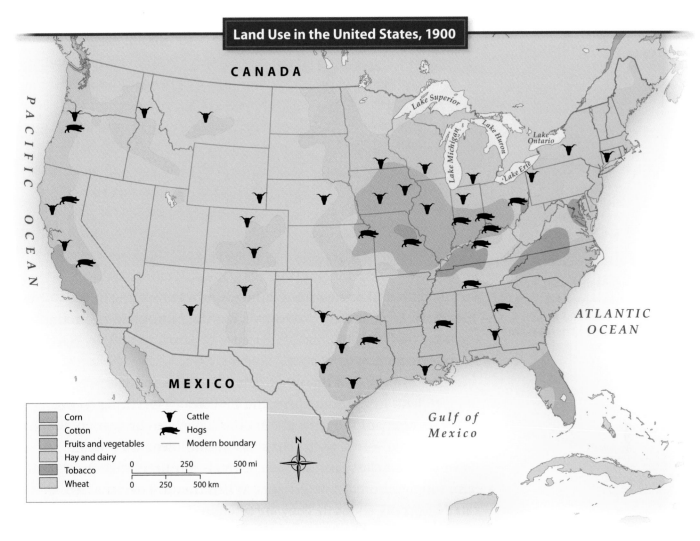

Land Use in the United States, 1900

CANADA

PACIFIC OCEAN

Lake Superior
Lake Michigan
Lake Huron
Lake Ontario
Lake Erie

ATLANTIC OCEAN

MEXICO

Gulf of Mexico

Corn		Cattle
Cotton		Hogs
Fruits and vegetables		Modern boundary
Hay and dairy
Tobacco
Wheat

0   250   500 mi
0 250 500 km

N

▲ In 1900, land in the United States was used in a variety of ways to feed a growing nation and compete in a world market.

That isn't really true. No one is plotting against the farmers on purpose. The big-money powers care only about themselves. They are working *for* their own interests—not *against* the farmers'. But their interests hurt the farmers. And their money gives them political power. The farmers have little money and little political power. Populism has arisen out of frustration.

Before the Civil War, life seemed simpler. Most people, then, were farmers who grew their own food, spun their own yarn, chopped their own timber, and had to buy little outside. Now farming has changed. Railroads and new equipment—and millions of acres of new farmland in the Great Plains—have led farmers toward larger farms and single-crop production. Farmers are growing big crops—of wheat, or cotton, or corn. Those crops are not just for themselves and

▲ New farming equipment, such as the Marsh harvester and binder, improved speed and efficiency on the big farms of the Midwest.

their neighbors: the American farmer is now competing in the world market. He is amazingly productive. But the more grain he produces, the more he floods the market. Because he farms so well, he is helping to drive prices down.

There is more to it than that. The farmer is no longer independent. In the South after the Civil War, everything seems changed. Many of the large plantations have been broken up. For the old aristocrats, losing their slaves has meant losing their wealth. A new merchant class wields power. Farmers must buy their goods and farm supplies from the merchants. When they are overcharged, they can do nothing about it. They are often in debt to the merchants. They must grow what the merchants wish. Many of the merchants are also bankers. Soon they own much of the farmland. Proud former planters have become tenants.

You can't be a modern farmer without modern equipment, especially on the big farms of the Middle West and Far West. Combines are needed to cut, thresh, and gather wheat. They are much faster and more efficient than human labor. To buy the new equipment, farmers must borrow from the banks. That puts them in debt. In order to pay the debt on farm equipment, to pay the mortgages on their property, and to pay railroad fees for shipping their crops, the farmers need cash. They need to sell their crops at a profit. They aren't doing that. They feel trapped.

In Kansas, 11,122 farmers lose their farms to the banks between 1889 and 1893. Even those who hang on are angry. After all, they want to enjoy all the new things—bicycles, electricity, and so on—that other Americans are enjoying. They don't have enough money to do so.

If there were more money in circulation it would help, they believe. And they are right. The Populist platform includes a monetary plan. Many bankers make fun of it. They don't think these farmers are smart enough to know anything about money.

The bankers are wrong. Farmers come by the thousands to farm meetings where they sleep in their wagons, or under the stars, share barbecues, and listen to speakers who talk of economic and national problems. The farmers listen, argue, and learn. Populism is a democratic movement, and an impressive one.

It would be easier for the farmers to pay the interest on their loans if more dollars were circulating and prices were higher. The Populists know how money can be used to help or hurt groups of people.

Making Money

A U.S. twenty-dollar double eagle gold coin ▶

You write a check for $100. You can cash that check if you have $100 in the bank. A check is just a promise to pay money that you already have. Dollars (paper money) printed by the government are like that check. They are our government's promise that it has something of equal value. That something used to be gold.

In the 19th century, anyone in the United States could exchange paper dollars for gold coins. A country that backed its money with gold was on the "gold standard" and usually had a sound currency. (*Currency* is a country's actual money in circulation—its paper bills and coins.) For the gold standard to work, the price of gold had to be fixed—the government said how many dollars it cost to buy an ounce of gold and stuck to that.

But a country on the gold standard can't print a lot of money. Gold is scarce—only a certain amount exists in the world. If you were on the gold standard, you couldn't print more money than you had gold to back it within your bank vaults.

During the Civil War, Abraham Lincoln needed money quickly. There wasn't enough gold. He issued a special kind of money, called "greenbacks." There was no gold to back them. The government promised to pay the value of the greenbacks.

That extra money in circulation created *inflation*. Inflation means rising prices. The more money people have, the more they can pay for goods and services. The people selling the goods raise their prices, and then it takes more money to buy something. So the more dollars there are in circulation, the less each dollar is worth.

After the war, Lincoln's greenbacks were gradually taken out of circulation. In 1873 the

▲ A one-dollar note, printed after Congress passed a law authorizing the treasury to issue paper money to finance the Civil War

nation returned to the gold standard. There was less money around. That caused *deflation*. There wasn't much money to pay for things, so people couldn't sell them. There were goods but no *demand* for them. When there's no demand, prices drop until goods are cheap enough for people to start buying them again. (*Depressions* happen when many people are out of work and so broke that they don't buy things no matter how low prices go.)

Falling prices meant less income for people like farmers. Farmers wanted more money in circulation. But there wasn't enough gold to let the government print more bills. The farmers thought the government should use silver to back its currency—in addition to gold. Naturally, silver miners also wanted the government to buy silver to back dollars. They wanted a *silver standard*.

In 1878, Congress listened to the farmers and miners. It voted to buy silver to back the nation's currency. People now had a choice: paper dollars, gold, or silver coins. At the same time, the Treasury—where the government keeps its money—had a *surplus*: gold and silver piled up, because the government had more money coming in (from tariffs and taxes) than it was spending. Since it now had a lot of gold and silver, the government could print more money. Prices went up—including the price of farm produce.

When Benjamin Harrison was president, Congress gave away most of the surplus in the form of pensions to Civil War veterans. It also raised tariffs (the taxes on imported goods) so high that the government's income from those taxes almost disappeared—people weren't willing to buy expensive foreign goods. That was the end of the surplus.

Soon money was scarce again and there was deflation. Farmers were earning less money because prices were dropping. That really hurt the farmers who had borrowed money for farm equipment. Many lost their farms.

Because money was in short supply, people who had money to lend could charge a lot of interest to those who wanted to borrow it. (*Interest* is the cost of borrowing money.) Deflation is hard on people who have borrowed money. They have less income but they still have to pay back loans at interest rates based on the old, higher prices.

To help the people who had borrowed, the Populist leaders wanted more money in circulation. They supported the *bimetal* (silver and gold) standard. Then they went even further. The Populists felt the money supply should be controlled by an elected board. They were asking for a new monetary system that would create money "in the name of the whole people." This concept—a democratic money system—was a huge break with tradition. The financiers hated the idea. Most Americans didn't understand it.

In the 20th century some of those Populist notions became law. A Federal Reserve System came into being, with a board (independent of political parties) that controls the supply of money. It had many elements of the plan the Populists proposed.

Hard Times

When Grover Cleveland stepped into the presidency for the second time, he walked into a beehive. It was 1893, and he got stung by a depression.

Remember, in those days, anytime you wanted to exchange your paper money for gold or silver, you could. But the supply of gold in the Treasury was way, way down. When Americans realized that, it created a money panic. People began turning in paper money for gold. Everyone preferred gold to silver. The gold reserve was being emptied. Then the stock market went zooming down. (So many people were selling the shares they owned in companies that the companies quickly lost value.)

Farmers had been in trouble for at least five years, what with droughts, a grasshopper plague, and falling prices. Now the rest of the nation began hurting. Badly.

◀ Investors at the New York Stock Exchange rush to sell their shares during the Panic of 1893.

When farmers stopped buying goods, because they had no money, manufacturers began to suffer. Soon the banks were in trouble, too. The banks took farms from farmers who couldn't pay their mortgages; then they tried to sell the farms. Someone had to pay back the money that the banks had lent. But no one was buying farms. That put the banks in trouble.

In the first nine months of 1893, 172 state banks, 177 private banks, and 47 savings-and-loan associations closed. By the end of the year the total was 500 banks. More than 15,000 businesses failed. And that was just the beginning. Railroad earnings were way down, and then the unthinkable happened: railroads began closing. The Union Pacific, and the Atchison, Topeka and Santa Fe were two of the 156 railroads that folded.

Mines were shut down, steamers stayed in port, factories closed their doors, and companies went bankrupt.

Many of the people who had worked in those banks, railroads, and factories were out of work, which made the depression more frightening.

Farmers could usually eat, but unemployed city workers were desperate. Unemployment was worse in some areas than others. The manufacturing states of Pennsylvania, New York, and Michigan were hit hard. One out of four people in Pennsylvania was reported out of work. In Michigan the figure was 43.6 percent. Nationally, one out of every five workers was said to be idle. In Chicago, 100,000 men were sleeping on the streets. Even those who had jobs faced cuts in pay and work.

What was going on in America? Was this the land of promise?

Congress passed a high tariff law (remember, a *tariff* is a tax on goods imported from abroad). That high tariff helped the business

---

Say MOR-gidge

When a farmer borrows money from a bank to buy a farm (or when anyone borrows money to buy a house or piece of land), the money he borrows—his debt—is called a "mortgage." It is a form of loan. The farmer has to pay back the bank for the loan in *installments*, a little at a time. If the farmer can't make his mortgage payments—if he *defaults*—the bank *forecloses*: it takes the farm instead of the payments. Now the bank has to sell the farm to someone else to make back the money it lent to the farmer.

◀ 1890—A line of unemployed men hoping for work

trusts by keeping foreign competitors out of the country. But it made goods expensive for most people. In addition, foreign countries, like England and France, weren't going to sit back and accept the tariff. They got even by not buying American wheat and corn. That, of course, hurt the American farmer again. First farmers had to pay high prices for home-produced goods that didn't have to compete with outside imports. Then they couldn't find markets to sell their crops because foreign countries were mad at them. And the high tariff stopped most imports from abroad, so the government got less income from taxes on foreign goods, just when the nation needed more money.

The business trusts weren't the only ones who wanted high tariffs. Most industrial workers believed that tariffs protected their jobs by making foreign goods more expensive than American-made goods. Without foreign competition, things made here were more likely to sell.

But the farmers were mostly Populists, and they were enraged by the high tariffs and high prices. The bankers and industrialists thought the tariff was needed to protect American industry and jobs. It wasn't easy for anyone to know who was right.

Gold and Silver

To *strike* means to "stop working in order to force an employer to pay higher wages or to meet other demands." If all the employees of a company go on strike at the same time, it may force the company to shut down, or find replacement workers (called "scabs"), or pay the higher wages.

Eighteen ninety-three was an awful year; 1894 was worse. Some 1,400 strikes were called in 1894. Workers were protesting low wages and poor working conditions. Many of them lost their jobs when they went on strike. You know they had to be hurting to risk that.

Jacob Coxey was a farmer, a quarry owner, a devout Christian, and a dedicated reformer. His great-grandfather fought in the American Revolution. He thought the government should help its out-of-work citizens find jobs. So, in 1894—when things had gotten really bad—he marched an army of unemployed men from Massillon, Ohio, to Washington, D.C. President Cleveland refused to see them. Crowds cheered the marching men; the police arrested Coxey.

President Cleveland didn't believe it was his job to do anything about the unemployed. Most leaders agreed with him. Employment and working conditions were thought to be the responsibility of business.

That summer, the highly profitable Pullman Company cut workers' wages for the fifth time. Pullman made railroad sleeping cars in a town near Chicago. When the company cut wages, it didn't

When the Pullman Company in Chicago repeatedly cut workers' wages but maintained their high rents, the workers went on strike. Some, like the man pictured here, lost their jobs and sank into poverty. ▶

▲ Rioting workers set fire to 600 freight cars at the Panhandle yards during the Pullman strike.

cut the fees it charged workers for rent, heat, and lights, or to use the company church. The workers were angry; they went on strike.

Soon the strike spread to 50,000 workers, throughout the railroad industry. The governor of Illinois said he could handle the situation, but Cleveland's attorney general didn't agree. (The attorney general had been a railroad lawyer.) He insisted the government take action against the workers and the union. Federal troops were sent to Illinois, which led to violence, deaths, and arrests.

Businesses and banks were failing everywhere, and there was a run on gold as people tried to make sure their money was in the safest currency—gold. The government's gold reserves were disappearing. President Cleveland blamed the country's money problems on an act of Congress—the Silver Purchase Act of 1890, which said that the government had to buy so many million dollars' worth of silver every year.

▲ President Cleveland called in the 15th United States Infantry Company C to help break up the railroad strike against the Pullman Palace Car Company.

The United States would leave the gold standard in 1933. Today you cannot cash in a dollar bill and get gold instead.

Cleveland led the nation back to a strict gold standard. The Silver Purchase Act was repealed. The president became known as a "gold bug." But it didn't help a bit. The gold reserves kept going down. And down. And down. That led to a crisis. The nation was in danger of going bankrupt.

Finally, in desperation, President Cleveland went to the country's leading financier—J. P. Morgan—and asked for his help. Morgan, with other bankers, gave the government gold in return for U.S. government bonds (which they soon sold at a profit). That helped stabilize the currency. But many Americans thought it was humiliating for the president of the United States to have to go to a private banker for help. The financiers seemed to have more power than the U.S. government!

Prosperity would soon return. Within a few years there were jobs and confidence in abundance. The experts would not agree on what had brought on the depression, or what brought recovery. The discovery of gold in South Africa, Canada, and Alaska helped. It put more money in circulation worldwide.

A satirical cartoon shows banker John Pierpont Morgan helping Uncle Sam. ▶

But in 1894 and 1895, everyone in the nation was concerned about money. No one knew that the hard times would soon disappear. People argued a lot about what was needed to bring back prosperity. Farmers and silver miners associated the bimetal policy with good times. If the Treasury were full of silver, it could print more money and mint more coins. More money in circulation, they believed, would bring happy days. Others—who called themselves "sound money" people—thought silver the road to financial disaster.

Gold in Alaska

Back in 1867, Secretary of State William Seward bought a big piece of land for the United States. Some people thought it worthless and overpriced. They called it "a large lump of ice." Seward spent $7.2 million, or about 2 cents an acre, to buy Alaska from Russia. Some Americans wanted Russia to keep it. They called the deal "Seward's folly." It turned out to be one of the world's great real-estate deals, like the Louisiana Purchase.

In 1896, when gold was discovered in the Klondike (in northwestern Canada, not far from Alaska), people decided that Seward was smart after all. It was the richest gold strike ever. It would change the history of western Canada, Alaska, and the whole Pacific Northwest. As news of the gold spread, a whole lot of people headed for northern Canada and Alaska.

Alaska, which became the 49th state in 1959, is huge. Put a tracing of Alaska on top of the lower 48, and you may be astonished at the size of our largest state. It has a coastline longer than that of all the lower states combined. Juneau (on the coast, off British Columbia) is its capital. In 1942, U.S. Army engineers hacked a 1,388-mile road through wilderness. That Alaska Highway has, for better and worse, brought trucks, oil rigs, and new people into a land of totem poles, caribou, and native cultures.

▲ Thousands of miners and prospectors climb through Chilkoot Pass in the rush to find gold in the Klondike region on the Yukon River in Alaska.

BIMETALISM, 1872

TAKE YOUR CHOICE

SILVER

THIS FACTORY IS CLOSED ON ACCOUNT OF A LACK OF FUNDS

MONOMETALISM, 1894

▲ Arguments about gold and silver raged in the mid-1890s. This cartoon, from a popular pamphlet published in 1893, depicts silver as the solution to the nation's financial woes. At left, the bimetal policy—in which the value of money is based on both gold and silver—is represented by a happy worker and thriving factory in the background. At right, the monometallic policy—in which the value of money is based only on the supply of gold—is represented by a closed factory and a family in poverty.

A stockpile of gold or silver in the Treasury isn't the only thing that determines a country's wealth. Its industry, resources, and people have much more to do with it. But you wouldn't have thought that back in 1895.

Gold and silver divided the nation. It was silver farmers against gold-bug industrialists and industrial workers. The fight got hot—very hot. Then into the fray marched a silver-tongued orator. He was young, handsome, and sincere. He wanted to be president.

Making a Mint

A *mint* is a place where you make coins. Today, the coins you use are made at the U.S. mints in Denver and Philadelphia. The U.S. Bureau of the Mint has gold warehouses (they're called "depositories") at Fort Knox, Kentucky, and at West Point, New York. Some commemorative coins are minted at West Point and at a mint and museum in San Francisco. Gold and silver coins (called "bullion") are minted at West Point. Paper currency is made by the Bureau of Engraving and Printing in Washington, D.C.

A Cross of Gold

If you were in school in the 1890s, and you wanted to impress your friends, you worked hard at oratory. Good speakers were heroes, even more than good athletes. Schoolchildren memorized Daniel Webster's speeches, and Abraham Lincoln's, too. They learned long poems and recited them at school assemblies. Boys and girls joined debating teams. They learned to speak out—loudly and clearly—and to make their speeches interesting.

Even with all that competition, William Jennings Bryan was the outstanding speaker in his grade school, high school, and college. He was a farm boy, and, like most of his Illinois neighbors, a devout Protestant who believed in the absolute truth of the words of the Bible. (Because his father was Baptist and his mother Methodist, Willy Bryan attended Sunday school *twice* every Sunday.)

Along with religion, something else was central to his being. It was a belief in the values of the American Constitution and of American democracy. William Jennings Bryan believed in democracy with the same intensity and purity he brought to his religion. People quickly realized that.

Bryan became a lawyer, moved to Lincoln, Nebraska, and soon impressed people there with his honesty and his sincerity. When he was just 30 years old, in 1890, he got elected to Congress. Bryan was a Democrat, and Nebraskans usually voted Republican, so it was a surprising victory.

In Congress he asked questions. Why do some people who work hard have lots of money, and other people, who also work hard, have little? Bryan went to the Library of Congress, got books, read them, thought about gold and silver, and formed opinions. When the Democrats, under Grover Cleveland, repealed the Silver Purchase Act, Bryan refused to go along with his party. He spoke out, he gave his reasons, and people listened.

Then he ran for the Senate, and lost. It was no disgrace for a man as young as he. It didn't slow him down a bit. He decided he would run for president.

The night before he gave his most famous speech, Bryan watched the delegates at the Democratic presidential convention cheering another candidate. "These people don't know it," he said, "but they will be cheering for me just this way this time tomorrow night." ▼

▲ This cartoon suggested that Bryan was a rabble-rouser who ruthlessly exploited the words of the Bible in his speeches.

Now that seemed laughable. He was unknown in most parts of the country. The Democratic Party leaders ignored him.

Bryan set to work. Someone said he had "superlative self-assurance." He took a job as editor of the *Omaha World-Herald*. That gave him a platform—a chance to write editorials that could be sent around the country. Then he went on a speaking tour: North, South, East, and West. When he spoke—well, he was magnetic. People were attracted.

These were the days before microphones. You needed a big voice to be heard. William Jennings Bryan had one. He discussed issues intelligently. He smiled and shook hands. He was always pleasant and friendly. He made complicated ideas seem simple. When he talked about gold and silver, people understood what he was saying. He was a silver man. He supported many of the reforming ideas of the Populists.

The Democratic convention gathered in a packed auditorium in Chicago. The delegates were to pick a candidate for president: someone to follow Grover Cleveland (who, as you know, was a gold bug). No one could agree on a candidate. Few even considered the young man from Nebraska—until he got up to speak about silver.

He led his listeners through the history of the struggle between the forces of silver and gold. On Bryan's tongue it became a struggle between good and evil. He was dividing the country between East and West. Between *hardy pioneers* and *financial magnates*. Between *city* and *country*. Between *labor* and *management*.

The crowd was caught in the energy of his words. He controlled them as a great actor controls an audience. He said:

Burn down your cities and leave our farms, and your cities will spring up again as if by magic. But destroy our farms and the grass will grow in the streets of every city in the country.

Cheers bounced off the walls like thunder off mountains. He wasn't finished. Now, when he spoke again, the audience was hushed. He talked of farmers and workers, and of the unfairness of an economic system that left the working classes burdened with debt. Then he came to the end of the speech and to words soon to be repeated around the nation. He was using religious images when, in a ringing voice, he said, *You shall not press down upon the brow of labor this crown of thorns; you shall not crucify mankind upon a cross of gold.* The convention went crazy.

The next day the Democratic Party nominated William Jennings Bryan for president of the United States.

The Populists, too, were swept up in the Bryan fever. They nominated the silver-tongued orator as their candidate for president.

But not all the Populists were happy about it. Tom Watson was furious. He thought the nation needed a third party and that the Populists should have their own candidate. If the Populists fused (joined) with the Democrats, Watson said, it would be the end of the Populists. So when he was asked to run for vice president on the Populist ticket, Watson was reluctant. But he finally agreed.

In the meantime the Republicans chose an Ohioan, William McKinley, as their candidate. He was an honest man, but his beliefs were different from Bryan's. He supported the gold standard and high tariffs. He was conservative and moderate, a quiet man, able to bring people together. He believed the future lay with the new business interests. He saw no reason for government to attempt to regulate or control business. If business prospered, he thought it would also benefit the poor and the farmers.

This election of 1896 was one of the most important in all of our nation's history. Americans had a real choice in 1896. Their decision set the direction the nation took in the 20th century. Here are some of the positions they took about issues:

▲ This election campaign poster (from Bryan's *second* campaign for the presidency, in 1900), reinforces the themes from his rousing speech to the 1896 Democratic National Convention—"NO CROWN OF THORNS, NO CROSS OF GOLD."

Democrats, Populists	Republicans
farmers	businessmen, some workers
silver	gold
"expanding money"	"tight money"
eight-hour day, child labor laws	leave-alone labor policies
income tax	no income tax
farm	city
Jeffersonian	Hamiltonian
liberal	conservative

What a campaign it was! Bryan had little money but he had his remarkable energy and voice. He crossed the nation by train and in just a few months gave more than 600 speeches. Sometimes he spoke 30 times in a day, making brief "whistle stops." Mostly he talked about silver.

In Canton, Ohio, William McKinley was engaged in a very different presidential campaign. He didn't go anywhere at all. He stayed on his front porch. People came to him. The railroads were supporting his candidacy, while corporations and banks sent lots of money. McKinley's good friend, Mark Hanna, organized things. Hanna was a brilliant organizer.

More than 120 million Republican pamphlets—printed in 10 languages—were distributed to voters. They made Bryan sound like a dangerous quack; 1,400 paid speakers went out around the nation speaking for McKinley and against Bryan. McKinley articles were sent free to newspapers. McKinley buttons, banners, and posters turned up everywhere. In 1896 the Republicans spent $4 million

North Dakota, South Dakota, Montana, and Washington all became states in November 1889. In July 1890, Idaho and Wyoming were admitted to statehood. And in January 1896, Utah entered as the 45th state.

In 1896, Democratic presidential candidate William Jennings Bryan crossed the nation in a whistle-stop railroad tour, sometimes giving dozens of speeches a day. ▶

on the presidential campaign; the Democrats spent $300,000. Today we are used to big, costly presidential campaigns. That was something new in 1896.

Maybe it was the money that made the difference. Maybe not. The American people had some tough issues to decide. To begin, there was the idea of democracy. Americans have never been sure how far to take democracy. Thomas Jefferson and Andrew Jackson had faith in the people. They wanted democracy to be as broad and direct as possible. They wanted the American people to make decisions for themselves. Others, like Alexander Hamilton and the McKinley Republicans, favored a more limited democracy, with decision-making power in the hands of the elected, the appointed, and the leaders of business, industry, and other interests (today we call them "special interest groups").

▲ As part of his "front porch campaign," in which the candidate stayed home and let supporters come to him, William McKinley speaks to a crowd from the front porch of his home in Canton, Ohio.

Many Americans wanted those reforms the Populists called for. They wanted laws to improve working conditions. They wanted shorter working hours; they wanted laws to prevent employers from hiring children for adult jobs. Many believed the railroads and the big utilities should be owned by the government and run for all people. Most wanted to see farmers helped.

But there were some things that were worrisome about Bryan. He was dividing the country into warring groups. He wasn't trying to bring the corporations and the common people together. He was picking a fight with the money interests. And he was supported by nativists and some other hate groups.

The business interests fought back and won. It was the corporation that would dominate the 20th century. Some say that the American people made that choice in 1896.

Some Bad Ideas

The election of 1896 was history. Bryan went on to run for president again and again and never made it. He became better known than some of the men who did become president.

And what of the Populists? What happened to them?

Tom Watson was right. Their party was dead. Not quite buried, but almost.

And Tom Watson? Ah, if only I didn't have to write the truth about Tom Watson. For his is a tragic story.

Remember young, idealistic Tom Watson, who began his political career by doing something no other party leader was doing: calling on blacks and whites to unite? For a while it happened. He brought the races together. When a black Populist leader was threatened by the racist Ku Klux Klan, Watson called for help. More than 1,000 farmers came in buggies and on horseback. This was the 19th-century South, and these were white farmers rushing to the aid of a black man.

By the turn of the century the Ku Klux Klan was a large, powerful, and widespread organization. It was not confined to the rural South, as some people imagined. This Klan parade took place in Long Branch, New Jersey. ▼

The farmers stacked their guns on Tom Watson's porch and made it clear they would not allow a lynching. The Klansmen got the message. There was no more trouble.

But the People's Party failed. It was too bad, since so many Populist ideas were soon accepted by both Republicans and Democrats. Tom Watson took eight years off from politics, and wrote books, and thought, and brooded, and came out a lesser man. Tom Watson ended his days as a bigot. He had been a champion of the common people; he became enamored of "white supremacy," prestige, and power. When he died, the largest bunch of flowers at his funeral came from the Ku Klux Klan.

By the turn of the century the Ku Klux Klan was a large, powerful, and widespread organization. It was not confined to the rural South, as some people imagined.

Watson wasn't the only Populist leader to take up bigoted theories. Sadly, it was a time when many Americans—and people in other nations, too—took racism seriously.

They were grappling with difficult problems. Life was unsettling in this age of extremes. In America, everyone could see that something was wrong, and not just on the farm. People were becoming too materialistic, too concerned with money and things. The economic system wasn't working well. Industry was ravaging the nation's resources. Thomas Jefferson's agrarian (farm-centered) world was vanishing, and the new world of corporations and capitalists didn't seem very noble. For the most part, presidents and congresses were weak and money magnates and city bosses strong. Railroads and new industries had changed the nation; laws and ideas hadn't caught up.

Some people had a simple solution to the new problems. They blamed others. First, they blamed the rich. Actually, the rich industrialists were no different from the poor farmers. Many were greedy, but so were many ordinary people. Some industrialists, like Carnegie and Rockefeller, who had abused and exploited others to gain power and wealth, were doing a surprisingly good job of sharing their wealth.

When blaming the rich didn't work, people looked for other scapegoats. Unfortunately, many turned racist. Some were anti-Catholic. Others were anti-Semitic (which means they blamed Jews for their problems). Many Americans became anti-immigrant. (Immigrants were competing for jobs. One Populist leader called them "foreign scum.") Some were anti-black. (It was at this time that

Racism and bigotry were appearing in other nations too. Japanese hated Chinese; Chinese hated Vietnamese; Greeks hated Turks; Turks hated Armenians; Germans hated the French; the French seemed to think they were superior to everyone. And people with different religions and different-colored skins looked down on each other.

the southern states wrote new constitutions that took the vote away from most blacks and poor whites.) On the West Coast, many citizens were anti-Asian.

Some Americans lost their way. Their wrong-headedness would hurt the nation. They didn't mean to be wrong. Few do. They were trying to define America. But it was as if they had decided to look through a telescope the wrong way. They narrowed the vision. They were looking backward to a past they thought was ideal. But things had never been quite the way they imagined them.

They thought America had once been just a nation of Protestant English farmers. They forgot all about the Native Americans—who had been a majority, and who arrived on the continent thousands of years before the first Europeans. They forgot about the Spaniards who had settled in Florida and South Carolina and New Mexico and Texas and California. They forgot the Poles, Italians, and Africans who had helped to create Jamestown. They forgot the Swedes in Delaware and the French in Louisiana. They forgot the Catholics in Maryland and the Jews in New Amsterdam. They didn't know their American history.

Those 19th-century bigots—whom we call "nativists"—were ignorant. They forgot that it was our English ancestors who had come up with the idea that all people are created equal. It was that revolutionary idea that was attracting immigrants to America from all over the world.

Leaving Sicily

If you look at a map and notice the boot that is Italy, you will see that the boot's toe is kicking a triangular rock. That rock is actually an island—the island of Sicily. In 1800 there were a million Sicilians; by 1900 there were 3.5 million. In many of the villages, there were just too many people to feed and house. Between 1880 and 1920, more than 3 million immigrants left Sicily and sailed for America. It has been called "one of the greatest mass migrations in history."

Italian immigrants on board a ship in New York harbor in 1900 ▶

An Italian immigrant family at Ellis Island, New York, waits to be processed after their long sea voyage in 1905. ▶

Because of that idea, America was attempting something amazing. We were taking peasants from German farms, children from Poland's shtetls, laborers from China's countryside, Italians from Naples's fishing boats, and former slaves from southern plantations—and expecting them all to get along together. Of course it wasn't easy. Revolutionary ideas never are.

Shtetl is a Yiddish word meaning village.

One thing neither the Populists, nor the Democrats, nor the Republicans understood was that the emerging political forces—the immigrants and the newly freed blacks—were helping to build a more fair and far richer America. But that wasn't clear to anyone at the end of the 19th century.

More Goods, More Challenges

What do you do when you need a shirt? You go to a store and buy one. Before the Civil War, you couldn't do that. Your mother, or someone in the family, had to make your shirt. If you had plenty of money, you could go to a tailor and have a shirt made especially for you.

During the Civil War, soldiers' uniforms were needed in a hurry. So uniforms were made in many sizes in factories. It was amazing—almost everyone could find something to fit. After the war, manufacturers started making clothing for civilians (people who weren't in the military). In the cities, new department stores began selling factory-made clothes, shoes, and things for the house and garden.

Do you remember how you felt when you were little and went into a big toy store for the first time? That's the way most Americans felt when they first entered a department store. The people who couldn't get to the big-city stores weren't left out. They could buy factory goods, too, because of Montgomery Ward's smart idea. Ward decided to sell merchandise through the mail. He printed a catalogue that showed pictures of the items

▲ An 1898 poster advertising the Montgomery Ward department store of Chicago

◀ Women's tailor-made suits featured in a 1902 mail-order catalogue

An early Sears, Roebuck catalogue, the "wish book" ▶

White Lily Face Wash, "the ladies favorite," at 37¢ per bottle.

The new department stores and the new catalogues brought wonders to the American household. Suddenly everyone wanted products from American factories. Those factories soon led the world with their good products and low prices. Now anyone could go into a store and buy a fine suit or dress. When immigrants got off their boats, all they had to do was go into a store to look American. Factories changed the way people lived and the way they worked.

Thomas Jefferson had wanted America to stay agrarian. That word *agrarian* means "farm-based." He wanted the United States to be a nation of small farmers who would have little need for government regulations. But there was no keeping the Industrial Revolution out of America. In 1920, half of all Americans lived in cities or towns. By then the United States was the leading industrial nation in the world, with 9 million factory workers.

Most of the factories were in cities or big towns. A new immigrant could get off the boat at Ellis Island, head for New York or Chicago or Cincinnati, and quickly find a job. A farm boy or girl, from Iowa or Wisconsin, could head for the city and find a world of activity—and a job, too.

The United States wasn't ready for the changes that cities and industry brought. There were new situations and problems that had not been faced before.

At the beginning of the 20th century, we were the greatest industrial power in the world. But a huge gap had opened—a chasm—between the opportunities available to rich Americans and to rural and urban poor. Giving everyone a chance: that was the great challenge to a nation that prided itself on its founding documents, which were all about fairness and equality of opportunity.

he had for sale. Soon another company, Sears, Roebuck, was doing the same thing. If you had the money, here are some items you could order from the 1909 Sears Roebuck catalogue (known as the "wish book"): men's two-piece bathing suits for $2.25, bathing trunks for kids at 20¢, official National League baseballs at 75¢, and

Harvest at Haymarket

When Cyrus Hall McCormick opened the McCormick Harvester Works in Chicago in the 1840s, he worked alongside his 23 employees. Of course, he knew them all by name. He cared about them.

A few years later, the McCormick factory was making more than 1,000 reapers a year. Cyrus still knew all 200 of his workers.

By 1884, the year Cyrus McCormick died, his plant was enormous. It covered 12 acres; 1,300 men worked 10-hour days, six days a week. Two huge steam engines supplied power in the modern factory. That year the company showed a profit of 71 percent. And McCormick no longer knew his workers.

That was typical of what was happening in America. Many of the new factories were owned by corporations—big-business companies. The owners of the corporations sometimes didn't even live in the same town as their workers. Some of those owners got very rich but refused to pay their workers a fair wage. Often they seemed to forget they were human beings. Steelworkers had to work 12 hours a day, six days a week, for little pay. Textile workers—many of them children—worked 60 to 80 hours a week.

In 1900, the average American worked 59 hours a week for 22 cents an hour. (You figure his weekly wage.) But then a new bike cost $14.65, a watch $3.65, a pair of shoes $1.95. You could have dinner in a good restaurant for less than a dollar.

◀ Working in a steel mill in 1900 meant long hours in intense heat and dangerous conditions.

▲ A coal miner deep underground, ca. 1900

▲ Even children worked in the mines. Mining boys often worked 10 hours a day, six days a week. Imagine working those hours every day, in the dark, bent double, deep underground.

Conditions were often dangerous. Miners worked underground with explosives but without safety regulations. In one year, 25,000 workers died on the job; many more were injured. Child workers had three times as many accidents as adults. If a person lost an arm in a job accident—and many did with the new machines—no one helped with doctor's bills. If a worker complained, he was fired.

Workers organized themselves into *unions* to try to fight for better conditions and better pay. The union was like a club for workers. People who worked together tried to help each other solve the problems they had in common. Sometimes they decided not to work unless they were paid better wages. In other words, they went on strike. Naturally, the owners hated strikes. They often fired anyone who joined a strike. Sometimes they hired police or soldiers to break a strike. Sometimes strikers were shot. Businessmen often took the law into their own hands. If they were powerful enough, they got away with it. Cornelius Vanderbilt was blunt when he said, "Law! What do I care about law? H'aint I got power?" He wasn't the only one who felt that way: Carnegie and Rockefeller hired their own police forces.

Workers began to demand their own power. The unions grew. Many Americans—especially the new immigrants—learned about democracy in the unions.

Workers (labor) and business owners (management and capital) often had opposing interests. Workers wanted good wages and owners wanted to keep their labor costs low. (There wasn't much long-range thinking. With good wages, workers could buy the products the industrialists were making, and everyone would profit.)

Sometimes the relationship seemed like war. It was big business versus the unions. And, because the situation was new, it was confusing.

Many people distrusted unions, especially because some unions were organized by socialists, who wanted the government to take over the businesses that affected most citizens, like railroads, electrical power, and telephones. (America had a tradition of individualism and private ownership; socialism seemed scary.) Some unions were led by *anarchists*. They didn't believe in any government at all, which wasn't a very helpful idea. And some unions did abuse their growing power. Many strikes were poorly planned and hurt workers more than owners. But some business leaders just wanted capitalism without regulations. And some got angry at the idea of workers having any rights and power.

In 1884, soon after his father died, Cyrus McCormick II announced that he was cutting his workers' pay. (Remember, his company made an enormous 71-percent profit that year.) A few months later the workers went on strike.

The workers in this shoe factory had few benefits and toiled long hours for little pay. ▼

A group of officers stand near a railway carriage in an emergency camp during the Pullman Strike in Chicago. The strike began when workers at George Pullman's railroad car manufacturing company protested against unfair wages and living conditions. ▶

McCormick hired other workmen to take their places. (They were called "strikebreakers" or "scabs.") Striking union men attacked the strikebreakers. McCormick hired armed guards. A crowd captured and burned the guards' rifles. A police captain (who was on the side of the workers) did nothing. Chicago's mayor wouldn't help either, so McCormick finally agreed to go back to the old pay scale.

But young Cyrus wasn't finished. The next year he installed expensive machinery that was designed to eliminate the most troublesome of the workers. At first the machines seemed to do just that. But he didn't plan on machinery problems. The machines broke down. The parts they turned out weren't as good as the handmade parts. The cost—to keep the machines operating—was more than double the old labor cost. McCormick didn't care; he thought he had broken the union and that seemed important to him now.

But the union wasn't finished. Myles McPadden, a union leader, convinced McCormick's workers to join two national unions: the Metalworkers Union and the Knights of Labor. The workers went to McCormick demanding higher pay and better working conditions.

▲ Samuel Fielden, a teamster, was speaking to the Haymarket crowds when a cast-iron bomb filled with dynamite suddenly went off.

In the meantime, McCormick had been busy. He gave money to the mayor and the police (that's called "bribery"). Then he closed his plant rather than meet the workers' demands. Four hundred city policemen protected the plant. McCormick hired strikebreakers so the factory could start production again. Now he was in desperate need of workers, so he agreed to let the scabs work an eight-hour day, which was one of the major demands of the strikers. Naturally, that enraged the strikers.

One day, some strikers attacked a group of strikebreakers as they left work. Police started shooting. Two men were killed and several wounded. The next day, more than 3,000 workers gathered in Chicago's Haymarket Square to protest the shootings. Most of the speakers were socialists; they were peaceful but angry.

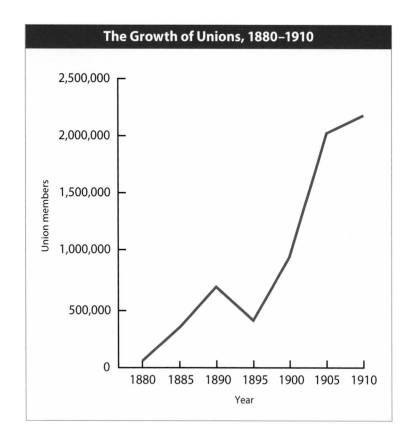

The Growth of Unions, 1880–1910

Union members

2,500,000

2,000,000

1,500,000

1,000,000

500,000

0

1880 1885 1890 1895 1900 1905 1910

Year

It is easy to give free speech to those with whose ideas you agree. But in America we believe in free speech for all, which isn't always easy. Should anarchists or neo-Nazis be allowed to speak?

Then it began to rain. Only 300 workers remained when 180 policemen marched into the square and demanded that the meeting be ended. The speaker was ready to go home. "We are peaceable," he said to the police chief and climbed down from his platform. Then something unexpected happened. A bomb was thrown at the policemen. No one has ever discovered who threw the bomb. One policeman was killed (six others died later of wounds). Police began firing their guns. Four civilians died. Many were wounded.

The nation was outraged. Most people were angry at the strikers. They seemed to believe that the union workers were all anarchists who were plotting to overthrow the government. Many Chicago workers were immigrants. Stories circulated about foreign conspiracies.

The Chicago police rounded up suspects. They arrested people without warrants to do so. Eight men were charged with conspiracy and murder. Four of those men had left Haymarket Square before the bomb was thrown. One of them reported that "there was not a syllable said about anarchism at the Haymarket meeting." It didn't matter. Fear was in the air. As someone said, "anarchism was on trial." The nation was afraid of foreigners and socialists and anarchists. No one wanted to hear the truth.

All eight men were found guilty. Four of them were hanged. One was sentenced to 15 years in jail. Two had death sentences changed to life in prison. One committed suicide in prison.

At the McCormick factory, the workers returned to a 10-hour day.

Workers, Labor (and a Triangle)

American labor laws lagged far behind those of almost every other industrial nation. Working conditions were often unsafe, factory pay was rarely fair, and workers had few if any benefits. In 1900, only one American worker in 12 belonged to a union.

Unions were feared by workers as well as managers, because many early labor leaders seemed too radical for most Americans. Then, near the turn of the century, a labor leader appeared who was a conservative thinker. No one could accuse Samuel Gompers of being a radical. He used American business methods to organize and negotiate for labor.

Sam Gompers came to this country from England when he was 13. His family was actually Dutch—they were Dutch Jews—but they had moved to London, where Sam's father tried to make a living as a

In 1900, American workers—represented here in a panel of a painting called *The Ages of the Worker*—led hard lives with few laws to protect their interests. ▶

▲ Luther Watson, 14 years old, lost his right arm in an industrial accident.

167

cigarmaker. He didn't have an easy time of it, especially as his family kept growing.

Sam was a bright boy and did well in school. After classes he went to Hebrew school and studied the Talmud, which he said "develops the more subtle qualities of mind, the student learns to deal with abstract problems, to make careful discriminations, to follow a line of reasoning from premise to conclusion."

He liked school and wanted to go on, but the family was desperately poor. Sam had to go to work. At age 10 he was apprenticed to a shoemaker. But he decided he'd rather be a cigarmaker, so he helped his father make cigars. Even that wasn't enough. The Gomperses were hungry when the Cigarmakers' Society (a union) came to the rescue. They had an emigration fund that helped members go to America. A civil war was being fought in America, but that didn't stop the Gompers family. They boarded a ship and headed for the New World.

The Gomperses lived in a New York City *tenement*. Tenements were apartment houses for the poor. Many were used as factories. Sometimes they were called "sweatshops," because they were usually hot and airless, and workers were "sweated"—forced to work long hours in cramped, dirty rooms with no provisions for safety, rest, comfort, or refreshment.

Sam's family lived across from a slaughterhouse and a brewery. A "penetrating, sickening odor" filled the neighborhood, as Sam later recalled. His father rolled cigars at home. Sam joined a debating club and began taking courses at New York City's Cooper Union, where he studied history, music, mechanics, economics, electric power, geography, astronomy, speech making, and more.

When he was 16, he got a job in a cigar factory. While the cigarmakers rolled the tobacco they liked to have someone read to them. The reader had to be smart. The cigarmakers wanted to educate themselves. They kept up with the latest news, they

> The *Talmud* is a collection of ancient writings on Jewish laws and traditions.

A tenement slum in New York (photographed by Jacob Riis) ▼

A group of women stitch articles of clothing in a New York City sweatshop.

had lively discussions, and they listened to good literature, too. Sometimes Sam Gompers did the reading.

After he got married and started his own family, he began to take an interest in the Cigarmakers Union. Gompers was a no-nonsense person who got results. His powerful voice and his good sense soon helped make him president of the Cigarmakers Union. It was a craft union, which means that all its members did the same kind of work. In 1886, he persuaded other craft unions to band together with the cigarmakers and form the American Federation of Labor. Gompers was named president, and for the next 38 years he worked for the A.F. of L. He made it a major force in the American industrial world.

Sam Gompers was a practical man. He wanted big changes, but unlike the anarchists and socialists, he did not call for society to be organized in new ways (which scared most Americans). Gompers stuck to labor issues such as working hours, wages, and job safety. He used strikes to get eight-hour working days, five-day work weeks, safety reforms in mines, and the right of workers to band together to negotiate (called "collective bargaining"). By 1901, the A.F. of L. had more than one million members.

"Show me the country in which there are no strikes," said Sam Gompers, "and I will show you that country in which there is no liberty." ▼

When the Irish Land League issued orders forbidding the Irish from supplying British land agent Captain Charles Boycott with provisions, it added a new word to the English language. That word came to America and became a tactic used by American labor. You know what the word is, don't you?

Gompers stayed out of politics. He knew that would divide the workers. He had only one goal—to improve working conditions in the United States. He wanted American workers to have the best possible wages and benefits. If workers earned good pay, he believed they would make everyone prosperous. Besides, he thought a fair labor policy led to a just society. "Show me the country in which there are no strikes and I will show you that country in which there is no liberty," said Samuel Gompers. (Do you agree with that statement? Why? Or why not?)

In earlier days, businesses were small. Usually owner and employee worked together. But in the industrial age, factories grew big and impersonal. Employers had almost unlimited power. They could lock employees in or out of the workplace. Their wealth often gave them the means to destroy unions, by hiring armed guards or buying unfavorable and often unfair publicity. The courts almost always favored the employers. That changed when unions acquired power and respectability. Then American workers began to reap the benefits of their own productivity. It might not have happened without leaders like Samuel Gompers.

The Triangle Shirtwaist Factory Fire

Workers were sometimes locked inside the buildings where they worked because the employers didn't trust them. If the doors were open some might stop working to go outside and get fresh air. So some doors were locked the day in 1911 when the Triangle Shirtwaist Company caught fire. Many women workers, who were sewing dresses, were trapped on a high floor. Some leapt out the window and fell to their death; some died in the flames: 146 young women perished on that day.

Workers were sometimes locked inside the buildings where they worked because the employers didn't trust them. When the Triangle Shirtwaist Company caught fire, many women workers were trapped. One hundred and forty-six women perished. ▶

Rolling the Leaf in Florida

In the 19th century, cigars were a big business. And the very best cigars were made from Cuban tobacco. Some businesspeople decided to ship Cuban tobacco leaves to Florida, offer jobs to Cuban workers, and make the cigars in this country. They would be just like Cuban cigars, but American-made and much less costly. So that was what they did.

In 1886 (the same year Sam Gompers founded the A.F. of L.), in the sleepy port town of Tampa, Florida, Don Vincente Martinez Ybor (EE-bor) opened a tobacco factory in a section of Tampa that was to be called Ybor City. Ybor soon helped make Tampa the cigar capital of the world.

Workers came from Cuba, Spain, Italy, Germany, and Romania. Twelve thousand of them were soon working in some 200 cigar factories. They created an industrial community and an immigrant city—and both were unusual in the Deep South. There was something even more unusual: men and women, blacks and whites, Christians and Jews all worked together around the cigar tables. "In those days we grew up together," Hipólito Arenas, an Afro-Cuban, reminisced about Ybor City. "Your color did not matter—your family and their moral character did." That may have been true in Ybor City (where 791 Afro-Cubans lived in 1900); it wasn't true in most of Florida, where color did matter.

Most of the workers spoke Spanish (and if they didn't, they soon learned that language). In the cigar factories the reader, who was called a *lector*, read in Spanish as workers rolled the fat cigars. It was a prestige job. The lectors were paid by the workers and made more money than any of the cigarmakers. The cigarmakers became very knowledgeable. While they rolled cigars they held discussions. They kept up with politics and, since many were Cuban, they worried and even got involved with what was happening in Cuba. A freedom movement was brewing on that island (more on that in a later chapter).

▲ Workers at the Tampa Cigar Factory in Florida (photographed by Lewis Hine in 1909)

Telling It Like It Is

"**M**other" Jones was a pugnacious little woman, and fearless. The worst things that could happen to a person had happened to her, so nothing else ever scared her. Her real name was Mary Harris Jones and she was living in Memphis, Tennessee, when her children caught yellow fever. In those days, before modern medicines, yellow fever was a killer. Mary Jones's four boys died. Then her husband died. She was all alone. She got her courage together, moved to Chicago, and opened a dressmaking shop.

Mrs. Jones had style, and she knew how to sew. She was becoming successful when, in 1871, Chicago had a great fire. Some say Mrs. O'Leary's cow kicked over a lantern and that started it. However it began, the whole city burned and Mary Jones's business with it. She was left with nothing. That decided her. If she was going to start over again, she wanted to do something important with her life. She wanted to help others. It was children she worked hardest to help.

Mother Jones was tiny—about five feet tall—with white hair (it turned white after her children died). She was called "mother" because she seemed like a nice old lady—until she opened her mouth.

▲ In Philadelphia, Mother Jones said the city's mansions were built "on the broken bones, quivering hearts and drooping heads of these children."

Inferno in Chicago

It was October 8, 1871, and Mrs. O'Leary left a kerosene lantern in her hay-filled barn on DeKoven Street. The cow kicked, the barn began blazing, and there was no stopping the flames. Chicago, a city of mostly wooden buildings squeezed together, quickly became an inferno. By morning, 18,000 buildings were gone. The fire is said to have reached 3,000° Fahrenheit. Buildings of "fireproof" masonry melted away. Cast-iron buildings turned liquid. Ninety thousand people (out of a population of 300,000) were left homeless.

The Chicago fire killed 250 people. Few people know that on the same day a fire in the forests of northern Michigan and northeastern Wisconsin killed between 1,200 and 2,400 people.

▲ Nearly a third of Chicago's 300,000 residents were left homeless by the terrible fire of 1871.

◄ Children as young as six and seven worked 12-hour days in textile mills.

▲ This young girl, dressed in rags, worked in a cotton mill.

She swore like a trooper, had the energy of a battalion, and spoke in ear-splitting tones. Clarence Darrow, a famous lawyer, wrote of her, "Mother Jones's…fearless soul always drew her to seek the spot where the fight was hottest and the danger greatest."

She wanted people to know of the plight of child workers, so she marched a group of young millworkers from Pennsylvania to New York. Most prosperous New Yorkers had never seen a mill child. "The toil of these children makes others wealthy," she explained.

"Here's a textbook on economics," Mother Jones said as she introduced little James Ashworth to a crowd. James's back was bent from carrying 75-pound factory loads. "He gets three dollars a week…working in a carpet factory 10 hours a day." Then she introduced Gussie Rangnew, "a little girl from whom all the childhood has gone." Gussie, whose tired face was like an old woman's, packed stockings all day long, day after day, summer, winter, spring, and fall.

Some people don't want to learn about unpleasant things. The police called Mother Jones a public nuisance. They arrested her. When the judge asked who gave her a permit to speak on the streets, she said, "Patrick Henry, Thomas Jefferson, and John Adams!"

Mother Jones was sent to jail—more than once. In jail she spoke of George Washington as a "gentleman agitator" who had fought the powerful English establishment. Each time Mother

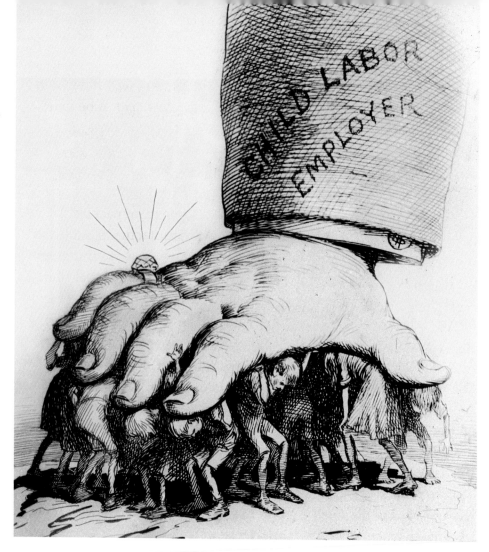

Mother Jones said, "The toil of these children makes others wealthy." How does this cartoon convey that idea? ▶

Jones got out of jail she went right back to speaking out for workers. "I'm not a humanitarian," she said, "I'm a hell-raiser." Actually, she was both. And she was very good at getting attention. Mother Jones made people think about America's working children. Here is part of what she wrote after going into a cotton mill in Alabama, where she worked along with the children:

> *Little girls and boys, barefooted, walked up and down between the endless rows of spindles, reaching thin little hands into the machinery to repair snapped threads. They crawled under machinery to oil it. They replaced spindles all day long; all night through…six-year-olds with faces of sixty did an eight-hour shift for ten cents a day: the machines, built in the North, were built low for the hands of little children…. At the lunch half-hour, the children would fall to sleep over their lunch of cornbread and fat pork. They would lie on the bare floor and sleep. Sleep was their recreation, their release, as play is to the free child.*

These children weren't slaves, but they might as well have been. This was another form of servitude. Something needed to be done. Laws were needed to keep children in school. Laws were needed to make working conditions safe for all workers. And there was something else—besides working conditions—that needed regulating: it was the products themselves.

Since there were no laws to prevent it, some meat packers put dangerous spoiled meat in hot dogs. Some manufacturers built toys that could hurt children. There were no laws about these things, because in the early days people bought meat from a butcher they knew. Toys were usually made at home. Now, with big factories and modern transportation, people were buying things made far from their homes.

Mother Jones wasn't the only one concerned. Writers were writing about the problems of unregulated business. Theodore Roosevelt called those writers "muckrakers," because they raked up muck and told people about it. They were important.

You can't clean up muck unless you know where it is. Eventually, laws were passed to protect children and make going to school compulsory. A pure food and drug act helped make our food safe. It was those who shouted out—like Mother Jones—who made those laws happen. "The militant, not the meek, shall inherit the earth," said Mother Jones. What did she mean by that?

In the 20th century, reformers and labor unions helped bring better wages and conditions to most of America's workers. Child-labor laws limited the hours that children could work. New laws said children had to go to school.

◀ Two girls wear banners with the slogan ABOLISH CHILD SLAVERY! in English and Yiddish.

Bread and Roses, Too

Officially they were the Industrial Workers of the World, but everyone called them "Wobblies."

Wobblies thought that all workers, not just skilled workers, should be in unions together. Their idealistic goal was one big union—all workers would belong to it—and they'd have one big strike that would stop everything, and the workers could take over and make the country a better place. The Wobblies hated Sam Gompers's American Federation of Labor. AFL members were skilled workers—the aristocrats of the working world—and not everyone was welcome. The Wobblies were democratic: any worker could join.

Utah's William "Big Bill" Haywood opened the Wobblies' founding convention in Chicago in 1905, when he proclaimed in his booming voice: "Fellow workers...this is the Continental Congress of the Working Class." Another important Wobbly founder was Eugene Debs, a lanky railroad man from Indiana. (Later, Debs became head of the Socialist Party, was sent to prison for opposing World War I, ran for president from jail, and got more than 900,000 votes.) Yet another Wobbly was Father Thomas J. Hagerty, a Catholic priest who had fought some battles for Mexican railroad workers. Hagerty said, "The working class and the employing class have nothing in common" (which didn't leave a whole lot of room for working out problems together).

In Lawrence, Massachusetts, early in the year 1912, the Wobblies had their finest moment. When the Massachusetts legislature passed a law saying that women and children were not allowed to work more than 54 hours a week, the owners of the Lawrence textile mills speeded up their machinery so the workers would produce as much in 54 hours as they had in 56. The workers had to work faster to keep up, but they didn't get paid more for their work.

In protest, some Polish women left their looms. Before long 25,000 millworkers had walked off the job. Most were foreign born—among them they spoke about 45 different languages. Many of the workers had come to Lawrence after reading advertisements in their native lands telling of opportunities in the mills. (One poster showed a Lawrence workingman leaving the factory with a suitcase full of gold.) When they got to Lawrence they found that their pay barely kept them from starving. They wanted more than just barely enough to eat. So they picketed with big signs that said, "We Want Bread and Roses, Too."

But they didn't have a real leader, so they appealed to the IWW for help. Big Bill Haywood was soon on his way east. He had no trouble communicating with gestures and sign language and his big heart. Elizabeth Gurley Flynn (a slim, pretty Irish dynamo) came, too; she had started as a strike leader for the Wobblies when she was only 16.

▲ Elizabeth Gurley Flynn became a strike leader for the Wobblies at the age of 16.

▲ An Industrial Workers of the World poster

I WILL WIN

And 26-year-old Joe Ettor, the son of an Italian immigrant family, took a leading role. He was a terrific organizer and spoke Italian and English fluently, with enough Polish, Hungarian, and Yiddish to get by. Ettor tried to keep the workers calm. He said to them, "You can hope for no success on any policy of violence.... Violence...means the loss of the strike."

There was violence at Lawrence—police violence. Strikers were the victims. Militia, special policemen, and Pinkerton detectives were brought to the city. Dynamite was discovered, strikers were arrested, and newspaper headlines screamed of anarchy. But it was soon found that the dynamite had been planted by the son of a former mayor, trying to frame the strikers.

One evening a group of strikers found themselves surrounded by armed police. A shot rang out and Annie LoPizza fell dead. Joe Ettor and IWW poet Arturo Giovannitti were arrested for the murder—although they were two miles away at the time. They were kept in jail for months, and kept out of their leadership roles.

Newspapers and magazines covered the strike. People all over the country began reading about Lawrence. Most Americans hadn't known about conditions in the mills. Some offered to care for strikers' children. People's hearts were going out to the Lawrence workers.

On the 43rd day of the strike, 40 children and their parents were gathered at the Lawrence railroad station. The children had been invited to Philadelphia, where families had arranged to "adopt" them until the strike was over. Suddenly the police appeared. A Boston newspaper reported what happened: "Police, acting under orders of the city marshal, choked and knocked down women and children, the innocent wives and babies of the strikers."

That was too much. Congress investigated. President William Howard Taft (whose wife attended the Congressional hearings) ordered an investigation of industrial conditions. Finally, the mill owners agreed to raise wages, pay overtime, and rehire the strikers. The Bread and Roses strike was over!

Ida, Sam, and the Muckrakers

On January 16, 1787, Thomas Jefferson wrote a letter to his friend Edward Carrington. He said:

The way to prevent…[errors] of the people is to give them full information of their affairs through the channel of the public papers, and to contrive that those papers should penetrate the whole mass of the people. …The basis of our government being the opinion of the people, the very first object should be to keep that right; and were it left to me to decide whether we should have a government without newspapers, or newspapers without a government, I should not hesitate a moment to prefer the latter.

The First Amendment to the Constitution, also known as Article I of the Bill of Rights, says:

Congress shall make no law…abridging the freedom of speech, or of the press.

> To *abridge* means to cut, shorten, or edit.

Our free press: some people call it the fourth branch of our government—an unofficial but very important branch.

Since early colonial times, Americans have been eager readers of newspapers and journals. But America's leaders have often become

Since early colonial times, Americans have been eager readers of newspapers. ▶

exasperated with that free press. No one likes to be criticized, and that is exactly what good journalists do.

Sometimes the media can be irresponsible, though libel laws usually control deliberate lying. (You can sue a newspaper if it lies and that lie harms you. A public figure must prove that the newspaper, or TV program, knew that what it was saying was false and that it had reckless disregard for the truth.)

Today when we use the word *media* it usually means any or all newspapers, magazines, radio, TV, and the Internet.

Jefferson never changed his mind about the importance of the press. And Americans have always understood that if we are to solve our problems we need *information*. A free press supplies that information.

At the turn of the century, America had unusually difficult problems to solve. The country was experiencing astonishing growth, industrialization and urbanization, an influx of many different peoples, and excessive government corruption. People needed to understand these phenomena to be able to deal with them. To understand them they had to have information.

Just when they were needed, some remarkable writers and editors appeared. They looked at America critically, fearlessly, and honestly—and they explained what they saw.

These writers were called *muckrakers*. *Muck* is dirt. Muckrakers were journalists who wrote about wrongs: about injustice, unfairness, and corruption.

◀ Nellie Bly in her traveling-around-the-world outfit in 1890. She loved stylish clothes.

A Woman Named Nellie Bly

Elizabeth Jane Cochrane was called "Nellie Bly," which was the way she signed her newspaper articles. Nellie got started when she wrote a sizzling letter to the editor of the *Pittsburgh Dispatch* (after reading it he hired her). She was soon writing for the most talked-about newspaper in the country, Joseph Pulitzer's *New York World*. Most women who were reporters—and there weren't many of them—were assigned to the cooking or household beat. Not Nellie Bly. She was a daredevil reporter who went around the globe to see if she could outdo the exploits of a character named Phileas Fogg in a popular novel by Jules Verne, *Around the World in Eighty Days*. She did it. When she decided to write about the treatment of the mentally ill, she pretended to be insane, got herself committed to an asylum, and wrote the best-selling series of articles "Inside the Madhouse." Later, Bly became the first woman to cover the European front in World War I.

In 1906, Upton Sinclair wrote a best-selling muckraking novel, *The Jungle*, about the city of Chicago, its horrible slums, and its stockyards and meat packers. He exposed the filthy ways of butchering and preparing meat, even worse than the grinding going on at this Chicago meat packing house. ▶

They went into slaughterhouses, where animals were killed and meat was processed, and they saw rats and dirt, and described what they saw. They wrote about city bosses and told how dishonest government cheated citizens of their rights and money. They wrote about the mighty industrial tycoons, about how some of them broke the law and got away with it, and why that cost the public great sums of money. And they wrote that in a democracy, all of these wrongs could be righted by the people, but only if the people are informed and take the time to vote.

The muckrakers had several things in common: they wrote unusually well, they did careful research, and they cared—really cared—about making this country a better place to live. They developed a new kind of journalism—*investigative journalism*—just at a time when publishing techniques made it possible to produce a good magazine, distribute it widely, and sell it for 10 cents. Everyone seemed to read the muckrakers' articles. And that made them very influential. They helped bring about change. Food-inspection laws were passed; antitrust laws were enforced; reforming mayors were elected to office.

Ida Tarbell was a muckraker—although she preferred to call herself a historian. Actually, she was both. And amazingly good at both callings.

Of all the muckrakers, Ida Tarbell was the most famous. When she was a little girl she heard women reformers say that if she wanted a career, she would have to give up the idea of marriage. Tarbell vowed never to marry—and she never did.

Ida became a teacher, but she found she didn't want to teach, so she went off to Europe.

She had a little money and a lot of adventurousness—and she could write. She believed she could write articles that would support her. That was what she was doing in France when the doorbell rang and Samuel Sidney McClure walked into her life.

Sam McClure came from an Irish family that had immigrated to the United States. His mother worked as a maid and washerwoman. Sam worked hard and made enough money to pay for college.

After college, he wrote for a biking magazine (bicycling was the new rage), and then he got a bright idea: he would start a syndicate (SIN-dih-cut) for writers. No one had ever done that before. He bought articles from very good writers and sold each article to several publications. The authors made more money than if they had sold to just one journal, and small papers and magazines were able to publish the best authors.

By now Sam McClure realized that what he really wanted to do was to be an editor. In 1892 he borrowed money and founded *McClure's* magazine. Not long after, he received an article from an unknown author. It was about paving the streets of Paris. That was an unlikely topic, but as soon as he started reading he said to an associate, "This girl can write. I want her to do some work for the magazine."

So he went to Paris, met the author, Ida Tarbell, and established one of the most productive collaborations in the history of journalism.

A fellow muckraker said Ida Tarbell was "beautiful with virtue—so generous, so modest, so full of kindness," and able "to infect her pages with [her] own shining love of truth." ▼

One of his colleagues said that Sam McClure "talked like a pair of scissors" and "gave the impression of a powerhouse of energy." ▶

A Boon to the Writers

Sam McClure could spot talent. Ida Tarbell was an outstanding writer. McClure suggested she write a book about Napoleon. When she did, *McClure's* ran a chapter each week. It was an inspired idea. People couldn't wait to read her chapters. McClure sold a lot of magazines.

Next, Tarbell wrote a *Life of Abraham Lincoln*. Again, *McClure's* ran chapters in each issue. And, again, people couldn't wait to get their copies of the magazine. *McClure's* circulation jumped from 120,000 to 250,000.

Then Ida Tarbell began looking at the world around her. She felt that the standards of her day were not at all the standards of her hero Abraham Lincoln. Many people—whether big business leaders, union leaders, political leaders, or ordinary citizens—seemed not to care about laws, or even about right and wrong. Money and power were their only goals. "A thing won by breaking the rules of the game is not worth the winning," she wrote.

McClure (most people now called him "S. S.") encouraged her to write a book about America's most powerful citizen, John D. Rockefeller, and his giant trust, Standard Oil. McClure didn't expect an exposé of ruthless business practices, but that was what he got. Tarbell spent four years writing two books that shocked the American people. She showed how Standard Oil took unfair advantage of its competitors. She showed how its uncontrolled power had spread into railroads, mining, and banking, and how that power affected the lives of most Americans. Tarbell was always proud that nothing she wrote was ever proved wrong.

Three years after her books were published, the Supreme Court dissolved the trust of the Standard Oil Company.

Ida Tarbell wasn't the only writer whom S. S. McClure encouraged. He had a knack for finding good writers. "I had to invent a new

An editorial cartoon depicting Standard Oil president John D. Rockefeller as the King of the World ▼

method of magazine journalism," he said. His method was to pay writers well and let them do careful, lengthy research. One of them, Ray Stannard Baker, wrote:

> *What a boon to the writer! To be able to take his time, saturate himself with his subject, assure accuracy by studying the subject at first hand and consulting every possible expert.*

Lincoln Steffens, another of *McClure's* writers, decided to investigate America's growing cities. He wanted to compare "the theories of ethics" (how people should behave) with the "actual conduct of men in business, politics, and the professions." He did that in articles that became a book called *The Shame of the Cities*.

Steffens went to St. Louis, Minneapolis, and Philadelphia, and found corruption. Then he studied New York and found it the best-governed city in America. Remember New York's Boss Tweed and his Tammany Hall gang of crooks? New Yorkers had booted them out and now had good government and schools. Most people assumed it was the poor who were the criminals in cities; Steffens showed that crime and graft were also found in the world of the middle class and rich.

Jack London, Booth Tarkington, Rudyard Kipling, Stephen Crane, Hamlin Garland, and Willa Cather were others of McClure's writers. If you have not heard those names, you will. They are all exceptional writers.

Because *McClure's* was so successful, other magazines began doing the same thing: hiring good writers and paying them well. Most of those magazines sold for 10 cents. It was a fine time for America's readers.

▲ The muckraking journalist Lincoln Steffens exposed political corruption in a variety of major American cities.

The cover of this issue of *McClure's* made both Sam McClure and Ida Tarbell famous. ▶

In Wilderness Is Preservation

Sometimes too much of a good thing turns out to be not such a good thing. We Americans were so rich in land, we became wasteful. It was the existence of the frontier that was in part to blame. The frontier—empty, inviting land—had a bewitching effect on the nation. It seemed as if it were endless, and that there would always be new land to settle, plant, and use up.

Thomas Jefferson thought America a land "with room enough for our descendants to the hundredth and thousandth generation." After 1890, most people knew that was not so.

In 1890 the U.S. Census Bureau said there was no more frontier. That was a shock. What did it mean?

▲ The lumber industry cut thousands of acres of old forest in the American West.

In 1890, the U.S. Census Bureau declared the frontier closed—a declaration borne out by this scene of people, wagons, and horses filling the streets of Guthrie, Oklahoma, in about 1895. ▼

It meant that the great stretches of habitable empty land were gone. The country was filling up. The frontier had been what is called a mixed blessing. It made hard work, cooperation, and resourcefulness important American traits. On a frontier it is what you can do—not who you are—that people care about. The frontier made America more democratic. But that frontier also made us wasteful, and it wasn't only land we wasted.

By 1890 the passenger pigeon was extinct; the endless herds of buffalo were being mowed down and would soon be gone; millions of acres of towering, ancient trees were gone or going; and mining was leaving mountainsides ravished and barren. A few citizens—a very few—began to talk of ways to preserve the land. One of them was John Muir.

> A *habitable* area is livable (as opposed to barren mountains, waterless deserts, soggy swamps, etc., which cannot support permanent human settlements).

An Early Conservationist

Picture a river eating its way through rock—for millions of years. That's how the Grand Canyon was formed by the Colorado River. The canyon is a mile deep (1.6 km), 4 to 18 miles wide (6.4–29 km), and 217 miles long (349 km). No human-made structure anywhere in the world is anything like that. Located in Arizona, it is one of the world's most spectacular natural wonders.

Ancient pueblos dot the canyon's walls and once must have made astonishing homes. A few Europeans stumbled onto the awesome canyon, but no one had mapped it, or traced the Colorado River from its headwaters through the canyon, until a geologist named John Wesley Powell led an expedition in 1869.

Powell had barely survived the battle of Shiloh in the Civil War. (He left an arm there.) This trip was equally dangerous. He wrote about his adventures and made Americans aware of the natural treasures in the West. Powell was among our first conservationists. He was anxious to preserve our natural wonders as national parks; others were more interested in promoting economic development. That conflict continues today.

▲ The Grand Canyon, formed by the Colorado River, is one of the world's most spectacular natural wonders.

John Muir was a naturalist; he studied nature (and loved it). Some other American naturalists were Thomas Jefferson, John James Audubon, and Henry David Thoreau.

Muir arrived in Wisconsin from Scotland at age 11. His new neighbors soon realized that he was a genius. It was his inventions that most impressed them. He invented a field thermometer so sensitive that it registered the heat of an approaching person or animal. He invented a wooden clock that struck the hours, started the fire in his stove, lit his lamp, and—with levers and wheels—raised the head of his bed and woke him in the morning.

He might have been another Thomas Edison, but an accident set him on a different path. Muir was working in a factory when a file flew into his eye. For a while he was blind and believed he would never see again. When he recovered he said he would waste no more time, but would live with nature. "God has to nearly kill us sometimes," he said, "to teach us lessons."

It was 1867. Muir was 29, and he wrote, "I set forth...joyful and free, on a thousand-mile walk to the Gulf of Mexico...by the wildest, leafiest, and least-trodden way I could find." He was embarking on the life he most wanted to live. "I might have been a millionaire," he said. "I chose to become a tramp." Muir believed that it was in nature that one can best answer questions of life and its meaning. He spent much of the rest of his life in the out-of-doors. He took other Americans outdoors with him in the journals he kept and the articles he wrote:

> As long as I live I'll hear waterfalls and birds and winds sing. I'll interpret the rocks, learn the language of flood, storm, and the avalanche. I'll acquaint myself with the glaciers and wild gardens, and get as near the heart of the world as I can.

In California's rugged Sierra Nevada mountains he felt at home—although he rarely stayed in one place. He climbed mountains, slogged through swamps, faced bears, panthers, and snakes. He never carried a gun; to kill was to disturb nature. He walked through much of Alaska, the Grand

▲ John Muir always hurried back to the mountains from the city shouting, "I'm wild once more!"

Canyon, and California's Yosemite Valley. Yosemite, carved by glaciers (as Muir discovered), has mountains, meadows, waterfalls, and cliffs. It has giant sequoia trees. "God himself seems to be doing his best here," Muir said of Yosemite. His writings helped make it a national park.

Three kinds of people were deciding the future of our national resources. There were those, like John Muir, who loved nature so intensely that they wanted to leave vast acres just as they were created, untouched by man. Others, who also cared about the land, thought land should be used, but wisely. They wanted foresters to harvest timber and plant new trees so there would be woods and forests for the future. But others seemed to care only about using land and lumber to make money. A congressman, in that last group, voted against a conservation bill. "Not one penny for scenery," he said. Many people agreed with him.

John Muir was alarmed. America's timberland was rapidly disappearing. Using a scientist's eye and a poet's tongue, he began to convince Americans that trees and birds and animals were too precious to destroy.

Thousands of tired, nerve-shaken, over-civilized people are beginning to find out that going to the mountains is going home; that wilderness is a necessity; and that mountain parks and reservations are useful not only as fountains of timber and irrigation...but as fountains of life.

Muir also said:

It took more than three thousand years to make some of the trees...trees that are still...waving and singing in the mighty forests of the Sierra.... Any fool can destroy trees.... They cannot run away.

John Muir believed that all the world is interrelated. "When we try to pick out anything by itself," he wrote, "we find it hitched to everything else in the universe."

◀ The naturalist John Muir helped convince President Theodore Roosevelt to create the Yosemite National Park.

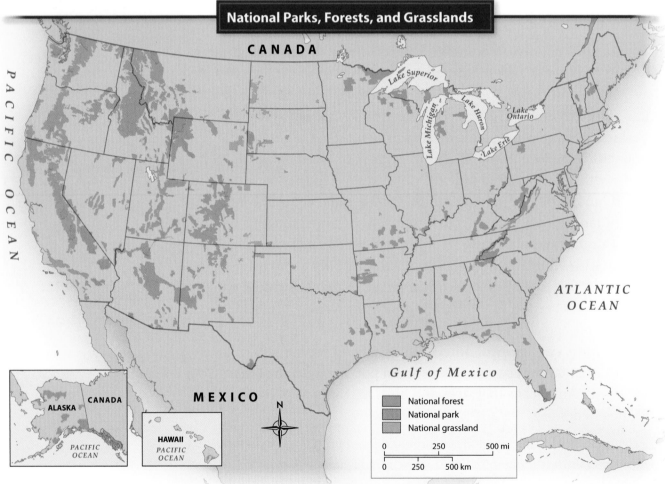

National Parks, Forests, and Grasslands

Legend:
- National forest
- National park
- National grassland

0   250   500 mi
0   250   500 km

▲ Today there are nearly 400 national parks in the United States, covering over 83 million acres of land. They are administered by the National Park Service under the U.S. Department of the Interior. The nation's 155 national forests and 20 national grasslands are administered by the Forest Service under the U.S. Department of Agriculture.

Parks for a Nation

When Abraham Lincoln was president, he signed a bill granting California the Yosemite Valley on condition that it "be held for public use, resort, and recreation...for all time." It was the beginning of an idea that would grow into national and state park systems.

Around 1870, some explorers feared that the spectacular Yellowstone area (in Montana and Wyoming) would be destroyed by homesteaders. Congress couldn't give the land to a state to preserve (Montana and Wyoming weren't states then), so, in 1872, when Ulysses S. Grant was president, Congress put one million acres under federal control as parkland. Settlers couldn't move in. In 1890 some other big areas were turned into national parks (including Yosemite, which now came under federal control). The railroads were big supporters of the national-park idea. They built large, rustic hotels for tourists in the parks, to encourage their passenger business.

Besides the undeveloped lands, there were some other areas that needed protection: Indian mounds, cliff dwellings, pueblo ruins, early missions, and other historic places. These were national treasures. The first step toward protecting them came in 1889 (Benjamin Harrison was president), when the Casa Grande ruins in Arizona were reserved from settlement. Finally, in 1916, when Woodrow Wilson was president, the National Park Service was created "to conserve the scenery and the natural and historic objects and the wild life therein...by such means as will leave them unimpaired for the enjoyment of future generations."

By that time there were 37 national parks; today there are more than 360. They are places where we celebrate history, find delight in nature, or are awed by natural wonders. Some are spectacular sites; some are gentle places. They include mountains, canyons, seashores,

▲ *Yellowstone Falls,* painted by Albert Bierstadt

volcanoes, and geysers. All are yours to enjoy—and preserve.

A great many historic places are run by the National Park Service. Thanks to that agency, you can take a ferry to Ellis Island in New York Harbor and you can imagine yourself an immigrant. Stand on the battlefield at Horseshoe Bend in Alabama and you'll see where Andrew Jackson fought the Creeks. You can tour Frederick Douglass's home in Washington, D.C. At Hopewell Village, Pennsylvania, you can see a 19th-century blast furnace smelt iron.

The National Park Service belongs to you. Don't miss out on something you own.

Jane Addams, Reformer in the Progressive Era

The 1900 census showed that America had 76.2 million people, 45 states, and territory that stretched from coast to coast. No other nation had ever grown so fast.

While most people still lived in rural areas, each year fewer and fewer Americans farmed their own lands. Many Americans had moved to the cities, where they found jobs and opportunities—but also crime, poverty, and other problems.

In response to these changes and problems, the Populists, who were mostly farmers, seemed to be saying, "Whoa," and "Hold on," and "Let's look at the old-time rural values." But the times were changing; America was changing with them.

Peaceful reform and change are difficult in any society. The powerful people in every nation are usually powerful because of the

Crowded, busy, dirty Mulberry Street in New York City, ca. 1900 ▼

Progressives fought to make a public school education available to almost all children and young people.

way things are. They don't want to see things changed. When William Vanderbilt canceled a mail train and was asked how it would affect the public, he replied, "The public be damned!"

Besides, change is unsettling for everyone. The important thing to remember about democracies is that when the people are ready for change, it usually comes about.

And so the Progressive Era was born. The Populists had made people aware of some of the nation's problems. The Progressives began to do something about them. They attempted to take the old rural values and make them work in the new urban order. For a while, Progressive ideas were accepted by both the Democratic and Republican parties. Intelligent, able people got involved with their government. They became mayors and governors and presidents. They became reformers and writers and lawmakers.

Progressives fought to see that children no longer spent their days working in fields and factories. They helped public schools grow until most children were assured of an education. For the immigrants pouring into the country, American public schools were a democratic wonder offering promise and hope for all.

There was one problem the Progressives put aside. It was the problem of racial prejudice. That was saved for later generations to face.

Progressives attacked the problem of long hours and low pay for workers, the problem of business monopolies, and the problem of the waste of our national resources. (You'll soon meet the first Progressive president.)

As you can see, Progressive reformers were busy on many fronts. Many focused their attention on solving the big problems in America's big cities.

America's cities in the 19th century were polyglot. A polyglot city is one where many languages are spoken.

America's cities were polyglot because they were filled with immigrants—diverse peoples from around the world, with their different languages and customs.

These immigrants weren't having an easy time of it. To begin, they didn't understand American democracy. Many had come to America to escape oppressive rulers. They thought of government as the enemy. They didn't realize that in America the government is supposed to be the people. That was why they often let city bosses control their lives. The boss answered their questions, helped them find jobs, or did other things to ease their adjustment to the new country.

The word *polyglot* comes from two Greek roots: *poly,* meaning "more than one," and *glossa,* meaning "tongue."

Working class people in American cities came from many parts of the world. ▶

Bosses did do many worthwhile things, but most of them paid themselves for those worthwhile things by stealing from the people. In Chicago a boss named Johnny Powers passed out free chickens and turkeys on holidays, so everyone loved him. Hardly anyone knew that he bought those turkeys with city money that was intended for schools. Powers also used city money to buy a house for himself and diamonds for his fingers. Since many of Chicago's citizens couldn't read English, it was difficult for them to know what was happening.

So when reformers tried to improve life in the cities, they had a fight on their hands. The bosses were popular. Many reformers were wealthy people who wouldn't live in the inner cities. They didn't know its polyglot population the way the boss did.

◀ Children crowd onto the fire escape of a tenement.

Children using a tenement alley for a playground in New York City ▶

▲ Jane Addams

Jane Addams was the best-known reformer of her day. She became the most admired woman in America. A visitor called her "the only saint the United States has produced." Well, she wasn't a saint, but she was an intelligent, determined, college-educated woman who got things done.

Addams's ancestors had come to Pennsylvania in the days of William Penn. By the time she was born the family had moved west, to Illinois. Her father, an Illinois state senator and friend of Abraham Lincoln, was a wealthy man. But that didn't mean she had an easy childhood. Jane's mother died when she was two. Then Jane got tuberculosis, a common disease in those days. It left her with a crooked spine. That handicap helped her understand people who had problems.

Still, Jane Addams could have had a life of parties and ease. She chose not to. She chose to do something important with her life. She chose to help others.

Children at Hull House in Chicago ▶

◄ Hull House offered painting lessons as well as English classes and many other activities.

She bought a redbrick house, with white columns on the porch, in Chicago, right in the middle of the slums. Then Jane and her friend Ellen Starr got to work with paintbrushes and rags and cleaned up the house. It had been built by a Mr. Hull, so they named it Hull House. All the neighbors were curious. Why would anyone live in the slums if they didn't have to? Chicago's slums were dirty and full of crime. But Addams didn't want to be an outsider. If she was to help people she needed to know them; she needed to be a neighbor.

Jane Addams turned Hull House into a place where people could learn to speak English, get care for their children, take painting lessons, go to a concert, exercise in a gym, or act on a stage. It was a place where they could get together with friends and take pride in their heritage. There were German nights at Hull House when German newcomers sang and danced and put on costumes from the old country. There were Polish nights, and Italian nights, and Russian nights.

▲ Hull House was one of a growing number of "settlement houses" in American cities.

Hull House was one of a growing number of "settlement houses" in American cities. It was so successful that it grew until there were 13 buildings and a staff of 65. About 50 people lived at Hull House. Some of them were writers or artists. Some were homeless. At dinnertime, the dining room might be filled with neighbors and political leaders and renowned philosophers.

Addams started clubs so that working boys and girls could have fun and learn, too. She worked to get child-labor laws passed to make it illegal for children to work long days. Chicago built its first public playground because of her efforts. She served on the Chicago school board and got new schools built.

When children committed crimes in the 19th century, they were treated like adults. Few people understood that children's problems are different from grown-ups'. Jane Addams understood. She helped establish the first juvenile court in the United States.

The Hull House neighborhood was full of garbage. Garbage stinks and brings rats. What did Addams do about it? She got herself appointed a city garbage inspector. Then she got up every morning at 6 a.m. and rode on a garbage truck, making sure the streets were clean.

Well-to-do Gilded Age women were expected to stay at home. Addams was breaking society's rules; that took courage. She had

Settling Down

Some Smith College graduates met in New York in 1887. They wanted "to do something concrete to solve social problems." They established the College Settlement in a New York tenement district. (They didn't yet know about Jane Addams in Chicago.)

Stanton Coit, an Amherst graduate who earned a Ph.D. at the University of Berlin, decided to use his training to help others. He came home and opened the Neighborhood Guild on New York's Lower East Side, and later, with Lillian Wald, founded the Henry Street Settlement in New York. By 1910, there were about 400 settlement houses in cities across the country.

plenty of it. She also had intelligence and energy. Maybe that's why she attracted so many thinking people to Hull House. A historian has written that "the Hull House community was perhaps the most formidable group of intellectuals and social activists gathered in this country since Jefferson's dinners at the White House."

Addams learned that reformers need to get involved in politics. That wasn't easy; after all, women couldn't vote or hold office. Still, she became active in presidential campaigns and in a world peace movement. In 1931, when she was 71, Jane Addams was awarded the Nobel Peace Prize—the first American woman to be so honored.

At Hull House, Jane Addams learned of "the struggle for existence which is so much harsher among people near the edge of pauperism." ▶

Problems of Progress

Thomas Jefferson had talked of America as a place where citizens are supposed to "pursue happiness. " But at the end of the 19th century life for some Americans wasn't very happy and, often, it wasn't their fault. The Industrial Revolution and the new capitalism had created a new kind of world—a wonderful world of new products and new opportunities. But no one was prepared for the misery and imbalance it also created. Mark Twain, the muckrakers, and others called attention to the imbalance created by the Machine Age and the unplanned growth of cities. Urban poverty was breeding crime and waste, along with a sense of unfairness. But the problems of poverty and injustice didn't get solved. They would haunt the 20th century; in the 21st century, there would still be Americans going hungry.

▲ A child rummages through a trash bin—a stark image of the persistence of urban poverty.

Politically Speaking

WHAT IS A DIRECT PRIMARY?

Candidates for political offices were nominated at party conventions, and those conventions were often controlled by party bosses. Now, if the candidates could be chosen by the people in party elections before the main election, you'd have direct primaries and a more democratic process. In 1896, South Carolina adopted the first statewide primary. After that, the movement spread quickly to most other states.

INITIATIVES AND REFERENDUMS

South Dakota was the first state (in 1898) to try the *initiative* (in-ISH-uh-tiv) *and referendum*. That fancy-sounding phrase means that voters get a chance to vote on some laws themselves (instead of leaving everything up to their legislators). If a specific number of voters petitioned to have a measure put on the ballot (the *initiative*), then voters could vote for or against it (the *referendum*). It was democracy expanding again. Can you think of good reasons why some people were against this idea?

AMENDMENT XVII

Article 1, Section 23 of the Constitution says: "The Senate of the United States shall be composed of two Senators from each State, chosen by the Legislature thereof, for six years." "Chosen by the Legislature thereof" was a process that bothered many Americans. They wanted to choose their own senators directly. It would be more democratic, but the Constitution would have to be amended. The House of Representatives voted for such an amendment; beginning in 1894, they voted for it three times.

Each time, the Senate defeated the measure. The senators liked the way they'd been chosen, but most Americans didn't. Finally, on the fourth try, the Senate agreed; in 1913 the 17th Amendment was ratified by the states. It says: "The Senate of the United States shall be composed of two Senators from each State, elected by the people thereof, for six years."

▲ The first American use of the secret ballot occurred in Boston, in an election held on November 5, 1889.

Part 3

Expansion, War, Boom, and Bust

From Teedie to TR

Theodore Roosevelt—who was called Teedie when he was a boy—was very rich and lived in a five-story house in New York City with his brother and his two sisters and his mother and father. Four or five servants (sometimes more) lived in the house, too. His uncle, aunt, and cousins lived nearby.

If you looked out the front door of the big house, onto East 20th Street, you could see cobblestones and horse-pulled carriages and hear city noises; but in the quiet backyard, flowers and strutting peacocks filled a block-long garden.

The Roosevelts were an old Dutch family, and had been New Yorkers since the days of Peter Stuyvesant. They were aristocratic and proper, and spent much of their time with wealthy families like themselves.

The Roosevelts all seemed to have something in common: it was energy and high spirits. They liked having a good time. They enjoyed laughing, playing games, and riding horseback. When Teedie grew up and became president, he brought more laughter to the White House than any president before or since.

Young Theodore was a studious boy and an astounding reader. All his life he read at least a book a day, and often more. He had an amazing memory. When he became president he surprised people with the wide knowledge he had from books. He also loved to write, and before he died, at age 60, he wrote some 150,000 letters. He wrote all his presidential speeches himself (most presidents have speechwriters), and he wrote more than 30 books.

But when he was a boy, Theodore Roosevelt expected to become a scientist. His special interest was nature, especially bugs and birds. He set up a natural-history museum in his house and kept detailed drawings and records of the animals he observed. Once a servant complained that she couldn't do the laundry with "a snapping turtle tied to the legs of the sink."

He was born just before the Civil War began, and his first memories were of playing soldier. Teedie pretended he was a Union soldier; his brother and sisters were not so sure which side

"This country will not be a permanently good place for us to live unless it's a good place for all of us to live," said Theodore Roosevelt when he became president.

Teedie in Paris, age 11, on his family's European tour: in Rome, "I…was given by Papa…a Roman vase and coin," he wrote. "Just think of it!!" ▼

to take. Theodore's father—Theodore, Sr.—was a strong supporter of Abraham Lincoln and the Union cause. Theodore's mother, Mittie Bulloch, was a Georgia girl who grew up on a plantation. She sympathized with the Southern cause. Perhaps it was because of his wife's feelings that Theodore, Sr., chose not to fight in the war. He did what many other rich Northern men did. He paid a substitute to fight for him. It was the only thing he ever did that upset his son.

The older Theodore, a glass merchant and a banker, was a philanthropist (fil-AN-thruh-pist), which means he spent much of his time and money helping others. He set up a program to help soldiers' families, he founded the Children's Aid Society, he helped start the American Museum of Natural History, he aided hospitals, and he worked on other good government causes. He believed that his wealth gave him a special responsibility to be a helpful citizen. His son called him "the best man I ever knew."

You can see that Theodore Roosevelt had an unusual childhood. When he wanted to learn more about animals and how to stuff them, his parents gave him lessons with a taxidermist who had hunted and worked with the famous artist and naturalist John James Audubon. When the Roosevelts wanted their children to learn about geography and art and history, they took the family on a year's trip to Europe. Teedie was 10. When he was 14, they spent a winter on a houseboat on the Nile River in Egypt. Teedie was given a rifle, and he shot and stuffed hundreds of birds.

Theodore Roosevelt in a studio photo, the Tiffany knife and sheath in his belt. ▼

Young Theodore's health was poor. He had bad asthma, terrible eyesight, and stomach problems. He was frail and sickly, and no one thought he would live long. His father told him he needed to build his body to match his mind. At age 11 he began lifting weights and doing exercises. For the rest of his life he boxed, rode horseback, hunted, and rowed. The weak, scrawny lad turned himself into a powerful, fearless man.

When he was 26, Theodore Roosevelt headed to the West. The North Dakota cowboys chuckled when they saw the young dude from the East with books under his arm. He wore a fringed and beaded buckskin shirt, fringed leather pants, silver spurs engraved with his initials, and alligator boots. Tucked in his belt were a knife and scabbard, custom-made at Tiffany's, the finest jewelry store in the nation. One day out on the range, the cowboys figured, and the city slicker would hightail it back East.

So a guide took him buffalo hunting. They were gone seven days, riding the wildest, loneliest, most difficult trails the Dakota Badlands had to offer. It rained most of the time; the days were hot and the nights were frigid. They were charged by a wounded buffalo, their food ran out, the dude fell into a bed of cactus, wolves frightened their horses, the horses had to be chased, and they woke one cold morning to find themselves sleeping in four inches of water. The guide, Joe Ferris, was close to collapse from exhaustion. But the worse things got, the more the dude seemed to enjoy himself. "By Godfrey, but this is fun!" he kept saying.

Roosevelt had dropped his childhood name, Teedie, and was now signing his letters "Thee," or "Ted," or "Theodore." Later, when he became president, people would call him "TR," or "Teddy." But he was little Teedie when he first dreamed of the West after reading adventure books by James Fenimore Cooper. He longed for adventure but he went west for another reason. He went to forget and to begin again. He had lived through a series of tragedies that no young man should have to face.

The Badlands is a high, dry region with deep gullies caused by heavy rain. That rain is nature's joke, because normally there isn't enough to make much of anything grow. When the rain does come, it is sometimes so hard it washes the land away. Badlands aren't good for agriculture or pasture, but they are hauntingly beautiful and full of tall earth columns and platforms.

Badlands National Park in South Dakota ▶

◄ Theodore Roosevelt riding a moose

The first tragedy came when he was a college student. He studied hard and passed the entrance exam for Harvard. He expected to be a scientist. Then his beloved father died. That changed his life, and his career, too. He decided to go into politics—to become a responsible citizen, as he believed his father would have wished him to do. Few people with his wealth and education entered politics. They were apt to look down their noses at the people who ran the country. Roosevelt was determined to be a reforming politician. When friends asked why he had gone into politics, he said he wished to be part of the governing—not the governed—class.

So when he left college, he became a legislator in New York's Assembly. And he got married, to sweet-natured Alice Lee. She was like a fairy-tale bride: blue-eyed, blonde, and beautiful. They were enchantingly happy. And then, on the same day—it was Valentine's Day, 1884—in the same house, Alice died giving birth to a daughter, and Mittie, Theodore's mother, died of typhoid fever. Mittie was 48; Alice, 22.

In his diary entry for that day, Roosevelt drew a dark *X* and wrote, "The light has gone out of my life." Three days later, he christened the baby Alice Lee and sorrowfully wrote in his diary, "my life has now been lived out." TR had no clue as to the full and productive life ahead of him; what he did have was resilience and energy, so he went west and threw himself into cowboy life.

Out west, TR learned to rope steers, wrestle calves, and ride bucking ponies. Once a pistol-toting bully threatened him in a bar. Roosevelt, as he later recalled, stood up, then "struck quick and hard with my right just to one side of the point of his jaw, hitting with my left as I straightened out, and then again with my right." Next day the bully left town on a freight train.

TR could ride 100 miles a day and then sit up all night on watch. If he found someone who could talk about books or ideas, he would talk and talk and talk.

Roosevelt fell in love with the bleak, haunting Dakota Badlands, a strange place of cliffs, ravines, and flat tablelands where survival wasn't easy—even for birds and animals. He may have understood that his was the last generation that would enjoy that frontier in its natural state.

When Roosevelt became president he did everything he could to save wilderness areas for future generations. He increased the national forests by 40 million acres, created five national parks, 16 national monuments, four national game refuges, and 51 bird sanctuaries. After hiking with John Muir, he made sure that Yosemite's forests of giant sequoia and redwood trees were saved "for the people's children and children's children." He helped make conservation a popular idea.

His first trips west did exactly what they were meant to do. They helped him begin his life again. When he went back east, he was ready to accept a new job, as police commissioner of New York. (Some people said roping steers was easier.) Now he was out walking the streets of New York with writers Jacob Riis and Lincoln Steffens. At night he could be seen in dangerous areas, making sure the police were doing their job. No police commissioner had done that before.

And he married a childhood playmate, Edith Carow. Together they raised a noisy, happy family of six children.

Teddy (then president) with John Muir at Yosemite ▼

◄ Albert Bierstadt painted these giant California sequoias in 1858.

The Spanish-American War

Spain's time as a great world power was behind her. Still, she remembered the glory days of Queen Isabella and King Ferdinand and clung tightly to colonies in Cuba, Puerto Rico, and the Philippine Islands.

In Cuba there were those, like the Americans in 1776, who wanted freedom to run their own country, especially as many of the Spanish officials seemed cruel and corrupt. So the Cubans rose up against the Spaniards. Naturally, most Americans sided with the revolutionaries.

Now this freedom movement came at the very time two rival American newspapers were fighting each other for readers. The Cuban story made exciting reading. Every day the newspaper headlines would boldly tell of atrocities in Cuba. When there was no real story to tell, eager reporters would make one up. That's called *yellow journalism* (good papers don't do it).

Anyway, with all the scare stories, the American people began screaming for war with Spain. They wanted Spain to clear out of the American hemisphere. But Spain didn't want to leave Cuba.

A Hero for All the Americas

José Martí, a poet and one of Latin America's greatest writers, dedicated his life to the cause of *Cuba Libre* ("free Cuba"). At 16 he was arrested and kicked out of Cuba. He went off to Spain, studied, and earned a master's degree and a law degree. After that he lived and worked in Mexico, Guatemala, Venezuela, and the United States (mostly in New York City). He wrote for American magazines and for Spanish publications. Martí said he was a citizen of the Americas.

Several times he visited Ybor City in Florida and spoke on the iron steps in front of the Ybor cigar factory. His listeners were electrified. He was a man everyone admired—except for those who wanted to keep Cuba Spanish. So when José Martí died in 1895 at age 42, on a battlefield in Cuba, people wept and called him a martyr and a great hero. Seven years later, Cuba became independent.

▲ José Martí dedicated his life to the cause of a free Cuba.

The screaming headlines of the *New York Journal* sold more than a million copies a day when the *Maine* blew up. Joseph Pulitzer's *World* sent its own divers to investigate the wreck in Havana harbor. ▶

▲ "Remember The Maine" became a patriotic slogan for many Americans who demanded war with Spain.

Spanish, Cuban, and American diplomats began meeting; they were trying to solve their differences quietly. Maybe they would have done so, if the *Maine* hadn't sailed into the harbor at Havana, Cuba.

The *Maine* was a U.S. battleship, and it had been sent to pick up American citizens if any trouble developed. Trouble did develop—on the *Maine*! The ship exploded! Sky high! Two hundred and sixty American sailors were killed.

A team of American experts said the *Maine* had hit a mine. Spanish officials said the explosion came from inside the ship. Seventy-eight years later, in 1976, an investigation proved the Spaniards were right.

The screaming headlines of the *New York Journal* sold more than a million copies a day when the *Maine* blew up. Joseph Pulitzer's *World* sent its own divers to investigate the wreck in Havana harbor.

Internal combustion had started a fire that reached some gunpowder on the *Maine*. In other words, it was an accident.

But in 1898 no one knew what had really happened. The newspapers played up the *Maine* story: they called it a Spanish attack. A headline in the popular *New York Journal* said WARSHIP *MAINE* SPLIT IN TWO BY AN ENEMY'S SECRET INFERNAL MACHINE.

The American people went wild. They demanded war. Congress wanted war. Theodore Roosevelt wanted war. William McKinley was president, and he had fought in the Civil War. He knew the horrors of war; he wanted no part of one. People started calling him a coward. They didn't realize it usually takes more courage to say no than yes. Finally McKinley gave in. War was declared on Spain.

Theodore Roosevelt, who was now assistant secretary of the Navy, resigned at once. He wanted to get into this war. He organized a cavalry troop, which trained in Texas. The cavalrymen called themselves "Rough Riders." (They got that name from the old Pony Express.) But when they got to the docks in Tampa, Florida, they found there was room on the ship only for officers' horses. The Rough Riders wanted to fight, even if they had to be foot soldiers. So they called themselves "Weary Walkers," and headed for Cuba.

In Cuba they fought fearlessly, TR most of all. He charged ahead with bullets flying around him. Along with the 9th and 10th black regiments, the Rough Riders fought their way up two important hills, Kettle Hill and San Juan Hill. The Spaniards were at the top of the hills, shooting down on them. When those Americans took San Juan Hill they went into the history books forever.

The war was short and popular. (It was over in 113 days.) Northerners and Southerners fought together; that helped heal some of the old Civil War wounds. Cuba won her freedom; Spain lost out. The United States took Puerto Rico as an American territory.

In the Pacific, Admiral George Dewey sailed into Manila harbor in the Spanish-held Philippine Islands and destroyed a Spanish fleet. The Philippines became American

In the late 1800s, naval officers and business people were arguing for a more powerful navy to protect U.S foreign markets. The most influential of these was Captain (later Admiral) Alfred T. Mahan. His book, *The Influence of Sea Power,* helped convince Congress to increase the navy's budget. By 1900, the U.S. Navy was one of the most powerful naval forces in the world.

The U.S. military met its recruitment goals quickly as American men responded to calls to enlist. ▶

YOUR COUNTRY CALLS YOU

R·M·WRIGH '98.

The Battle of Manila in the Philippines during the Spanish-American War ▶

To *annex* means to bring land into a larger territory.

territory; so did Guam and Wake Island. At about the same time, American businessmen in the Hawaiian Islands asked the United States to annex those islands. We did.

Some native Hawaiians, and many Filipinos, wanted to be independent—they wanted to form their own nations. They weren't given a choice. American expansionists wanted the islands. The Filipinos decided to fight. They fought the United States valiantly. It took 75,000 soldiers—four times the number that fought in Cuba—to conquer the Filipinos.

Senator Henry Cabot Lodge said:

We must on no account let the islands go: the American flag is up and it must stay.... Manila with its magnificent bay is the prize and pearl of the East.... It will keep us open to the markets of China.

A Harvard professor called the Philippine fight an "unrighteous war." Samuel Gompers called it "an unjust war." But few Americans agreed.

Theodore Roosevelt came home from Cuba a hero. New Yorkers soon elected him governor. As governor, he worked so hard and did such a good job that the political bosses hated him. They didn't know what to do—TR was trying to put them out of business! Then one of them got a bright idea. Why not nominate TR as vice president of the United States? That way he would be out of New York and out of their hair. Roosevelt was ambitious; he was delighted to run for vice president on the Republican

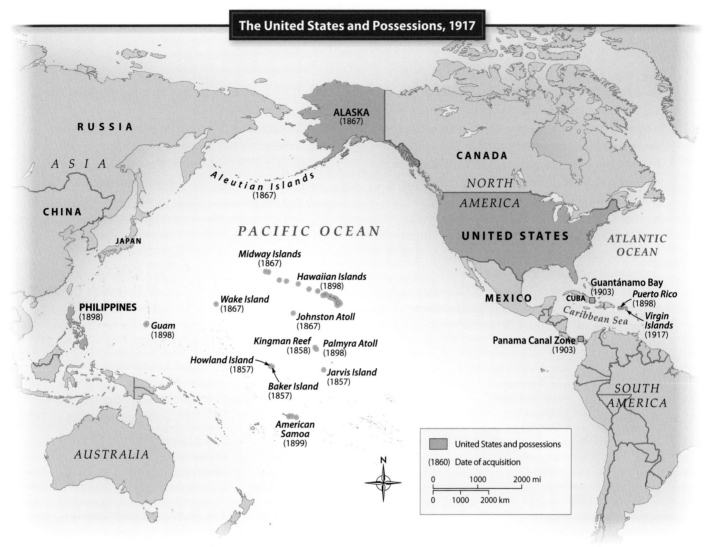

The United States and Possessions, 1917

RUSSIA

ASIA

CHINA

JAPAN

ALASKA
(1867)

Aleutian Islands
(1867)

PACIFIC OCEAN

CANADA

NORTH
AMERICA

UNITED STATES

ATLANTIC
OCEAN

Midway Islands
(1867)

Hawaiian Islands
(1898)

Wake Island
(1867)

Johnston Atoll
(1867)

PHILIPPINES
(1898)

Guam
(1898)

Kingman Reef
(1858)

Palmyra Atoll
(1898)

Howland Island
(1857)

Jarvis Island
(1857)

Baker Island
(1857)

American
Samoa
(1899)

MEXICO

CUBA

Guantánamo Bay
(1903)

Puerto Rico
(1898)

Virgin
Islands
(1917)

Caribbean Sea

Panama Canal Zone
(1903)

SOUTH
AMERICA

AUSTRALIA

N

United States and possessions

(1860) Date of acquisition

0   1000   2000 mi

0   1000   2000 km

ticket with William McKinley (going for a second term). They were elected easily. No one knew an assassin had a bullet ready for President McKinley.

Theodore Roosevelt was hiking in the Adirondack Mountains when a messenger ran puffing up the mountain with a telegram. McKinley was dead. Roosevelt was 42, younger than any president before him. His first day in the White House was his father's birthday. That, he believed, was a good omen.

Mark Hanna didn't see anything good about it. He was a political insider who had been persuaded to help get TR out of New York and into the "safe" job of vice president. "Now look!" Hanna said to New York's Senator Platt. "That damned cowboy is president of the United States!"

▲ By 1917, the United States controlled territories in North America, the Caribbean, Central America, and the Pacific.

Expansionism Is Imperialism

Expansionism is a big word, which is appropriate, because it means the practice (by a nation) of getting bigger. Should nations grow and grow as much as they can? In the past, many nations have felt the only way to be great was to do just that. How does a country grow? Usually by getting land from others.

Isn't that wrong? Well, in the past, many good people believed that they were helping or improving the other nations that they grabbed. Besides, it was the way nations had always become powerful. At the turn of the century, many Americans thought expansion would bring glory, prestige, and power to the United States. They believed America's ideals were so great that they should be forced on other people. It was a popular way to think.

Expansionism was also called *imperialism*. Imperialism is the policy of expanding a nation by claiming foreign lands. Theodore Roosevelt was an imperialist. He always liked to do things in a big way.

But some people—like Mark Twain and ex-President Cleveland—thought differently. The people who were against expansion were called anti-imperialists. Their view was not very popular. They believed it was America's destiny to be different from other nations. They thought the United States should stick to its own affairs. They agreed with Thomas Jefferson's principle "that we should have nothing to do with conquest."

Senator Albert J. Beveridge, from Indiana, thought the United States should expand wherever it could. He saw the spoils of the Spanish War as a path to world power. Here is what he said in 1898:

> *Those who do not want the United States to annex foreign lands tell us that we ought not to govern a people without their consent. I answer, "That rule of government applies only to those people who are capable of self-government." We govern the Indians without their consent. We govern our territories without their consent. We govern our children without their consent....*

◀ This 1904 cartoon depicts the imperialist ambitions of the United States as an American eagle with wings spread from Puerto Rico to the Philippines.

Carl Schurz, a former senator, was an anti-imperialist. He didn't think the United States should annex foreign territories. This is what he said in 1899:

Our government was, in the words of Abraham Lincoln, "the government of the people." To make this republic the example and guiding star of mankind was the noblest of ambitions. Such was our ambition just a short year ago.

Then came the Spanish War. When our forces occupied foreign territory, a loud demand arose that the conquests, even the Philippines, should be kept. "Why not?" was the cry. Has not the job of the republic almost from its beginning been one of territorial expansion? The question is not whether we can do such things, but whether we should do them.

The 19th century was an imperialist era. Most Americans wanted to join the imperialist competition. But when it came to China we had something else to say. Great Britain and Japan had gotten there first. We complained and demanded that China be open to all who wanted to trade with her. We wanted an "open door" to China's rich markets. (An *open door* means a policy where all nations have equal opportunities to trade in a region.) We also wanted an open door in Latin America.

America's citizens would do a lot of thinking about "imperialism" and "isolation" and "world responsibility." It would be difficult to find the right road.

◄ A group of soldiers in the Spanish-American War stand to defend their camp with bayonets at the ready.

Aloha Oe

Mark Twain called them "the loveliest fleet of islands that lies anchored in any ocean." He was talking about the Hawaiian Islands, which are moored in the middle of the Pacific Ocean. But the first American missionaries to the islands—led by Hiram Bingham of Vermont and Asa Thurston of Massachusetts—didn't see loveliness. They came to save souls and were horrified by what they found.

"The appearance of destitution, degradation, and barbarism among the chattering, and almost naked savages…was appalling," wrote Bingham. It was March 30, 1820, and Hawaii would never be the same again.

The islands are actually mountains—volcanic mountains—built up from the sea bottom. Poking above the water like a crescent of jewels in the enormous Pacific, they include eight major islands and 124 islets. Polynesian sailors discovered them long before Magellan set sail, maybe a thousand years before. How they did it is still a mystery. The Polynesians came from the Marquesas Islands (more than 2,000 miles away) and they had no compasses or maps or sextants. But they were skilled navigators, and they traveled back

The Na Pali Coast of Hawaii ▼

and forth across a vast triangle of ocean—from New Zealand to Tahiti to Easter Island to Hawaii. For those long voyages, they lashed together two huge canoes, using cords made from coconut fiber, and rigged them with sails woven of leaves. Some of their vessels held 200 people.

The Polynesians settled the islands and, for about 900 years, kept in contact with their home islands. Then the voyages stopped. Those who had come to Hawaii were on their own. By this time, powerful chiefs and priests were ruling what was a feudal society. Just as in Europe, the feudal lords bickered and fought in brutal wars that were often over land rights.

But fighting was only one part of the story. The Hawaiians developed a rich oral culture (there was no written language) that passed on myths, historic tales, and practical knowledge. On irrigated plantations, they grew taro (an edible root) and cultivated groves of coconut and banana trees. The Hawaiian religion was centered on a system of *kapus*—taboos. These were complicated rules of daily life that couldn't be broken. If you did break a *kapu*, you were insulting God. That usually meant death.

The first European to discover the Hawaiian Islands was said to be a 16th-century Spanish explorer. But he didn't leave a written record of that contact, so he doesn't get credit.

The name *Hawaii* is sometimes written with an apostrophe between the two i's: *Hawai'i*. This reflects the native pronunciation of the word—the simplest way to describe it is that it sounds like a slight pause or hesitation: "huhwye…ee." Both spellings are correct: the spelling here is *Hawaii*, without the apostrophe. *Ka'iulani* is the way a Hawaiian princess's name is often written.

▲ English captain James Cook presents sheep and goats to Hawaiian natives. Peaceful relations soon turned violent and Cook was killed.

Sandalwood is yellowish and aromatic, and especially fine for carving and making furniture. It produces an oil used in some perfumes. Sandalwood trees (there are several varieties) are native to tropical Asia.

England's Captain James Cook does. It was 1778, and Cook was looking for a northwest passage through the American continent. He sailed up the west coast of North America. When he reached Icy Cape in the Bering Strait, he turned south; he needed supplies and food. That's when Cook ran into those gorgeous islands. He named them the Sandwich Islands, after a British aristocrat, the Earl of Sandwich, who was helping to pay the bills for his trip.

At first the Hawaiian people thought Captain Cook was a god. They treated him with awe. But that soon changed to anger, after fighting began between sailors and natives. The details of what happened are still disputed, but not the outcome: Captain Cook was killed.

The outside world now learned of the Hawaiian Islands. Ships soon came calling. In the Hawaiian Islands they could find food, wood for ship repairs, and a place to rest. New England whalers began to spend their winters in Hawaii. Merchants vied for the islands' rare sandalwood, which was prized in China. (It was soon depleted.) Fur traders, on their way to Asia, made Hawaii a stopping point.

The greatest of Hawaii's rulers was Kamehameha I. Using guns and persuasion, he united the islands by 1810. A shrewd businessman, Kamehameha promoted trade with the foreigners and earned a fortune for his kingdom. He paid attention to the new ideas the foreign sailors brought with them, but he also guarded and encouraged traditional Hawaiian ways. When Kamehameha died in 1819, his son, Liholiho, succeeded him.

Liholiho became Kamehameha II, but he was a weak king, and often drunk. It was his mother who held real power. She wanted to end the *kapu* system. The *kapus* kept Hawaiians fearful and kept women subservient. Men and women were not allowed to eat together. The Queen Mother planned a big official dinner; foreign guests were included. Kamehameha II sat down between his mother and another royal female. The king began to eat. The women ate, too.

Nothing happened. The gods did not send bolts of lightning. But the Hawaiians at the dinner felt as if they had been struck by lightning. They couldn't believe what they were seeing. Then, all over the islands, people who had lived in fear started breaking every rule they could. And nothing happened. Except that now there were no rules, no laws, no customs to turn to. Kamehameha II officially abolished the old religion and ordered the destruction of all idols and temples. Then he and his wife sailed off to England. They came home in coffins, victims of measles.

Imagine that everything you've ever believed is suddenly wrong. Your leader is gone. Where do you turn? The Hawaiians were lost.

And that was just when those missionaries, Hiram Bingham and Asa Thurston, arrived. They found many Hawaiians receptive to Christianity. The Hawaiians turned to the Americans for advice on laws, on other matters of government, and even on dress and ways of life. The missionaries, who were horrified by many native practices, brought their own rigid ideas and values. They wanted the Hawaiians to wear clothes that covered their bodies. And they outlawed the hula dance because the movements seemed indecent to them. (The hula dance wasn't tourist entertainment: it was a religious ritual.) Their intentions were good, but they destroyed much of the native culture.

The religious missionaries weren't the only newcomers who came to the islands. Merchants, and others who saw opportunity, began arriving. Europeans came as well as Americans. Planters established big sugarcane plantations. By the middle of the 19th century, there were frame houses, schools, churches, stores, taverns, and written language—Western culture was taking over. Some of that culture—like drinking, using guns, and trading for profit—would destroy many Hawaiian traditions. Some of it—like schooling and writing—would help preserve what survived.

In 1848, a Hawaiian land commissioner introduced the Western idea of private ownership of land; much of the islands' territory was soon bought up by the newcomers. (That land exchange was called

In this early photograph, an American missionary stands behind two Hawaiian princes, Alexander Liholiho and Lot Kamehameha, dressed in Western attire. ▼

Japanese workers harvest sugar cane in Hawaii. ▶

the Great Mahele.) Then the outsiders (called *haoles*) began to want more than just land; they wanted political power.

The diseases they brought to the islands helped their cause. The Hawaiians had no immunity to Western diseases; for them they were killers. Much of the native Hawaiian population got wiped out. That meant there were few workers for the sugarcane plantations. So the planters brought in Chinese laborers; they were followed by Japanese, Filipino, Korean, Portuguese, and Puerto Rican workers.

The Americans and the Europeans attempted to get along with the native Hawaiians and the other Asian peoples, but they never considered them equals—not for a minute. Today we would call them racial bigots; then, their ideas reflected their times.

In 1891, a new ruler came to the throne. Her name was Queen Liliuokalani. A brilliant, determined woman, she intended to restore power to the Hawaiian people. Liliuokalani worked secretly on a new constitution. Only native Hawaiians would be able to vote.

But the world had changed; Liliuokalani didn't understand that business interests now had more power than kings and queens.

And the planters weren't going to let a native leader make rules for them. Especially a woman! They employed thousands of workers. They determined Hawaii's economy. Asa Thurston's grandson, Lorrin, led a revolution. The American minister to Hawaii (the government's secretary in charge of Hawaiian affairs, not a religious leader) had U.S. Marines land at Honolulu. A new government was set up; its leaders (the *haoles*) appealed to Washington; they asked that the United States annex the islands.

President Grover Cleveland didn't know what was going on in Hawaii, and he was a cautious man. The queen's niece, Princess Kaiulani, arrived in Washington and told the president that her country had been wronged; Cleveland sent a congressman to the islands to investigate. The congressman's report wasn't what the revolutionaries expected. It advised that, in the name of justice, the monarchy be restored.

But that didn't happen. Queen Liliuokalani had tried to return to a past that was no more. On July 4, 1894, Sanford B. Dole, a leading businessman, proclaimed himself president of the Republic of Hawaii. Liliuokalani was imprisoned in the royal palace (for eight months). The Hawaiian monarchy was finished.

Manifest Destiny soon brought Hawaii under U.S. control. That idea—that the United States has a mission to spread democracy—was used to justify American expansion, even where it wasn't wanted. So, despite some strong opposition in Congress, President William McKinley signed a resolution annexing Hawaii to the United States. It was 1898, and the American flag now flew over the islands.

The more you read history the more you will notice that sometimes the right things happen for the wrong reasons, and vice versa. The Hawaiian story is complicated and filled with emotional and often heartrending moments. All those people who came to Hawaii—the Asian workers, the missionaries, the planters, and those simply lured by the beauty of the place—created an astonishingly diverse society where people of all backgrounds have come to power. In 1959, Hawaii became the 50th state.

▲ Liliuokalani, the last queen of Hawaii, was an early advocate of women's rights. She composed more than 200 songs, including the well-known "Aloha Oe."

Hawaii is now the southernmost state in the United States. Of the eight major islands that make up Hawaii, Oahu is the most populous. Honolulu, the state capital, is a port of the island of Oahu. Hilo, the second-largest city, is on the island of Hawaii.

In Hawaii today, there is no majority racial group—everyone belongs in a minority. The term "Hawaiian" is reserved for those of Hawaiian/Polynesian ancestry, who now make up about one-eighth of the total population (about 1.2 million people). People of Asian origin comprise 62 percent of the population; whites make up 33.3 percent.

Teddy Bear President

Roosevelt made a great president. But you knew he would. He was "deelighted" to be president, he said. It was a "bully" job, he added. No president has ever had such a good time at it—and worked so hard, too.

The people loved him; the press did, too. He was always doing things that made good stories. Like the time he went hunting for bear but refused to kill a helpless little bear. When that story got out, a candy maker in Brooklyn, New York, made a toy bear and called it a "Teddy bear." He sent it to the president and asked his permission to use the name on more bears. Theodore Roosevelt said yes, and soon people were calling him "Teddy" Roosevelt. He hated that nickname, but he was stuck with it. The candy maker became a toy maker and got rich. Everyone wanted those bears, and that's how teddy bears came to be. (That first teddy is now in the National Museum of American History, in Washington, D.C., where you can see it.)

Reporters found TR's children were worth writing about, too. Alice, the oldest and a teenager, sometimes kept a snake in her purse. Quentin, the youngest, stood on the second-floor White House balcony and dropped a huge snowball on a White House guard. It knocked the guard over. All six children roller-skated in the basement, slid down the banisters, and played hide and seek in the attic. Sometimes government business waited while the president played tag with them.

But Theodore Roosevelt wasn't just fun and games. He was a strong president. He brought his energy, habit of working hard, and intelligence to the job. He helped see that pure food and drug laws were passed. He found ways to control some of those corporations that were acting

Roosevelt couldn't seem to get enough of "the people." On New Year's Day in 1907, anyone who wanted to could go to the White House and shake their president's hand (anyone who was clean and not drunk). Roosevelt set a record that day: he shook 8,150 hands.

Theodore Roosevelt said that being president was a "bully" job—by which he meant, superb, first-rate. ▼

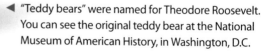

◄ "Teddy bears" were named for Theodore Roosevelt. You can see the original teddy bear at the National Museum of American History, in Washington, D.C.

as if they were above the law. The biggest of them had turned into "trusts." Congress had passed the Sherman Antitrust Act, but no one had enforced it. TR went "trustbusting."

One day in 1905 a struggling poet named Edward Arlington Robinson went to his mailbox and found a letter from the president. It offered him a job that would allow him time to keep writing poetry. Theodore Roosevelt invited the great black educator Booker T. Washington to the White House for dinner. Some prejudiced people objected; that didn't stop TR.

President Roosevelt was responsible for the building of the Panama Canal. That created a water passageway from the Atlantic Ocean to the Pacific Ocean at the midsection of the American continents. Just think about that. It took most ships more than two months to make the trip from San Francisco to the East Coast by sailing through the Straits of Magellan at the tip of South America. Cutting through Panama was like unlocking a door between the oceans.

"We demand that big business give the people a square deal," said TR. "When anyone…in big business…endeavors to do right he shall himself be given a square deal."

▲ A 1903 cartoon illustrates Teddy Roosevelt's determination to see a canal dug across Panama, regardless of the opposition.

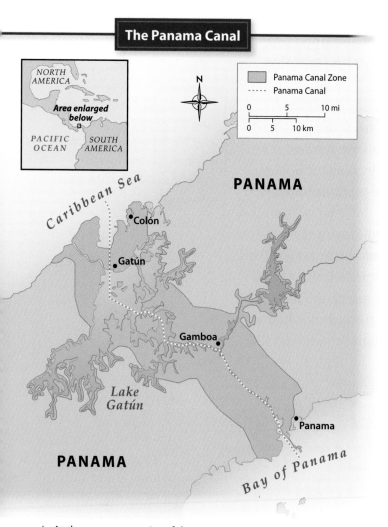

The Panama Canal

NORTH AMERICA

Area enlarged below

PACIFIC OCEAN

SOUTH AMERICA

N

Panama Canal Zone
Panama Canal

0   5   10 mi
0   5   10 km

Caribbean Sea

PANAMA

Colón

Gatún

Gamboa

Lake Gatún

Panama

PANAMA

Bay of Panama

Look at Panama on the map. It should be a simple thing to take some steam shovels to Panama and dig out a canal, shouldn't it? Ha. Digging that canal was a nightmare. The map does not show thick jungle, but that was only one of the things the canal builders had to contend with. The worst problem may have been the tiny mosquitoes that carried malaria and yellow-fever germs. Nearly 6,000 men died, mostly from disease. There were also accidents and political hassles and enormous engineering problems. It is worth going to the library and finding a book about the building of the Panama Canal. It is some story. Without Theodore Roosevelt it would have been even more difficult.

He had a favorite saying: *Speak softly and carry a big stick.* It was an African proverb, and TR was always quoting it. He believed that if you show you are strong no one will pick on you. The big stick he wanted for the nation was a strong navy. He helped build one.

▲ At the narrowest point of the Isthmus of Panama, only 30 miles separate the Atlantic and Pacific Oceans. (An *isthmus* is a narrow strip of land connecting two larger land areas.)

Tugboats pull a ship through the Panama Canal in 1915. ▶

Roosevelt talked a lot about war and soldiering, but his presidency was a time of peace. He was a good diplomat and was able to deal well with other countries. After he helped settle a war between Japan and Russia he was given the Nobel Peace Prize. He gave the prize money to the nation; he said it belonged to the American people (even though it came at a time when he could have used it himself).

Today we think that Roosevelt's most important contributions as president were in the field of conservation. We can thank him for saving many of the public lands that we enjoy today.

He did one thing he later regretted. When he was elected president on his own in 1904 (remember, he first got the job because McKinley was killed), he said he would not run for a third term. When his second term was up he was only 50, and he loved being president. The American people loved having him as president. But he had given his word. So he didn't run for reelection. Instead, TR went off to Africa to hunt big game.

"San Francisco is gone!"

On April 18, 1906, a major earthquake rocked the city of San Francisco and the coast of northern California. The earthquake started the damage, but the fires that resulted were much more devastating—and there was no water available to put them out. In a news report in *Collier's Weekly*, Jack London wrote:

The earthquake shook down in San Francisco hundreds of thousands of dollars' worth of walls and chimneys. But the conflagration that followed burned up hundreds of millions of dollars' worth of property.... Not in history has a modern imperial city been so completely destroyed. San Francisco is gone!

A 1906 earthquake caused devastating fires in San Francisco. ▶

Henry Ford

Not many people get to change the world they live in. Henry Ford did. He did it because he had an idea he believed in, and he never gave up, even when people laughed at him.

Henry Ford's idea was this: to build an automobile so cheap that almost everyone could own one. A car that would cost about the same as a horse and buggy. Ford said that store clerks, schoolteachers, carpenters, farmers, librarians—ordinary people—would be able to buy his car.

Now, to any reasonable person at the turn of the century, the idea of an inexpensive car seemed nonsense. Henry Ford went to J. P. Morgan's bank (the biggest bank in the nation) and asked for a loan to get started. The sensible bankers turned him down. Automobiles, they told him, were for rich people.

Back then, cars were called "horseless carriages." If you were wealthy and liked new gadgets, you might own a Stanley Steamer, powered by a steam engine, or you might have an electric car, powered by a battery. The trouble with the steam engine was that it sometimes blew up; the trouble with the battery car was that it often needed recharging.

In his workshop in Dearborn, Michigan, Henry Ford built his first car in 1896—here he is, driving the Quadricycle. ▶

Henry Ford was a tinkerer—he loved to design and make things. He believed he could design an inexpensive car powered by a liquid fuel. A farmer's son, he had energy to burn and a head filled with ideas. When Ford was a boy he took apart—and put together again—every watch he could find. Ford became an apprentice in a machine shop. Then he got a job with Thomas Edison's company. He told Edison his idea about an inexpensive automobile powered by liquid fuel. Edison encouraged Ford. "Young man, keep at it," he said.

Ford tinkered away and designed several cars. Then he designed a car he called the Model T. It was a car that worked well and was easy to build. Henry Ford needed to find a way to build it so the cost would be very low.

Ford took Eli Whitney's idea of interchangeable parts and adapted it to cars. All the Model Ts were exactly alike. The parts of one Model T could be used on any other Model T. Then Ford took the factory system and made it work better than it had ever worked before. An architect named Albert Kahn supplied many of the ideas for Ford's factory.

In the old days, before modern factories, skilled workers, called artisans, built products by hand from beginning to end. In the new factories, workers made only one part of a product—the same part every day.

"The man who puts in a bolt does not put on the nut; the man who puts on the nut does not tighten it," was the way Ford described his factory system. Workers hated it. It made work boring, but it made car building very efficient. In Henry Ford's factory a wide, moving belt, called a "conveyor belt," brought the car parts to the worker. He didn't even have to move. With this system—called the "mass-production assembly line"—cars could be built quickly by relatively unskilled workers.

The first Model T, which came out in 1908, cost $850. Many Americans could afford that. In 1915, Henry Ford drove his millionth car off the assembly line.

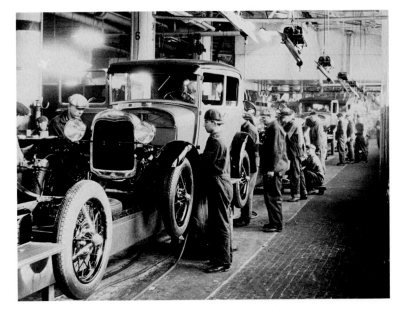

Workers on a Ford factory assembly line—one of Ford's colleagues said, "Mass production and its intensification into automation stems directly from what we worked out at Ford... between 1908 and 1913." ▼

Americans packed their picnic baskets, donned their traveling clothes, and set off in their new automobiles. ▶

People bought gasoline for their cars in a store, usually where they bought kerosene for their lamps. Then, in 1913, a drive-in gas station opened in Pittsburgh. The owner thought the first day's business was terrific: he sold 30 gallons of gas!

Factories were soon mass-producing not only cars but also appliances like this electrically driven washing machine. ▼

By 1916, the price of the Model T had dropped to $360. Now there was no question about it: Henry Ford had made a democratic car! You didn't have to be rich to own one. People who had never been farther than they could walk now got in their cars and went traveling.

Henry Ford showed that making products for average people was much more profitable than making products for rich people. There are only a few rich people, but there are many, many average folks. Ford's idea led to the building of American factories that were soon turning out washing machines, refrigerators, and other appliances, at prices ordinary people could afford. Those ordinary people driving around in their cars would eventually need motels and want supermarkets. Automobiles created industries that no one had foreseen.

Henry Ford understood that if ordinary people were going to buy the new products they needed to earn reasonable wages. So, in 1914, when the average American worker earned $2.40 a day for a nine-hour day, Henry Ford announced that he would pay his workers $5 for an eight-hour day. That was an astonishing decision. It was also smart. That $5 a day meant that workers at the Ford Motor Company could afford to buy Ford cars. Henry Ford was creating his own customers. Soon other manufacturers and businessmen followed his thinking. America became a nation of consumers. Ford, who always enjoyed simple living, helped bring about our complex modern way of life.

Henry Ford created a revolution. He wanted to build a car "for the multitude." He did that—and more, too. He helped bring democracy into the marketplace.

The Birdmen

Suppose, tomorrow, you open your front door and there before you is a flying saucer. A spaceman steps out and smiles. The next day you tell your friends what you saw. Do you think they will believe you?

Today, it is hard for us to understand what people thought when they first heard that men had flown. Mostly, if they hadn't seen it themselves, they didn't believe it. Why, if people were foolish enough to say men could fly, the next thing they might say was that someday men would walk on the moon!

But on December 17, 1903, two men flew. They were brothers from Dayton, Ohio, and they owned a bicycle shop. Neither had graduated from high school. Their names were Wilbur and Orville Wright. It was not luck that made them the first persons in all of history to build and fly an airplane that lifted off the ground with its own power. It was hard work and determination. Before they built that plane they studied all that was known about flying. They thought, argued, and experimented. They built a wind tunnel and tested 200 differently shaped wings. Then they drew plans and built carefully.

The first machines the Wright brothers tested at Kitty Hawk were gliders. They experimented on these before trying a powered plane. ▶

When they flew, it was from Kill Devil Hill at Kitty Hawk, on North Carolina's Outer Banks, islands that run like a row of beads along the Carolina coast.

Today the islands are filled with tourists and hotels and cottages, but in 1903 Kitty Hawk was empty beach, and Kill Devil Hill a big sand dune—and a good place to test an airplane.

On that windy December day, Orville won the toss of a coin. He got to fly first, lying flat on his stomach on the wing of the kite-like biplane. Wilbur ran beside him; the plane lifted a few feet above the sand and stayed in the air for 17 seconds. The brothers took turns and flew four flights that day. The longest lasted 59 seconds. It was enough. They had flown.

Orville and Wilbur went home to Dayton and set to work. They knew they could fly, but they also knew their plane needed improving. Besides, they needed to learn to be pilots; they needed time in the air.

So they flew around a big pasture in Ohio. Neighbors saw them and talked about the flights. But only a few other people believed that men were actually flying. In 1904 a group of newspaper reporters came to see for themselves.

Now, the Wright brothers were not daredevils. They were very methodical and precise. They did everything as well as they could. They checked and tested and checked and tested again, each time they flew. That made sense. They didn't want to get killed.

When the reporters arrived, the brothers were having mechanical problems with the plane. The reporters stayed two days. The Wright brothers wouldn't fly on those days; the plane wasn't ready. The reporters left. Some wrote that the Wright brothers were fakes.

One writer did stay and see them fly. He was the editor of an apiary journal. An *apiary* (AY-pee-ary) is a place where bees are raised for their honey. Yes, you read that right: the first long article about the Wright brothers' flight was in a beekeepers' magazine!

> A *biplane* has two wings, one above the other, a bit like a box kite.

Wilbur and Orville Wright on Flyer I, 1910 ▼

Finally, in August 1908, Wilbur went off to Europe and flew his plane at a racetrack in France. This time he sat on the wing (instead of lying on his stomach). There were 24 witnesses. They went wild—hugging and kissing him and throwing their hats in the air. They begged Wilbur to fly again the next day. But it was Sunday, his sabbath, and he wouldn't do it. On Monday, 4,000 people were at the racetrack to watch him fly. *"Il vole, il vole"* ("He flies, he flies"), they cried—and that soon became the title of a popular French song.

A month later, in Virginia, Orville showed Americans that people could fly. He lifted his plane into the air and swung around an army field one and a half times before he landed. The crowd of watchers rushed forward "screaming as loudly as they could, overwhelmed by the miracle that had taken place before their eyes."

Try to imagine that scene in 1908. For thousands and thousands of years, men and women looked at birds and dreamed that they, too, could lift themselves into the air. Some tried. They had built gliders, or hot-air balloons that floated on the wind. What the Wrights did was different. They didn't depend on the wind. They used their intelligence to build a machine that conquered the skies. They solved the problem of flight.

Suddenly the two shy brothers were celebrities. They were carried in parades and toasted at banquets. Kings and presidents invited them for visits. Stores sold Orville and Wilbur caps. Now everyone believed it— people could fly!

Who were these brothers who had made it happen?

In Dayton they were known as the minister's sons. Wilbur had planned to be a minister himself, but in his senior year in high school he was hit in the mouth by a fast-moving hockey puck. Besides knocking out teeth, it hurt him seriously.

Three problems needed solving in order for people to fly. Scientists call them *lift*, *propulsion*, and *control*. The Wright brothers needed to find a way to *lift* a plane into the air and keep it there; they needed to *propel* the plane forward; and they needed to *control* the flight—to turn, to climb, to land. Those problems had baffled some of the greatest scientific minds of all time. The Wright brothers solved them.

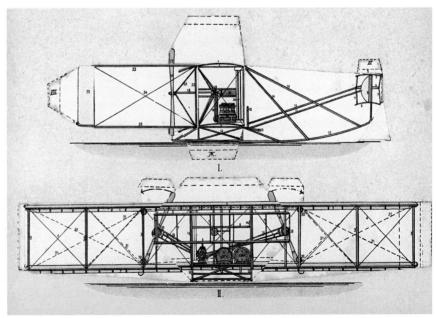

A diagram of Flyer I, in which the Wright brothers made their historic first flights in December, 1903 ▼

It seemed a terrible tragedy—he gave up his hope of being a minister—but it turned out to be a lucky break for the rest of the world.

Wilbur was the older and more serious of the boys. Orville had a mischievous side. Their father had given them hardworking habits. Their mother taught them mathematics and how to make things. When the boys wanted a sled—one that would win races—she taught them about wind resistance and streamlined design. Then she helped them make a plan—on paper first—and taught them to build a model.

They loved to argue back and forth, and out of those arguments came good ideas. They enjoyed making and fixing things. They went into the bicycle business. Bikes, back at the end of the 19th century, were high-tech items. The brothers built their own bikes and made them faster and better than their competitors'. Still, they wanted to do something special.

On September 3, 1900, Wilbur Wright wrote this to his father:

It is my belief that flight is possible and while I am taking up the investigation for pleasure rather than profit, I think there is a slight chance of achieving fame and fortune from it. It is almost the only great problem which has not been pursued by a multitude of investigators, and therefore carried to a point where further progress is very difficult. I am certain I can reach a point much in advance of any previous workers in this field.

It was just three years after Wilbur wrote that letter to his father that he and Orville flew. Five years after that (in 1908), people believed it had happened.

If men and women could fly, anything might be possible.

◀ A crowd watches as Orville Wright flies over Templehof Field in Berlin, Germany, in 1909.

William Howard Taft

William Howard Taft didn't want to be president. Theodore Roosevelt picked him for the job. And Taft's wife was determined that he have it. When she was 17 she said that the man she married would be president.

Campaigning for the presidency in 1908, Taft joked about his size. When Yale University offered him a professorship of law, which is called a "chair," he said a chair wouldn't do but a "sofa of law" might be all right.

Taft was a huge man: he weighed more than 300 pounds. He was also sweet-natured and capable. After college he became a lawyer, and then the first American governor of the Philippine Islands.

He was a good governor, who gave the Filipinos much control of their own affairs. Theodore Roosevelt named him secretary of war. What he really wanted was to be chief justice of the Supreme Court, and one day he would have that job and handle it well. But his wife wanted to be First Lady, so he ran for president.

President William Howard Taft was a man of great talent, experience, and girth. ▼

▲ Helen Taft wanted to be First Lady, and got her wish.

As president, Taft did more trustbusting than TR, and he helped get some good laws passed. But after Teddy Roosevelt, people found him dull. His presidency seemed boring. Besides, as time went on, Taft turned control of the Republican Party over to the conservative party leaders. They were called the "Old Guard." They didn't want change or reform, although most Americans did. Many people wanted progressive leadership.

Some of Roosevelt's friends were alarmed. They wrote the ex-president and told him he was needed at home. They wanted to see him become president again. Teddy didn't need much urging.

Now the politicians and financial leaders who headed the Republican Party were alarmed. They didn't want TR as president again. No one could control that man! They'd been happy when he went off to Africa. J. P. Morgan had said he hoped that "the first lion he meets does his duty."

In 1912, the Republicans nominated William Howard Taft for a second term and turned their backs on TR.

Theodore Roosevelt started his own party—the Progressive Party—and ran for president anyway. (Sometimes it was called the Bull Moose Party because Roosevelt once said he felt "like a bull moose.")

People who usually voted Republican were confused. Some voted for Taft; more voted for Roosevelt. But the Republican vote was divided. For the first time since Grover Cleveland—and for only the second time since before the Civil War—a Democrat was elected.

He was Woodrow Wilson, and he wasn't at all like TR or Taft. Wilson was a scholarly, serious man. He had been president of Princeton University. People didn't love him as they had Theodore Roosevelt, but they did respect and admire him. They believed in him, and were right to do so. He became one of the nation's great presidents.

◄ Democratic candidate Woodrow Wilson won the election of 1912 against a divided Republican Party.

Some Political Theory: A Discussion

This is not a free country. Hold on—what am I saying? Of course this is a free country.

No, it isn't. No country is completely free.
Are you free to kill your neighbor?
Are you free to steal?
Are you free to destroy property?

When people get together and form a government, they make rules—laws—that limit freedom. Usually those limits help protect other people's freedom. In this country we try to have as few limits as possible. It is a trick finding a comfortable balance between freedom and restraint.

It isn't as easy as you might think even to agree on what freedom means. "The world has never had a good definition of the word liberty," said Abraham Lincoln.

We all declare for liberty, but using the same word we do not mean the same thing. With some, the word liberty may mean for each man to do as he pleases with himself and the product of his labor; while with others the same word may mean for some men to do as they please with other men and the product of other men's labor.... The shepherd drives the wolf from the sheep's throat, for which the sheep thanks the shepherd as his liberator, while the wolf denounces him for the same act.... Plainly the sheep and the wolf are not agreed upon a definition of liberty.

The problem of defining freedom is one that concerns every generation. People in the Gilded Age were suddenly confronted with a need for new laws and regulations to control new industries and handle the great numbers of people living in cities. They worried about losing their freedom.

What is the proper balance between laws and freedom? ▶

We have many more laws today than Americans had in 1900. Does that mean we have less freedom? Possibly. But that is not necessarily a bad thing. Conditions are different today from what they were 100 years ago.

Besides, we have found that some people abuse freedom. They harm other people. In the past, some enslaved others. We need laws to protect some citizens from others.

We have found that without laws, some businesspeople act dishonestly or unfairly. We need to protect the consumer. We need laws to ensure fair business practices.

Should people be free to cut down forest trees or pollute the atmosphere? Are we taking away a person's freedom if we don't allow him to litter?

Today some people say that American citizens should not be allowed to have handguns. Others say that would be a terrible loss of individual freedom. What do you think? Can you think of ways laws protect you from yourself? (How about speeding laws, drug laws, antismoking laws?)

James Madison said, "If men were angels, no government would be necessary." But people aren't angels and government is necessary. The idea is to make laws as fair as possible.

Madison said that the great difficulty was this: "You must first enable the government to control the governed; and in the next place oblige it to control itself." Most Americans worry about government that is too big and too active. It is something to worry about.

During the Gilded Age, the government began to do something besides protecting people and their rights. Government began actively to help people—children, army veterans, the poor, the working class, consumers, farmers, small businessmen. That was a new role for government. How active should the government be in helping citizens? That became an important question for citizens.

The government had often helped businesses and farmers with tariffs and money policies. Now the government was *regulating* business. It broke up trusts that were unfair to their competitors. Do you think the government should do that?

Today we have laws that make child labor illegal. Other laws say that an employer must pay at least a certain minimum for an hour's work. Another law says that employers may not make most people work more than eight hours without extra pay. With those laws the government has changed the way we live. Do you think that is the proper role of government?

Questions about the role of the government caused much discussion and disagreement during the Gilded Age. They still do.

At the U.S. Capitol in Washington, D.C., lawmakers meet in Congress. The actions of these lawmakers, and the proper role of government, continue to be topics of heated debate. ▼

A Schoolteacher President

When Thomas Woodrow Wilson was nine he was still having trouble learning his ABCs. When he was 10 he could read—but not well. Some of the people who knew him thought he was not very smart. Did they turn out to be wrong!

Woodrow Wilson's parents had faith in their son, but what was even more important, he seems to have had faith in himself. Today we believe he had a learning disability—probably dyslexia—which made it difficult for him to learn to read. In those days no one understood about learning disabilities. Wilson had to solve his own problem. He did.

Sometimes problems can become strengths. If Theodore Roosevelt had not had severe asthma when he was a boy, perhaps he would not have turned into a powerful man who loved "the strenuous life." If Woodrow Wilson had been able to read easily, perhaps he would have been less determined to study and learn.

Wilson was never able to read quickly, but that didn't stop him from becoming a college professor, president of Princeton University, governor of New Jersey, and president of the United States.

"My best training came from my father," he said when he was grown up. His father was a Presbyterian minister who read aloud to his son and taught him to think clearly and write exactly. He assigned the boy subjects for speeches and essays and gave him suggestions to improve them. Woodrow Wilson became a brilliant speaker and a distinguished writer. But the most important thing the Reverend Wilson gave his son was a sure sense of what is right and what is wrong, which guided Woodrow Wilson all his life.

He was born in Virginia, four years before the Civil War began. The family soon moved to Georgia. His earliest memories were of war and grown-up discussions of politics, battles, and democracy. He was the son, grandson, and nephew of ministers. It was expected that Tommy (his childhood name) would become a minister, too. But from an early age it was politics that interested him.

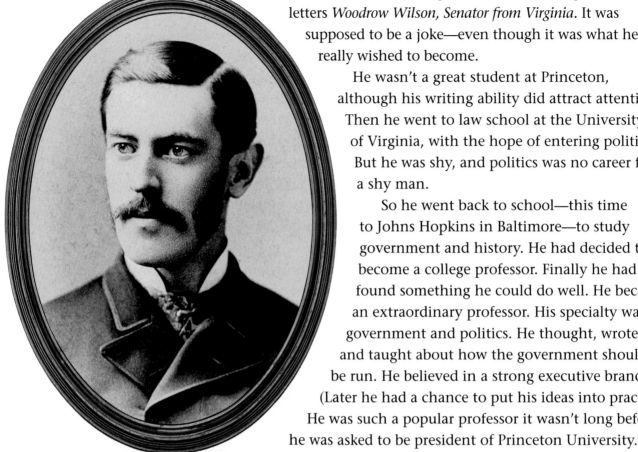

▲ Woodrow Wilson as a graduate student in 1883 at The Johns Hopkins University, where he studied history and political science

When he went to college at Princeton, he signed his letters *Woodrow Wilson, Senator from Virginia.* It was supposed to be a joke—even though it was what he really wished to become.

He wasn't a great student at Princeton, although his writing ability did attract attention. Then he went to law school at the University of Virginia, with the hope of entering politics. But he was shy, and politics was no career for a shy man.

So he went back to school—this time to Johns Hopkins in Baltimore—to study government and history. He had decided to become a college professor. Finally he had found something he could do well. He became an extraordinary professor. His specialty was government and politics. He thought, wrote, and taught about how the government should be run. He believed in a strong executive branch. (Later he had a chance to put his ideas into practice.) He was such a popular professor it wasn't long before he was asked to be president of Princeton University. Woodrow Wilson was determined to make Princeton one of the best universities in the world. He did just that. People began talking about Princeton's unusual president. And that got him into politics, where he had always wanted to be. He ran for governor of New Jersey.

The state's government was a mess. Its citizens were disgusted with the corruption. Naturally, the political bosses didn't want to change things. But they wanted people to think things were changing. The bosses wanted a governor who would look good but whom they could control. Woodrow Wilson seemed perfect. He was well-known, and his fine manners made him seem meek. The bosses were sure a college president wouldn't know much about the real world of politics. They thought he would be easy to push around. So they backed him for governor. Were they fooled! Woodrow Wilson had steel in his bones and brains in his head. When he believed he was right he wouldn't bend or budge.

Wilson promised to clean up politics in New Jersey. Then he proceeded to do it. He became a reforming governor. The bosses tried to stop some of his reforms; Wilson spoke out and explained the issues to New Jersey's citizens. Remember, he was a great speaker. He asked the people to back him. They did. It was democracy at work. The bosses couldn't believe what was happening. Most were forced to retire. New Jersey became a model state (for a while). People everywhere began paying attention to Wilson-the-politician.

President Woodrow Wilson ▼

In 1912 he was elected president of the United States. He knew just what he wanted to do as president—after all, he had been teaching about the presidency. He thought the president should be a strong leader. He believed in progressive goals. He wanted to improve working conditions, help the farmers with their problems, change the banking system, control monopolies, and lower tariffs.

Other leaders had wanted to do those things, too, but Congress and the special interests had stopped them. Wilson did exactly what he had done in New Jersey. He explained the issues to the American people. He told them to write their congressmen.

▲ Thousands gather to witness Woodrow Wilson's inauguration.

▲ The spark that ignited a world war—the Archduke Ferdinand of Austria-Hungary and his wife, Sophia, are assassinated in Sarajevo, Bosnia, in June 1914.

When the people speak out, Congress listens. When President Wilson explained the issues, America's citizens understood and responded. Soon there were new and lower tariffs, a new banking system, and controls on the giant trusts. Wilson did what he had promised. He began to deal with the problem of the differences between rich and poor. He made our democracy reflect the wishes of the people, which was what Thomas Jefferson and James Madison had intended.

But Wilson wasn't perfect. He did nothing about the racism that was a poison in American life. (He seemed to accept it.) He did not (until late in his life) believe in giving women the vote. Sometimes he was too sure of himself, and he wasn't good at understanding the other side's view of a problem.

Wilson's ideas on foreign affairs were different from those of the presidents who came just before him. He was not concerned with making America powerful. He was not interested in treaties that gave unfair advantages to American business. He was not an imperialist. He thought that nations, like people, should not be selfish. He believed the United States should help other nations become democratic. Mostly, he hoped to stay out of foreign affairs.

Woodrow Wilson wanted America to fulfill the vision of the Founders. He wanted the United States to be great because it stood for the right things. He was getting things done in the nation when something happened that he hadn't expected. An archduke was assassinated in Europe, which started a war. A war that changed the whole world.

War

It was called the Great War. (Later it became the First World War.) It began in Europe in 1914. At first, the Central Powers (Germany, Austria, and Turkey) fought the Allies (England, France, and Russia). Before it was finished, many other nations were involved. It was unnecessary—as most wars are—and came about because of national pride and the struggles of huge empires for power and territory and economic gain.

Like the Civil War in America, it became ugly and hateful. Nine million men died—more than the whole population of New York City today. It left scars and wounds that refused to heal. It changed the fate of the world. But no one knew that when it started.

In England, young men hurried to enlist—afraid the war would be over before they got a chance to fight. No one believed it would last long. Wilson called the war "a distant event." He, too, thought it would soon be over.

German soldiers flee French artillery fire during the Battle of Verdun, one of the longest and most devastating battles in the history of modern warfare. ▼

Armies on both sides dug themselves into trenches and fought on for four years. ▶

▲ In the Great War, airplanes battled in the skies—the first time planes were used in warfare.

That was a big miscalculation. World War I was worse than anyone could have dreamed. Many of those 19th-century inventions, which people thought would prevent war, were turned to killing. Airplanes shot at each other overhead, machine guns cracked their deadly staccato, submarines ejected killer torpedoes, and poison gas turned men blind or unable to breathe.

But the killing machines didn't seem to make much difference. It was men—huge armies of men—that determined the outcome. Armies of men who dug themselves into trenches and shot at enemies in other trenches. Both sides fought on, stuck in bloody mud, for four years. They wasted a generation of young men.

The United States had the vast Atlantic Ocean as a moat to keep it isolated from Europe's troubles. Washington and Jefferson had warned the nation to stay away from the Old World and its problems. Most Americans had no interest in Europe's fight. But America was now a world power. It became harder and harder not to be involved.

Woodrow Wilson wanted to be a peacemaker. He tried talking to leaders on both sides; he tried to end the war. But Germany insisted on being given French and Polish land before it would stop fighting. France and Russia (which ruled most of Poland) wouldn't agree to that.

Woodrow Wilson believed America should stay out of the battle. He wanted the nation not to take sides—to remain neutral. He remembered the Civil War from his southern childhood. He knew how awful the effects of war could be. But when German troops marched on peaceful Belgium, many Americans became angry.

Then, when German submarines, called U-boats, began sinking ships—even passenger ships—Americans were horrified. In past wars there had been rules of fair play: ships were given warning and passengers allowed time to get into lifeboats. The submarines gave no warnings.

Meanwhile, Mexico was having a revolution (some called it a civil war). When Mexican bands began raiding small towns and ranches in the United States, President Wilson sent General John Pershing south of the border. For a while it looked as if the United States might go to war with Mexico. And that was exactly what Germany hoped.

> The Germans called their submarines "U-boots" ("U-boats" in English) short for *Unterseeboot*, or "under-sea-boat."

The Sinking of the *Lusitania*

On May 1, 1915, the German Embassy in Washington placed an advertisement in the leading New York newspapers. The ad said, "Travelers intending to embark on the Atlantic voyage are reminded that a state of war exists between Germany and Great Britain…vessels flying the British flag…are liable to destruction." This warning was published next to an advertisement for a British passenger liner, the *Lusitania*, "Fastest and Largest Steamer now in Atlantic Service."

That same morning the luxurious *Lusitania* set sail for England, filled with tourists, business people, and others who wanted to get to England. (You couldn't go by plane then.) Many of the voyagers were nervous about the trip—but passenger ships had traditionally been safe from military attack. Six days later, within sight of the Irish coast, most were preparing for a festive last evening dinner. A German submarine, the U-20, was about to cancel the meal. A single torpedo was fired without warning. Eighteen minutes later the *Lusitania* was beneath the waves. Of 2,000 passengers, 1,198 drowned, innocent victims of war. Among the passengers killed were 198 Americans. The captain, who had ignored official warnings and instructions, was washed from the deck and saved.

In 1917, Germany declared war on all ships that went near England or France. Eight U.S. ships were sunk.

Nearly 1,200 people died when a German U-boat torpedoed the *Lusitania* in 1915. ▼

▲ A German submarine sinks a British fishing steamer.

After more than two years, the war in Europe was eating soldiers and national economies and getting nowhere. U-boat warfare was making many Americans very angry with Germany and its allies. More and more people in the United States began to side with the Allies. The United States was under increasing pressure to enter the fray on the side of Britain and France. Americans sold war supplies to the Allies. But President Wilson still seemed determined to stay neutral. In 1916 he campaigned for president on a platform of peace.

Then, on January 16, 1917, the German foreign minister, Arthur von Zimmermann, sent a telegram to Mexico City. Before it was read there, the telegram was intercepted by British intelligence and decoded by their astonishing cryptographers (code readers). The Zimmermann Telegram (as the message is known) suggested an alliance between Germany and Mexico. It was a German plot to make Mexico fight against the United States. When they won the war, as Germany was sure they would, Germany would give Texas and New Mexico to Mexico as a prize for entering the war.

On the night of March 31, 1917, Woodrow Wilson got out of bed and took his portable typewriter to the south veranda of the White House. Mrs. Wilson brought him a bowl of milk and crackers from the kitchen. Then, in the quiet of early morning, the president typed out a message that was to become famous.

It was a declaration of war. Wilson said our nation had no selfish aims, and it didn't. America wanted no territory—no gain for itself.

The present German submarine warfare against commerce is a warfare against mankind. It is a war against all nations.... We are accepting the challenge.... The world must be made safe for democracy.

On April 2, Wilson went before Congress and spoke his message. It was a fearful thing to lead this great, peaceful people into war, he said:

...into the most terrible and disastrous of all wars, civilization itself seeming to be in the balance. But the right is more precious than peace, and we shall fight for the things which we have always carried nearest our hearts—for democracy, for the right of those who submit to authority to have a voice in their own governments, for the rights and liberties of small nations, for a universal dominion of right by such a concert of free peoples as shall bring peace and safety to all nations, and make the world itself at last free.

The congressmen cheered and cheered.

But not all of them. For three days a few impassioned congressmen attacked the president's decision. It would turn out that Wilson, and the American people, had been misled by propaganda; they didn't really know what was going on in Europe and they didn't think American troops would be needed.

▲ On June 5, 1917, conscription began—every American male between 21 and 30 had to register to be drafted into the armed forces.

1917—cheering soldiers begin their journey to France, knowing little of the horrors that await them in the Great War. ▼

World War I, 1914–1918

Legend:
- Allies
- Central Powers
- Neutral nations
- Trench system
- Major battles

0   200   400 mi
0   200   400 km

ARCTIC OCEAN

Barents Sea

Norwegian Sea

SWEDEN

NORWAY
Oslo
Helsinki
Stockholm
Petrograd (St. Petersburg)

Jutland (1916)

DENMARK
Baltic Sea

GREAT BRITAIN

North Sea

Copenhagen

Moscow

RUSSIA

Lusitania (1915)

London

NETHERLANDS
Berlin
Minsk

BELGIUM
GERMANY
Warsaw

ATLANTIC OCEAN

Paris
LUXEMBOURG
Prague
Kiev

Western Front
E U R O P E

FRANCE
SWITZERLAND
Vienna

AUSTRIA-HUNGARY

ROMANIA
Black Sea

PORTUGAL

ANDORRA
Madrid
Sarajevo

Lisbon

SPAIN
Corsica (France)
ITALY
Rome

SERBIA
MONTENEGRO
ALBANIA
BULGARIA
Istanbul

ARMENIA

OTTOMAN EMPIRE

Sardinia (Italy)

Gallipoli (1915)

SPANISH MOROCCO (Spain)
Algiers

GREECE
Athens

A S I A

Sicily (Italy)
Tunis

Crete (Greece)
Cyprus (Great Britain)

MOROCCO (France)

TUNISIA (France)

M e d i t e r r a n e a n   S e a

ARABIA

ALGERIA (France)

Malta (Great Britain)
Tripoli

Cairo

A F R I C A

N

LIBYA (Italy)

EGYPT (Great Britain)

Red Sea

▲ The Central Powers faced a two-front war—major battle lines formed on both their eastern and western borders. More battles were fought in France than in any other nation.

"We're Coming Over..."

If you want to understand people, start with the music they make. And, in 1917, we were a singing nation. We sang in church, we sang in school, we sang at work, and we sang when we marched off to war. George M. Cohan (1878–1942) and Irving Berlin (1888–1989), two spectacularly successful songsmiths, provided patriotic tunes for a nation at war. Berlin was a soldier and, at the same time, he wrote and produced a musical, *Yip, Yip, Yahank*. You don't have to be in the army to relate to one of its songs, "Oh, How I Hate to Get Up in the Morning." (In 1942—during another war—the show was staged on Broadway as *This Is The Army*.) Berlin's "God, Bless America," may be the most popular song ever written in this country. "There's No Business Like Show Business" and "White Christmas" are two of his other hits.

George M. Cohan wrote about 500 songs, acted in more than 1,000 productions, and wrote or co-authored some 80 plays. Everyone sang his "Yankee Doodle Dandy," "Give My Regards to Broadway," and "You're a Grand Old Flag." But the most popular of all was "Over There." It's what the soldiers sang when they sailed across the ocean to fight in a war that President Wilson told them would make the world safe for democracy.

Over there, over there
Send the word, send the word over there
That the Yanks are coming, the Yanks
*   are coming*
The drums rum-tumming ev'rywhere.

So prepare, say a pray'r
Send the word, send the word to beware
We'll be over, we're coming over
And we won't come back till it's over
*   over there.*

More than 20 years after he wrote "Over There," George M. Cohan received the Medal of Honor. ▶

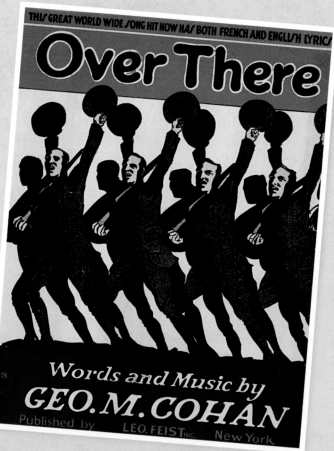

War's End

In Europe, in 1918, on the 11th hour of the 11th day of the 11th month, it suddenly became quiet. The cannons were still. For the first time since 1914, men could hear each other without shouting. The Great War—soon to be known as World War I—was over.

It had been a horrible war. Nine million men died. It was not fought soldier against soldier, like medieval battles of knights in armor. The new weapons of killing—machine guns, tanks, long-range artillery, grenades, and poison gas—led to mass slaughter. "War," wrote one soldier, "is nothing but murder."

But now the guns were silent; the dying was finished.

In Washington, D.C., even though it was six o'clock in the morning, America's 28th president, Woodrow Wilson, was up and at his desk. Because he was considerate, and feared his clackety typewriter would wake his wife and staff, he sat and wrote these words with a pen on White House stationery:

> *Everything for which America has fought has been accomplished. It will now be our fortunate duty to assist by example, by sober, friendly counsel, and by material aid, in the establishment of just democracy throughout the world.*

No one could buy his way out of service in World War I (unlike the Civil War). And for the first time women served officially in the armed forces.

Soldiers blinded by mustard gas move past the bodies of dead comrades in this painting by the American artist John Singer Sargent. ▼

They were the words of a high-minded leader. The slim, frail, bookish man had proved to be a great war president. In amazingly fast order he had turned a peaceful nation into a strong fighting force. The country's factories had gone from making corsets, bicycles, and brooms to production of guns, ships, and uniforms. In just over a year—beginning in April 1917—more than a million American men had been drafted into the army, trained, and sent overseas. And just in time. In Europe the fighting had been going on for three years; both sides were near collapse.

The Central Powers (Germany, Austria-Hungary, and the Turkish Ottoman Empire) were on one side, against the Allies (Britain, France, Russia, Japan, and Italy), with a few other nations involved, too. The war—awful, dreary, bloody—had begun in Europe for selfish reasons. It ended up making

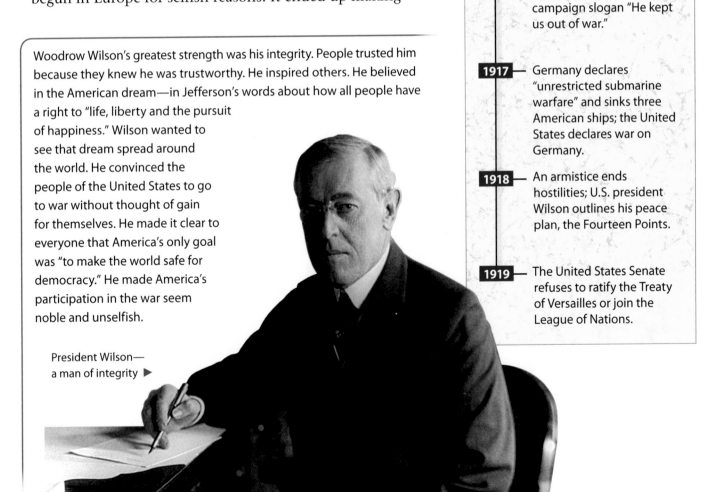

Woodrow Wilson's greatest strength was his integrity. People trusted him because they knew he was trustworthy. He inspired others. He believed in the American dream—in Jefferson's words about how all people have a right to "life, liberty and the pursuit of happiness." Wilson wanted to see that dream spread around the world. He convinced the people of the United States to go to war without thought of gain for themselves. He made it clear to everyone that America's only goal was "to make the world safe for democracy." He made America's participation in the war seem noble and unselfish.

President Wilson—
a man of integrity ▶

The Great War

1914 — The assassination of Austria-Hungary's Archduke Ferdinand sparks war between the Allies and the Central Powers; the United States proclaims neutrality; the war quickly becomes a stalemate.

1915 — A German U-boat sinks the British passenger ship *Lusitania*, killing almost 1,200 people, including 128 Americans.

1916 — American president Woodrow Wilson wins reelection with the campaign slogan "He kept us out of war."

1917 — Germany declares "unrestricted submarine warfare" and sinks three American ships; the United States declares war on Germany.

1918 — An armistice ends hostilities; U.S. president Wilson outlines his peace plan, the Fourteen Points.

1919 — The United States Senate refuses to ratify the Treaty of Versailles or join the League of Nations.

An *armistice* is a truce that brings an end to fighting, before the official signing of a peace treaty.

nations and people cruel, and bitter, and angry, and it led to another terrible war.

On November 11, 1918, it was still dark, but the news of war's end was too good to wait for daybreak. Whistles tooted, church bells rang, and sirens blared. Before long the streets across the nation were filled with people cheering, shouting, hugging, and kissing. America had gone to war and the world was going to be a better place because of it, or so it seemed on that Armistice Day.

In November 1918, people celebrated the end of the Great War. ▼

Fourteen Points

The innocent, optimistic, sure-of-itself 19th century didn't actually end in America until the First World War began. The real start of the 20th century came in 1917. No question about it, the war changed things. It changed people. They began to question old ideas that had never been questioned before. Hardly anyone seemed sure of anything.

Except Woodrow Wilson. He was like an old-time Puritan, convinced of God's grace and very sure of himself. Wilson would do everything possible to lead his nation and the world on a path of righteousness. His father had been a minister; he had the preacher's genes. He spoke eloquently and told the world how to behave. Unfortunately, some people don't like being told what to do—even if the teller is right.

Before the war ended Woodrow Wilson came up with "Fourteen Points" on which the peace was to be based. Wilson didn't believe in revenge; he believed in the power of kindness. He said he wanted "peace without victory," with no punishment for the losers. Now that was a startling statement in a nation that had cheered Ulysses Grant when he called for "unconditional surrender." But Woodrow Wilson had grown up in the defeated South. He knew about the hatreds that can come after a war. He didn't think an enemy needed to be shamed, or made poor. He intended to lead the world toward a generous and lasting peace.

Wilson's Fourteen Points may have been the most forgiving peace plan ever. Under the Fourteen Points, people all over the world were to determine their own fate—by vote. It was called "self-determination." Self-determination was to end the old imperialist system that let winning nations grasp foreign colonies. The Fourteen Points also called for

- free trade (that means no tariffs)
- an end to secret pacts between nations
- freedom of the seas
- arms reduction
- the forming of a world organization—a League of Nations

▲ Enormous crowds gathered to greet Woodrow Wilson when he arrived in Europe for the Versailles Peace Conference.

Wilson expected this league to guarantee freedom to all the world's peoples and keep the peace between nations.

Leaflets describing the Fourteen Points were dropped over Germany from those new vehicles that had been used, for the first time, as instruments of war: wood-framed airplanes. The German people—who were tired of the war and close to rebellion—read the leaflets, hoped for peace, and soon forced their ruler, the kaiser (KY-zer), to flee the country.

With the war over, Wilson set off for Europe, the first American president ever to do so while in office. He wanted America to lead the world to a just peace, and he wanted to be the peacemaker. The European people were wild with admiration for Woodrow Wilson. They greeted him with flowers and cheers. They called him the savior of the world.

Too bad he went, say some historians. Others say it would have been worse if he'd stayed at home. Everyone agrees: Wilson didn't get what he wanted. Perhaps because of that, the Great War, which was called the "war to end wars," didn't end anything. It turned out to be World War I. Another world war—which was much worse—followed 21 years later.

What went wrong? Why didn't Wilson get his just peace?

Was it because he was too sure of himself? Or because he didn't worry enough about jealous politicians, at home and in Europe? Was it the tragedy of his health? (Before he left the presidency, he exhausted himself, lost contact with reality, and became unable to fight for his beliefs.) Maybe it was all of those things—and more, too. After four years of war, many Americans seemed to have stopped caring. Most just wanted to get on with their lives; some didn't want to be bothered by ideals; others were disappointed that we hadn't smashed the enemy. Besides, President Wilson's sermons were getting tiresome.

France's crafty old premier (prime minister), Georges Clemenceau (cleh-mon-SO)—who was called "the Tiger"—said, "God gave us his Ten Commandments and we broke them. Wilson gave us his Fourteen Points—we shall see."

What Clemenceau saw was that France did, indeed, want revenge. Germany had invaded France twice within his memory (in 1870 and 1914). Two generations of young Frenchmen were dead. The French countryside was devastated. The French wanted protection and repayment for what they had suffered. They, and England and Italy, wanted—and got—a hard peace. They were angry with Germany.

The peace treaty was signed at a gorgeous French royal palace called Versailles (vair-SY). Some of Wilson's most important points got thrown out of the window at Versailles. Germany was

▲ British Prime Minister Lloyd George, French Premier Georges Clemenceau, and U.S. President Woodrow Wilson walk together in Paris during negotiations for the Treaty of Versailles.

blamed for the whole war and given a huge bill for war costs. The Germans (who had surrendered, in part, because of their faith in the Fourteen Points) felt betrayed. But the 14th point, which meant most to Wilson—the League of Nations—was saved. He believed that the League would right the wrongs of the Old World order.

And it might have done so, if the nation that was now the most important power in the world had joined the League. (What nation could that be?)

American treaties with foreign powers must be agreed to by two-thirds of the members of the Senate—a simple majority won't do. At first, most Americans believed in the League of Nations. But there were strong senators who hated Wilson. Some were Republicans who were anxious to win the next election; they thought that a triumph for Wilson would hurt their party's chances.

When Wilson went to Europe he brought many advisers with him; they were either professors or Democrats. None were prominent Republicans. That wasn't wise or generous on Wilson's part. Some Republican senators began to fight the idea of the League. Many Americans, Democrats as well as Republicans, worried about America getting involved in Europe's problems.

No Clear and Present Danger

Americans had roots in many different countries. Because of hereditary ties to other nations, the issue of possible disloyalty began to concern the U.S. government. As a result, in 1917 Congress passed an Espionage Act. In 1918 it passed a Sedition Act. (*Espionage* is spying; *sedition* means "inciting others to rebel.") Those acts were meant to ban speech that might harm the war effort.

The First Amendment guarantees free speech. Were these acts unconstitutional? Or do things change in wartime? Clearly, war demands national unity.

When anarchists threw 5,000 antiwar leaflets from a New York hat factory, and were arrested and convicted, the case was appealed all the way to the Supreme Court.

The court upheld the convictions, but two justices—Louis D. Brandeis and Oliver Wendell Holmes, Jr.—disagreed. Holmes said that speech may be punished only if it presents "a clear and present danger" of producing evils that the Constitution tries to prevent. "Now nobody can suppose," Holmes wrote, "that the surreptitious publishing of a silly leaflet...would present any immediate danger." His opinion was that "the defendants were deprived of their rights under the Constitution of the United States." Today, the concept of *clear and present danger* is used as a test of whether speech should be censored. Holmes became known as the "Great Dissenter."

▲ Oliver Wendell Holmes, Jr.

Woodrow Wilson knew that the problems of any one part of the globe were now the problems of all peoples. America could not hide from world responsibility. So the president decided to do what he did best: explain things to the American people. That had worked for him before. But, in those days before radio and TV, it meant getting on a train and giving speeches. Wilson crossed the country; he gave three or four speeches a day talking about the importance of the League of Nations.

It was too much for his health. Wilson had been working hard. In Paris he had been ill and had acted strangely. In Pueblo, Colorado, he was so sick he could not finish his speech. Then he had a stroke. He was never the same again.

Those who opposed the League in the Senate were now able to defeat it. The United States did not join the League of Nations. You can imagine how Woodrow Wilson felt. He believed that without a strong league to enforce peace, there might be another war—and that it would be much worse than the Great War. "What the Germans used were toys compared to what would be used in the next war," he said.

But we didn't listen. The United States embarked on a period of "isolation." We tried to stay away from the rest of the world and its concerns. We would learn that could no longer be done. Like it or not, the United States was now a world leader.

I can predict with absolute certainty that within another generation there will be another world war if the nations of the world do not concert the method by which to prevent it.
—Woodrow Wilson, on a 1919 speaking tour

◀ As he crossed the country to urge support for the League of Nations, President Wilson drove himself to exhaustion and ill health.

The Influenza Pandemic

In 1918, a deadly strain of influenza began to spread rapidly. It was an epidemic; no, it was worse than that. It was a *pandemic*, which means a disease that spreads across many nations. This one went around the globe.

It lasted about nine months, and, worldwide, killed more than 20 million people. That was more than the total of deaths during the four years of the Great War. Mysteriously, it struck at about the same time in India, and Russia, and China—no major nation escaped. In the United States there were more than half a million victims. In the last week of October in 1918, 2,700 American soldiers died fighting in Europe; that same week, 21,000 Americans died at home of the flu.

On one terrible day in Philadelphia, almost 1,000 people died. Neither doctors, nor hospitals, nor cemeteries could handle the awful burdens put upon them. In those days before the discovery of modern medicines, there was little doctors could do.

The disease soon departed as mysteriously as it had arrived. It left the country exhausted. Wasn't a war trouble enough? Everyone had worked hard supporting the war effort. Americans had done astonishing things in factories and on the farms. They'd fed Europe with an amazing harvest of grain; they'd armed the Allies. Citizens had given up luxuries and even some necessities to help others. That flu epidemic was the final straw.

Soon a new word was being used. It was *normalcy*. That's what people wanted. They wanted to go back to the good old days before the war. But time won't march backward.

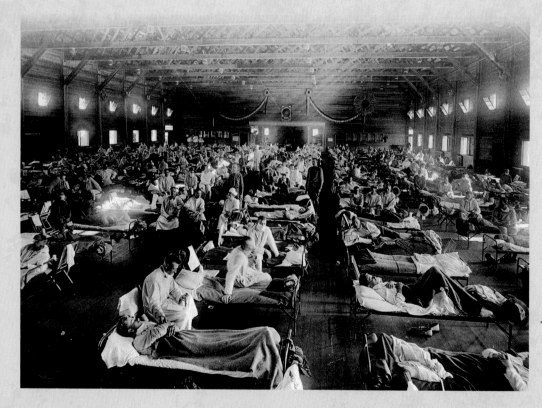

◀ The influenza pandemic of 1918 killed more than 20 million people worldwide.

The Prohibition Amendment

The soldiers who came home from Europe in 1919 had exciting things to tell. They'd been to Paris and had seen fancy nightclubs, stunning buildings, and splendid boulevards. Some bragged about their heroism in battle, which was understandable; you had to be tough—or lucky—to be a survivor. A few came home without arms or legs. Some didn't want to talk about the war at all.

The returning soldiers were surprised to find that America had changed in the year they'd been gone. They noticed one thing right away. It had to do with beer and liquor. During the war it was considered unpatriotic to drink alcohol. Beer is made from grain, and grain was needed to feed soldiers. Now that the war was over, many people wanted to put an end to all liquor drinking. It would make the world a much better place, they said.

The Constitution does not give Congress the right to tell people what they may eat or drink. If someone wants to drink poison, only a state can make laws to try to keep him from doing so.

Many people say that alcohol can be a kind of poison. No one disagrees that drinking too much is harmful.

Drunkenness was a special problem in early America. Most drinking was done in saloons, where women were not admitted. Some men took their paychecks, went to a saloon, drank up, and then went home drunk, with no money left for their families. Reformers decided to attack the problem. Some of them believed in *temperance*, which means "moderation." Others believed in *prohibition*, which means "outlawing all drinking."

Some women's groups fought for prohibition. Several religious groups—especially Methodists and Baptists—joined the battle. Many states became *dry*. In a dry state it was against state law to buy or sell liquor. Some people wanted to go further. They wanted the whole nation to be dry. A constitutional amendment was needed.

A federal agent destroys a barrel of whiskey during Prohibition. ▶

253

After the Prohibition amendment was passed, Congress needed to provide for its enforcement. That was done with a law called the Volstead Act. Prohibition didn't make it illegal to drink, or even to buy liquor; it just made it illegal to sell it.

The 18th Amendment made it illegal to sell liquor, but people still found ways to buy it in places like this illegal bar, called a speakeasy. ▼

It was the Progressive Era: people thought that laws could help make people perfect—or close to it. It took about 20 years to get the 18th Amendment passed, but finally it was done. The Prohibition amendment became law in 1920. The amendment made it illegal to sell liquor anywhere in the United States. Most people thought it a very good idea. All but two states passed the Prohibition amendment.

It didn't work. Many people who wanted to drink kept drinking—although per capita alcohol consumption did fall during Prohibition years. Per capita (pur CAP-i-tuh) is Latin, and means "by heads" or per person. In other words, the total amount of liquor consumed in the U.S., divided by the number of people in the U.S., showed there was less alcohol drunk during Prohibition than before. But there was a problem—many new kinds of people began drinking.

Some people, especially some women and young people, who had not drunk before, decided to try it. Prohibition wasn't supposed to do this, but in some crowds it made drinking fashionable. (Maybe it had to do with disillusionment after the war. Writers were calling this a "lost generation." People weren't really lost, but they were confused about right and wrong.)

Since selling liquor was now a crime, gangsters took over that activity. People who sold liquor were called "bootleggers." (Some of them stuck flasks inside high boots.) Ships running whiskey from foreign suppliers to coastal ports were called "rumrunners." Illegal bars, where drinks were sold, were called "speakeasies." (If people spoke loudly, and the police heard them, the bar would be raided. So they spoke "easy.")

No one expected it, but Prohibition made crime a big business in the United States. Americans learned that some kinds of prohibition must be done by persuasion and education. Laws and force don't always work.

Another amendment was needed to get rid of the Prohibition amendment. The 21st Amendment was passed in December 1933. It ended what was a well-meaning experiment. The experiment had failed.

But how do you get people to stop doing something that isn't good for them? Do the lessons of Prohibition apply to drugs? Some people say we should make it legal to buy drugs; then criminals could not earn big money selling drugs. Others say that would encourage people to use drugs. What do you think?

◀ Patrons of a New York City bar raise their glasses to celebrate the repeal of Prohibition in December 1933.

The Constitution of the United States, Article V

The Congress, whenever two thirds of both Houses shall deem it necessary, shall propose Amendments to this Constitution, or, on the Application of the Legislatures of two thirds of the several States, shall call a Convention for proposing Amendments, which, in either Case, shall be valid to all Intents and Purposes, as Part of this Constitution, when ratified by the Legislatures of three fourths of the several States, or by Conventions in three fourths thereof.

What does all that mean? Read it slowly and it isn't as difficult as it may seem. What it means is that the men who wrote the Constitution—James Madison, Gouverneur Morris, Ben Franklin, John Adams, and the others—understood that a constitution needs to be adaptable. The Founding Fathers wanted people in the future—you and me—to be able to change the Constitution. But they didn't want to make it too easy to change. If they did that the Constitution wouldn't have much lasting value: it would get changed all the time.

So they came up with the idea of amendments as a way to change the Constitution. It has been more than 200 years since the Constitution was written; hundreds of amendments have been proposed, but only 27 have been passed.

For an amendment to succeed, two-thirds of the Congress must pass it—that means two-thirds of both the Senate and the House of Representatives. Then three-fourths of the states must also approve the amendment. (The Constitution may also be amended if a constitutional convention is called by three-fourths of the states—that has never been done.)

Remember, we have a federal form of government. Power is shared among the national government in Washington, D.C., and the state governments. The Constitution lists all the things the president, Congress, and the courts can control. Any powers not listed in the Constitution belong to the states.

Mom, Did You Vote?

We're heading back in time—just a bit. It is 1917, and some women are marching in front of the White House. They carry a big banner that says 20 MILLION AMERICAN WOMEN ARE NOT SELF-GOVERNED. In Europe, American soldiers are fighting for democracy; these women feel they should fight for it at home.

Day after day, for months, the women march in front of the president's house. They are peaceful and respectful, but persistent. Some people don't like it; they say the suffragists shouldn't annoy the president during wartime. The police tell the women to leave. "Has the law been changed?" asks Alice Paul, leader of the group. "No," says the police officer, "but you must stop."

"We have consulted our lawyers," says Alice Paul. "We have a legal right to picket."

The next day two women, Lucy Burns and Katherine Morey, are arrested. Other arrests soon follow.

In 1917, in front of the White House, women marched for the right to vote. Many were arrested and put in jail. ▼

On the Fourth of July a congressman speaks to a large crowd gathered behind the White House. "Governments derive their just powers from the consent of the governed," he says. Police keep the crowd orderly and protect the congressman's right to free speech.

In front of the White House a group of 13 women silently holds a banner with those very same words from the Declaration of Independence. Some are young women, some white-haired grandmothers; all are arrested. The women are taken to court and fined. They refuse to pay their fines—to do so would mean to admit they are guilty. They do not believe themselves guilty of any crime. The police take them to jail. More women are arrested. Anne Martin speaks out in court:

> *As long as the government and the representatives of the government prefer to send women to jail on petty and technical charges we will go to jail. Persecution has always advanced the cause of justice. The right of American women to work for democracy must be maintained.*

More women go to jail. They are separated from each other. Prison conditions are awful. For 17 days Ada Davenport Kendall is given nothing to eat but bread and water. Some women are held in solitary confinement. Some who go on hunger strikes are held down and fed against their will. Anne Martin, Lucy Burns, and Elizabeth McShane are force fed. Burns is bruised on her lips and face; McShane throws up. Now the women have become interested in prison reform, as well as in women's suffrage. One woman writes that it is "necessary to make a stand for the ordinary rights of human beings for all the inmates."

In the White House, Woodrow Wilson has other concerns. He is fighting a war—that war for democracy. Wilson says he isn't against women's suffrage—in fact he is for it—but, like many men, he thinks that most other issues are more important.

The women keep marching. All kinds of women. Rich and poor. Could it be that they understand democracy in a way the president doesn't?

Many Americans—men and women—don't bother to be active citizens. Many don't vote. The whole point of a democracy is that it gives everyone power. Those who don't vote give up their power.

Lucy Burns served more time in jail than any other American suffragist for her protests for women's rights. ▼

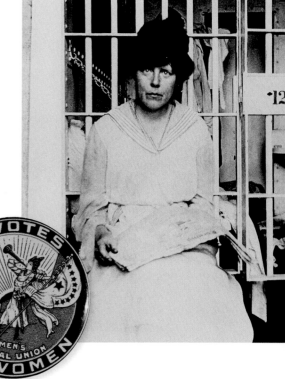

A pin shows the wearer's support for women's suffrage. ▶

Mrs. John Rogers, Jr., is arrested. She is a descendant of Roger Sherman (a signer of the Declaration of Independence). Like her plain-speaking ancestor, Mrs. Rogers says what she thinks. She tells the judge:

> *We are not guilty of any offense…. We know full well that we stand here because the president of the United States refuses to give liberty to American women. We believe, your honor, that the wrong persons are before the bar in this court…. We believe the president is the guilty one and that we are innocent.*

Now, isn't that what America is all about? The right of every citizen to speak out—even against the president.

Mrs. Rogers's cause is just, but her comments aren't quite fair. It is Congress that is holding things up, not Woodrow Wilson. But the president hasn't helped. Finally, he does. He urges Congress to pass the 19th Amendment. The proposed amendment says, "The right of citizens of the United States to vote shall not be denied or abridged by the United States or by any state on account of sex." It is known as

Young and old, rich and poor—women of all kinds came together to support the cause of women's suffrage. ▼

In 1920, the 19th Amendment guaranteed all American women the right to vote.

the Susan B. Anthony amendment. This battle for women's suffrage is not something new. Susan Anthony and her friend Elizabeth Cady Stanton began the fight in the mid-19th century. They spent their lives fighting for women's rights. So did Carrie Chapman Catt, the head of the National American Woman Suffrage Association.

Many men and women have worked hard for this cause. Most are people you have never even heard about. In Tennessee, Harry Burn was 24 and the youngest representative in the legislature when he got a letter from his mother. "Don't forget to be a good boy," wrote his mother, "and help Mrs. Catt put the 'Rat' in ratification."

The Tennessee legislators were trying to decide whether to approve the 19th Amendment or not. Half were for women's suffrage, half were not. Burn held the deciding vote. He followed his mother's advice. It was 1919, and Tennessee was the last state needed to ratify. The following year, 1920, America's women finally went to the polls.

Female Takeover

In 1920, the women of Yoncalla, Oregon, got together and made plans to take over the town government. They didn't tell anyone, not even their brothers or husbands. Men outnumbered women two to one in this community of fewer than 350 persons, but the women all voted. According to *Literary Digest*, they were "stirred by the alleged inefficiency of the municipal officials, and swept every masculine officeholder out of his job." When they went to the polls they elected an all-women's slate of town officials. Mrs. Mary Burt became the new mayor. The out-of-a-job former mayor, a Mr. Laswell, was said to be "much surprised."

Red Scare

Russia fought with the Allies in World War I until the Russian people decided they'd had enough of the war. It was more important, as far as they were concerned, to solve their own problems. They wanted to get rid of their ruler—the tsar (ZAR). They wanted to end the big gap between rich and poor in Russia. They wanted what Americans had wanted in 1776. They wanted freedom. So they had a freedom revolution.

At first, it looked as if they might get freedom. The people who overthrew the tsar (in 1917) were trying to create a democratic government. Then a revolutionary named Vladimir Lenin, who was living in Europe in exile, came back to Russia. That man changed the fate of Russia and the world. He became dictator of Russia. He didn't believe in democracy.

Bolsheviks attack the Winter Palace in Petrograd during the October Revolution in 1917. ▼

Things had been bad in Russia when the tsar was ruler. They got much worse under Lenin and the ruler who followed, Joseph Stalin. Lenin and Stalin brought totalitarianism to Russia. They brought repression, murder, state control, and misery. They brought an economic system called communism.

Lenin took Russia out of the war. That let Germany move troops from eastern Europe to France. It made the Great War tougher for the Allies.

What does all this have to do with U.S. history? A lot. You see, the world had become smaller. Not smaller in size, but in accessibility. At the beginning of the 19th century, it took at least two years for a ship to go from Salem, Massachusetts, to China and back. Now, with the telephone, communication was almost instantaneous. Modern technology meant that the ideas of one nation could spread quickly to others.

Some people in America were scared by Russia's ideas. They were afraid of communism. Others were attracted to those ideas. Under communism, most property and goods belong to the state. People are expected to share. That sounds noble; it just never seems to work unless forced upon people. Communist nations have not been free nations.

After the world war, some people were scared that communists wanted to take over in the United States. There were a few communists in this country—but they were not successful. Most American people were not attracted to communism.

In that same postwar time, there were also some *anarchists* in America. Anarchists don't believe in government at all. You don't

▲ Vladimir Lenin (left) and Joseph Stalin (right) brought totalitarianism to Russia.

Sacco and Vanzetti

Nicola Sacco and Bartolomeo Vanzetti were accused of murdering a paymaster and his guard at a shoe factory in South Braintree, Massachusetts. Did they do it? Even today, no one is sure. But they were convicted and executed. Sacco and Vanzetti were anarchists, and many said it was radical beliefs that were on trial. The trial was a *cause célèbre* (which, in French, means "a famous happening").

Nicola Sacco (right) and Bartolomeo Vanzetti, Italian-American anarchists, were convicted of murder and robbery in 1921 and executed in 1927. ▶

have to be very smart to realize that anarchy doesn't work. But when the anarchists looked around and saw poverty, war, and evil, they thought that this was the fault of governments. Some may have really believed that the answer was to do away with all governments. A few tried to do that by setting off bombs intended to kill government leaders. That, of course, was criminal behavior. Newspapers made big headlines of the bombs. Many Americans were frightened. But what A. Mitchell Palmer, President Wilson's attorney general, did was irresponsible and criminal. (He got away with it—but not in the history books.)

Palmer went on a witch hunt. The witches he went after were communists and anarchists. He took the law in his hands, and, in two days of raids in major cities (in 1920), agents invaded homes, clubs, union halls, pool halls, and coffee shops, rounding up nearly 5,000 people, who were held in jail, not allowed to call anyone, and treated terribly. Those without citizenship papers were sent out of the country—to Russia. Most weren't guilty of anything.

Communists are sometimes called "reds." Mitchell Palmer took advantage of America's fear of communism. He helped create a "red scare." He hoped it would make him president. During the red scare, Americans were not free to speak out about communism. They weren't free to criticize the government. Some people's lives were ruined.

Witch-hunting turns up every once in a while in American history. (It happened in Salem, Massachusetts, in colonial days; it happened after World War II with a senator named Joe McCarthy.) The good thing is, it never seems to last long. Persecution for ideas is not the American way.

The First Amendment (part of our Bill of Rights) says: *Congress shall make no law…abridging the freedom of speech.* Does that mean that communists and anarchists are free to speak out here—as long as they do not engage in criminal activity or plot to overthrow the government?

Thomas Jefferson wrote: *Truth is great and will prevail if left to herself, and errors cease to be dangerous when it is permitted freely to contradict them.* He believed that when everyone's ideas are heard, people will make wise choices. Do you agree with him?

Communists were called *reds* after the red flag of the Communist International, which was the worldwide communist organization.

In 1789, Congress passed an alien law. It kept certain people from emigrating to the United States. A sedition law made it a crime to speak against the government. People were jailed for their ideas. The people who supported those laws said they wanted to keep "dangerous foreigners" out of the country. At the time, the foreigners they feared were French.

Soft-Hearted Harding and Silent Cal

When Woodrow Wilson signed his last official papers as president, his face was ash white. He had always been slim; now he seemed shrunken, like a dry reed. Just two years earlier, Wilson had been the world's hero. Now he was ill and ignored. His country seemed to have no use for him or his ideas, and he knew it.

The new president—our 29th—Warren Gamaliel (guh-MAY-lee-ul) Harding, had been elected enthusiastically by the people. If a movie director were casting a president's part, he might pick Harding. The man *looked* presidential. His hair was silver, his eyebrows black, his skin tanned bronze, his voice golden. He was handsome, well groomed, and distinguished looking. He was also a good-natured, pleasant man.

"We must strive for normalcy," said Warren Harding. After the stormy war years, that was just what Americans longed to hear.

Two years and five months later, Harding was dead, and the nation wept as it had not done since the death of Abraham Lincoln. In his lifetime, Warren Harding was one of the most popular presidents ever.

He is said to have died of heart failure, but perhaps it was of a broken heart. For he knew, before he died, that his friends, whom he trusted with important government jobs, had betrayed him and the nation. It was a terrible scandal.

A Few Firsts

Loudspeakers were used at Warren G. Harding's inauguration for the first time in the event's history. Harding was the first president to address the nation over the radio. Florence Harding, along with being First Lady, also managed a lot of firsts. She was the first president's wife to fly in an airplane and the first to hold press conferences for women reporters. She worked, successfully, to found the first rehabilitation penitentiary for women (that's a jail where prisoners are helped to change their criminal behavior rather than just punished for it). And she spoke out for women's equality in sports, schools, employment, and politics.

Warren G. Harding ▶

This cartoon from 1924 shows Washington officials racing down an oil-slicked road to the White House, trying desperately to outpace the Teapot Dome scandal.

The scandal in the Harding administration centered on some naval oil reserves, including one at Teapot Dome, near Casper, Wyoming. (Geologists call a swollen upward curve in the earth's surface a "dome.") Congress was concerned that the military services have enough oil in case of emergencies, so it had set aside certain oil-rich areas for government use. Harding had appointed men who gave secret rights to those government oil lands, meant for public use, to individuals and private companies. These men, whom Harding trusted, gave away priceless oil reserves, laughed at the conservationists, and took bribes from business and criminal interests. They became very rich.

And what did the American people think when they heard the news? At first they were angry at the senators and journalists who told them. Later, they became angry when they thought about Harding. Before long, historians were calling him the worst of all presidents.

He wasn't the worst. He created the Bureau of the Budget, reduced the national debt, cut taxes, and appointed black men to public office.

Warren Harding, as I said, was a pleasant man, always gracious and considerate. But he may not have been tough enough, or smart enough, to handle the presidency.

When Harding died, thrifty, Vermont-born Calvin Coolidge became president. He had been an active governor of Massachusetts and, like most Vermonters, he didn't waste words. When a woman told him she had bet someone that she could get him to say more than three words to her, he responded, "You lose."

He started out as an energetic and decisive chief executive. In his first message to Congress he called for federal laws to punish "the hideous act of lynching," and for more attention to education, minimum wages for women workers, and other progressive measures.

Business and Idealism

In a speech, Calvin Coolidge said, "The business of the American people is business…" In the thriving nation at the time, many agreed, without ever hearing the rest of his speech. Coolidge went on to say, "The accumulation of wealth cannot be justified as the chief end of existence…. So long as wealth is made the means and not the end, we need not greatly fear it." He added, "I cannot repeat too often that America is a nation of idealists. That [idealism] is the only motive to which they [Americans] ever give any strong and lasting reaction."

Do you think he was right?

But then something terrible happened. Coolidge's son, 16-year-old Calvin Jr., died of blood poisoning, which developed from a toe blister he had gotten playing tennis. Coolidge was overwhelmed with grief. He couldn't concentrate. He developed an assortment of illnesses, including severe depression. His work suffered.

Still, the times were prosperous, he was popular, and almost no one, besides his wife and close friends, knew what was happening to him. Today, he is mostly remembered as a president who didn't say or do much—but that was part of his philosophy, since he was against active government. "Perhaps one of the most important accomplishments of my administration has been minding my own business," he said. The argument between active government and stand-aside government continues today. Most Americans at the time thought Coolidge a splendid president.

▲ Calvin Coolidge

Being President: One Tough Job

A president has to make hard decisions. If you are president you need to appoint good people to the cabinet and to thousands of administrative jobs. You need to be a leader of the armed forces. You need to make a huge budget to run the country. You need to come up with ideas for domestic policies that will make the country prosperous and happy. You need to make foreign policies to guide the nation in its relations with other nations. You need to get along with Congress. You need to get along with the states and their governors. You need to be a role model for millions of citizens with differing ideas and desires. Being president is an enormous, complicated job.

The President's Roles	
Chief of State	represents the nation at home and abroad
Chief Executive	leads the executive branch of government, appoints cabinet secretaries, sets policy on how to enforce the law
Chief Diplomat	directs foreign policy
Commander in Chief	makes military decisions, commands the military
Chief Legislator	suggests laws, can veto bills
Chief Economic Leader	plans the government's budget, monitors the economy
Chief of Party	supports party's goals and members, raises campaign funds

The Roaring Twenties

Some called the decade of the 1920s the "Roaring Twenties," some called it the "Jazz Age," and some the "Dance Age." Whichever you chose, it seemed like a time of fun and change.

More people had more money than ever before. And, mostly, they were intent on having a good time. Hardly anyone seemed to worry that some people were left out of the prosperity boom.

In 1919, before the '20s began their roar, women's ankles sometimes could be glimpsed beneath long skirts. Those ankles, however, were modestly hidden beneath high-topped shoes. Then skirts started going up, and up, and up.

That made it a tough time to be the parent of a girl. It wasn't easy to be a girl then either. Most young women were cutting their hair—short. They called it "bobbing." Some parents wouldn't allow it. Short hair seemed indecent to the older generation, but up to the minute to those who did it. The girls who weren't allowed to cut their hair felt old-fashioned.

A 1920s couple does the popular new dance called the Charleston. ▼

In the Roaring Twenties, women—like this flapper, dressed for a day at the beach—began to assert their individual freedom both in their dress and their actions. ▼

Some daring women were wearing bathing suits that left their legs uncovered. Police arrested women on the beaches for doing that. And makeup! "Nice" women started wearing lipstick, rouge, and powder. The older generation worried. "What is the world coming to?"

Those girls who bobbed their hair and wore short skirts and lipstick were called "flappers." They did other things, too. They drove automobiles, got jobs, went to the movies, read romantic novels, played Ping-Pong, and danced. My, did they dance! It was the big thing in the '20s. And the big dance was the Charleston. (In New York City, Gimbel's department store advertised special Charleston dresses that swung loose on the body. The price was $1.58.) When you danced the Charleston you swung your arms, kicked up your heels, knocked your knees together, and moved frantically.

Frantic is a good word to describe the '20s. The idealism of the Wilson years seemed to have come to nothing. After the war, everything was supposed to be better. But anyone could see that it wasn't. And there was the Prohibition idea. Americans wanted to have a good nation—where all people behaved themselves and didn't get drunk—but that wasn't working either. If you read the newspapers you could see that criminals were becoming rich and powerful selling liquor. So a lot of Americans in the '20s figured that the best thing to do was to forget about ideals and have a good time—frantically.

It was a materialistic age. People concentrated on making money and buying things for themselves. Successful businesspeople became national heroes. There were more rich people than ever before in American history. No one seemed to notice, however, that there were also growing numbers of unemployed people—people who were desperately poor. And many farmers were in terrible trouble.

But for most Americans, the times seemed good. The stock market—like women's hems—went up and up and up. Land values boomed. People were able to buy things they never could buy before.

▲ A magazine cover captures the frantic spirit of the Twenties.

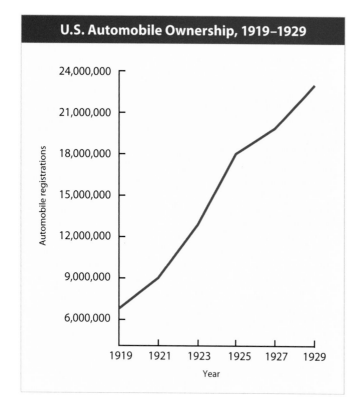

U.S. Automobile Ownership, 1919–1929

In 1920 the car was a novelty. Ten years later, almost every family had a car. Many Americans who didn't have indoor toilets in their homes had motorcars in their yards. The automobile was becoming a necessity.

Before the war, life had been slow paced; now change was coming with cyclone speed. Ordinary people owned radios and listened to comedy shows and the nightly news. In Florida, in 1924, a schoolboy named Red Barber heard radio for the first time at a friend's house. Barber was so excited he stayed up most of the night listening to news from around the nation. It was a new experience. "A man...in Pittsburgh said it was snowing there...someone sang in New York...a banjo plunked in Chicago...it was sleeting in New Orleans." (Red Barber later became a radio sports broadcaster.)

By the late 1920s, many Americans owned cars. The automobile sped up the pace of American life. ▶

The Scopes Trial

Dayton, Tennessee, 1925—in this dusty town of 1600 citizens, a court case called the "monkey trial" became the best-known trial of the decade.

A young schoolteacher was on trial for teaching the theory of evolution in his classroom. The theory of evolution traces life on earth through millions of years of development from one-celled creatures to plants and animals to humans. (Since apes and monkeys turn up near humans on the evolutionary ladder, jokesters came up with the "monkey" label for the trial.)

In 1925 Tennessee had passed a bill stating that it was "unlawful for any teacher...to teach any theory that denies the story of the divine creation of man as taught in the Bible, and to teach instead that man has descended from a lower order of animals." That state law told schools that they should teach the Bible's version of creation—that the world was created in six days and that humans were part of the Creation from the very beginning.

Critics argued that it was unconstitutional to impose a church doctrine on public schools. The American Civil Liberties Union (founded in 1920 to protect civil rights) said it would pay the legal expenses of any teacher who wanted to test the law and keep teaching from their science textbooks. In Dayton, 24-year-old John Scopes taught evolution in his high school biology class and was arrested.

When William Jennings Bryan heard of the trial, he volunteered to be the prosecutor, in favor of the Tennessee law. Everyone knew Bryan—he had run for president three times. He was kind, well liked, and a fundamentalist Christian who believed in the exact words of the Bible.

Clarence Darrow volunteered to defend Scopes. Darrow was a brilliant lawyer, a friend of the underdog, and an agnostic (someone who is not sure if there is a God or not).

It was an angry trial, full of bad feelings, and it didn't settle much of anything. Bryan won the case: the courts agreed that Scopes broke Tennessee law. (That law stayed on the books until 1967.)

Long after the "monkey trial," the issue of the separation of church and state kept coming up. In 1968 and again in 1987, the Supreme Court ruled that laws requiring the teaching of creationism (the Bible's story of Creation) are in violation of the First Amendment. For many citizens, those Supreme Court decisions did not decide things. In this debate, both sides claim ownership of truth.

◀ Clarence Darrow (left) and William Jennings Bryan (right) in an unusually calm moment at the often angry Scopes Trial in 1925.

Walt Disney's *Steamboat Willie*, which introduced Mickey Mouse in 1928, was the first animated film with sound. ▼

▲ In the 1920s, people flocked to movies, like this silent film, with live musicians playing the score.

Young people were flocking to the movies and, in 1927, the first talking picture, *The Jazz Singer*, starring Al Jolson, opened.

The following year, in Hollywood, California, a young filmmaker named Walt Disney produced the first animated sound film, Steamboat Willie, and introduced a little mouse named Mickey to the American public.

Suddenly, America seemed filled with artistic geniuses: musicians George Gershwin and Aaron Copland; writers Ernest Hemingway, William Faulkner, and F. Scott Fitzgerald; and artists Mary Cassatt, Grant Wood, and Thomas Hart Benton. And those are just a few of the names.

A Writer for the Jazz Age

Francis Scott Fitzgerald, a young Minnesotan (named for an ancestor, Francis Scott Key), had a tough time in school—but he loved to write. In a short life (he died at age 44), Fitzgerald wrote five novels (including one of the greatest American novels, *The Great Gatsby*), more than 150 short stories, and many essays. Hardly anyone described America of the 1920s and '30s as well as he did. It was he who labeled the times the "Jazz Age." His characters tried to turn life into a glittering party and then couldn't understand why they weren't happy.

Harlem (a part of New York City with a rapidly growing black population) began vibrating with artistry. It was contagious. Playwrights, poets, musicians, artists, and actors, all living within a few blocks of each other, were sharing ideas. Langston Hughes, Claude McKay, and Countee Cullen began writing poetry. Zora Neale Hurston and Jean Toomer wrote novels. Jacob Lawrence and Romare Bearden painted pictures. And Duke Ellington and a whole lot of other people made music. Artistic excellence was something that the segregationists (who believed that different races should be kept separate) couldn't suppress. And Harlem, during this time known as the "Harlem Renaissance," exploded with creativity.

▲ Marcus Garvey came to the United States from Jamaica in 1916 to launch his Universal Negro Improvement Association. Garvey, the most influential black leader of the 1920s, promoted self-help and race pride and urged blacks to return to their African heritage.

Migrating North

Between 1910 and 1920, more than one million black people headed north. Working conditions in the South were awful, schools were worse, and most blacks couldn't vote. The North held the hope of better jobs, better schooling, and a chance to get ahead. New York's black population (centered in Harlem) increased by 66 percent in that 10-year period. Chicago's black population (centered in the South Side) increased by 50 percent. That black migration—from field to factory, from rural to urban—continued through most of the century. Jacob Lawrence painted the migration in a series of paintings that are small in size but powerful in impact.

▲ Jacob Lawrence's *The Migration of the Negro, Panel No. 1* (1940–41). "There is absolutely nothing before them on the farm," said a government report on Southern labor, "no prospect…but to continue until they die." Instead, they fled.

Jazz: An American Original

People in the 1920s were crazy about jazz. In fact, the 1920s are sometimes called the "Jazz Age." Today, many people call jazz America's most original art form.

The roots of jazz are in New Orleans, down in Louisiana at the mouth of the Mississippi River. New Orleans had, and has, an unusual mixture of peoples. The city was settled by the French in 1718. (In 1803, President Thomas Jefferson bought New Orleans as part of the Louisiana Purchase.) The French language stuck. Some of the sounds and words of that language can be heard in New Orleans even today. Many of the French and Spanish men who came to New Orleans in the 18th century married African American women.

Their biracial children, called Creoles, often spoke French or Spanish as well as English.

Out of the sounds of New Orleans, and the mixed heritage of its people, a new music arose. It was called "jazz," and it was uniquely American music, unlike anything heard in the world before. It combined the rhythm and drum beat of Africa with the instruments and heritage of Europe. It added a dash from the spirituals of the black Protestant churches and much from the talents of some black musical geniuses who could be heard in street bands and nightclubs. In the 1920s jazz began to spread: first to Chicago, then across the country, and then around the whole world.

Louis Armstrong ▼

▲ Many of the early jazz leaders—such as Joe "King" Oliver (back row, on cornet, with his Creole Jazz Band)—were trumpeters, probably because the trumpet could be played while marching, and because its sweet, high sound carried over the street noise. Kneeling, front, is Louis Armstrong.

The best way to learn about jazz is to listen to it. You could start with one of the greatest jazz performers: Louis Armstrong. Louis grew up poor in New Orleans. Then someone gave him a trumpet. He was born to play the trumpet. People began calling him "satchelmouth," because his cheeks seemed to hold a suitcase full of air. "Satchmo" was soon playing on riverboats that went up and down the Mississippi. Then he went to Chicago and began making history. Satchmo had a big grin, but when he played the trumpet he closed his eyes and blew clear, heavenly tones.

No two jazz performances are exactly alike. Composers who compose European-style music write down notes and expect musicians to play those notes just as they are written. That isn't so in true jazz. An important part of jazz is *improvisation.* Improvising means doing your own thing. Jazz musicians talk to each other with their instruments. It is something like African drum talk. One musician leads with a theme. Then someone answers that theme. He plays the theme his own way. Then maybe the first musician improvises with another variation on the theme. Soon the whole band is playing with it. It isn't easy to do it well.

In New York City in the late 1920s, jazz provided the soundtrack to nightlife in Harlem. At the popular Cotton Club, crowds danced to the music of Duke Ellington's band. But the club was segregated: the customers were white, the musicians black.

Some African American musicians went to Europe, especially to Paris, where they joined

▲ The Cotton Club in Harlem

a colony of writers and artists; all were part of a cultural moment where creative talent mattered more than anything else. Everyone in Paris seemed to be listening to jazz. George Gershwin, who was there, put a jazz beat into his groundbreaking *An American in Paris.* Gershwin and Aaron Copland (called the "dean of American composers") studied with France's great music teacher, Nadia Boulanger.

Picturing the Early Twentieth Century

At the beginning of the 20th century, most American artists were painting elegant, refined portraits and scenes and showing their best work at exhibitions at the National Academy of Design. Then along came some artists who broke the rules. They painted working people. They made pictures from real life: down-to-earth, open-hearted paintings. They were following the lead of some boldly realistic 19th-century painters—especially Thomas Eakins (AY-kinz) and Winslow Homer— except that this new group concentrated on urban scenes.

Finding vitality in shabby streets and down-on-their-luck people, they were called the "Ashcan artists." The name was meant as an insult; the art establishment wanted nothing to do with them. Their paintings weren't "pretty"; it was "new" art, and a threat to the old.

When John Sloan sent some of his etchings to be exhibited at the National Academy, they were rejected as "vulgar." So was most of the Ashcan art. (Today it's in museums.)

The group's leader was Robert Henri (HEN-rye)—a superb teacher as well as a fine painter. Edward Hopper was one of his students. Over and over, Hopper painted the loneliness of city life with scenes of people who don't seem to be doing anything—and yet they haunt your mind.

Edward Hopper (1882–1967) sold his first painting at the Armory Show; he didn't sell another one for 10 years. This work, one of his most famous, is called *Nighthawks*. ▶

Robert Henri's bold realism, his strong brushstrokes, and his sensitivity to the environment seemed innovative and daring until you looked at the art that was being done in Paris. Artists there were breaking all the old rules. Alfred Stieglitz (STEEG-lits) brought European art to his small New York gallery at 291 Fifth Avenue even before the Armory Show scandalized the nation. That gallery, called "291," became a center for the best in new art.

Stieglitz was a photographer at a time when photography was making huge technological leaps. Stieglitz was determined to make people aware that great photographs can be great art.

Besides that, he cared about art in general. When he found an artist whose work he liked, he would do everything he could to be of help. And artists often need help—especially if they are breaking new ground. Modern artists were looking at the world

The Armory Show

It was a cold winter day in 1913 when the doors opened at an old, drafty armory on 25th Street and Lexington Avenue in New York City, and people got to see some new paintings and sculpture (including many from Europe). American art was never the same again. Some of the paintings in the Armory Show were done by Henri Matisse, Paul Cézanne, Pablo Picasso, Paul Gauguin, and Vincent van Gogh. Today we know them all as great artists, but in 1913 their work was unlike anything most people here had seen before. Matisse was part of a French group called Les Fauves, or "the wild beasts." Many viewers thought it a good title for all the artists.

One painting, by Marcel Duchamp, was called *Nude Descending a Staircase*. Classical paintings often showed naked figures reclining on couches. This painting showed what seemed to be a bunch of sticks—or maybe a figure; it was hard to tell—but something very active was happening on the canvas. Before, art had always more or less imitated reality. These paintings were completely different. Many American artists were profoundly changed by the new modernism on display at the Armory Show.

Marcel Duchamp's *Nude Descending a Staircase* puzzled and outraged many viewers at the Armory Show. Former president Theodore Roosevelt compared it to a rug in his bathroom. ▶

▲ Many of the Americans who went to Paris clustered around Gertrude Stein. She was a writer who had an eye for art, and she seemed to know everyone famous—like Picasso, who painted her portrait.

through unusual lenses. They distorted line and shape and color playfully and didn't worry about realistic conventions. They looked for inspiration everywhere. Stieglitz's 291 gallery showed the best of their work. It held the first serious exhibition of children's art in the United States. It exhibited African American art. And it showed some startling new paintings from Europe. Both Stieglitz and Henri helped make the Armory Show happen.

Stieglitz believed American artists were creating major works of art, and he said so in an arts magazine he published. He encouraged and exhibited works by John Marin, Marsden Hartley, Arthur Dove, Elie Nadelman, and Max Weber (never charging them a fee or profiting from any of their work). The most important of all the artists he guided and helped became his wife. She was Georgia O'Keeffe.

O'Keeffe grew up in prairie Wisconsin, went to high school in traditional Virginia, studied art in Chicago, arrived in New York in 1914, married Stieglitz, and eventually moved to New Mexico, where she fell in love with its earth and sky and mountains. "I found I could say things with color and shapes that I couldn't say in any other way—things I had no words for," wrote O'Keeffe.

The Avant-Garde

Both Robert Henri and Alfred Stieglitz challenged traditionalists and gathered followers. Both art leaders lived in New York, and, between the two of them, they dominated the world of *avant-garde* American art in their time. *Avant-garde* is a French word; it literally means "the vanguard"—the troops who move at the front of an army. In modern times, avant-garde artists are those who are in the forefront of a movement, at the cutting edge, ahead of their time.

Alfred Stieglitz, a leader of the American artistic avant-garde, helped guide the early career of Georgia O'Keeffe, who painted *Blue and Green Music* in 1921. ▶

In the early part of the 20th century, the hub of artistic innovation was not in New Mexico, where O'Keeffe worked, nor even in New York, which drew many American artists. In the Western Hemisphere, Europe was the center of the art world and Paris was the center of Europe. Paris was the place to be if you were an artist, a writer, or a musician. Marc Chagall came from Russia, Pablo Picasso from Spain, Amadeo Modigliani from Italy, sculptor Elie Nadelman from Poland. Almost every American artist of significance (including Henri and Stieglitz) came, even if only for a short time. In Paris, the "modern" painters didn't attempt to copy life; they seemed to be reinventing it with color and imagination.

In the early 20th century, many Americans were slow to embrace the new art. They associated modern art with dangerous ideas that seemed to be coming from foreign lands and, sometimes, from New York. But there were three contemporary artists whose work did become popular: Thomas Hart Benton, John Steuart Curry, and Grant Wood.

When *Time* magazine put Thomas Hart Benton on the magazine's cover, overnight the three artists became stars. *Time* called them "earthy Midwesterners." Only Iowa-born Grant Wood actually lived in the Midwest. Curry lived in Connecticut and Benton had a studio in New York. But they all did have Midwestern roots. And they painted an idyllic America. They became known as "Regionalists."

This is Grant Wood's *American Gothic* (1930). Wood got his sister Nan to pose with a dentist from Cedar Rapids. Why do you think he is holding a pitchfork? The painting hangs in the Art Institute of Chicago. ▶

Everyone's Hero

During the Roaring Twenties, America fell in love with organized sports. Working hours were changing, and more Americans had more leisure time. They could go to ballparks or listen to games on radio. (Red Barber was now one of their favorite sportscasters.) They could also play sports themselves. When the Great War ended there were very few tennis courts or golf courses in the nation. Some states didn't have any at all. Those sports were mainly played by rich folks. By the end of the '20s, golf courses and tennis courts were popping up everywhere. Americans were hard at play.

Sports stars became American heroes. One, George Herman Ruth, didn't look like a hero. His body was shaped like a barrel with spindly legs sticking out of its bottom. His face wasn't much to look at either. In the middle was a mashed-in nose.

But none of that mattered, because Ruth—who was known as "the Babe"—turned beautiful when he stepped onto a baseball field. He was the most famous ballplayer of all time.

He had an awful childhood. He wasn't an orphan, as some books say, but his parents, who ran a tavern, didn't care for him much. So he spent most of his time on the streets of Baltimore, got in trouble, and, at age eight, was sent to a Catholic boys' home (where he played a lot

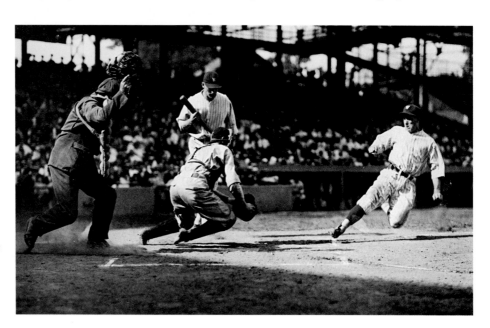

In the 1920s, Americans, who had more leisure time, packed into ballparks to enjoy watching sports. Here, Bucky Harris of the Washington Nationals slides into home plate in 1925. ▶

of baseball). He was tough—he had to be—but not bitter or angry. Actually, he was funny and friendly, and had all the instincts of a natural ham actor. He loved playing baseball, he broke all its records, and he was always himself, which means no one could predict what he would do or say next. The crowds adored him.

Ruth was a lefty—a southpaw—and he started out as a pitcher (in 1914) with the Boston Red Sox. He was sensational. But he could also hit—harder and farther than anyone. So Boston had him pitch some days and sometimes had him play first base. In 1918 he was about the best left-handed pitcher in the game, and that year he also led the American League in home runs.

But Boston needed money, so they traded him to the New York Yankees. The Yankees put him in the outfield. Pitchers play only every three or four days. An outfielder plays every day. The Yankees were counting on Babe Ruth's hitting.

Were they ever right! Before Ruth, baseball had been a low-scoring game. Pitchers were the stars, and batters did a lot of bunting and base-stealing. Ruth made it a hitter's game.

The all-time home-run record—set in 1884—was 27 home runs in one season. In 1920, Ruth hit 54 home runs. People came to the ballpark just to see those homers. Other ballplayers began holding the bat the way he did and swinging with all their might. Scores began going up. High-scoring games are a lot more exciting than pitchers' duels. The fans went wild. Baseball teams agreed to switch to a lively ball that went farther than the ball they had been using. The game got really exciting.

In 1921, Babe Ruth hit 59 home runs and scored a total of 177 runs. Yankee baseball attendance doubled. In 1923, the New York Yankees built big, beautiful Yankee Stadium. They used the money that came from increased attendance. It was called "the house that Ruth built."

▲ Babe Ruth had the most famous swing in the history of baseball. At Ruth's funeral in 1948, an old newsman said, "I stopped talking about the Babe for the simple reason that I realized that those who had never seen him didn't believe me."

Black Sox

Babe Ruth was a godsend for a national game deep in scandal. In 1919, members of the Chicago White Sox (forever after known as the "Black Sox") took money from gamblers and lost the World Series on purpose. Only a larger-than-life figure like Ruth could distract the millions of baseball fans from the ugly scandal and restore the game's innocence. Ruth, with his prodigious hitting, flamboyant behavior, and childlike enthusiasm, was just what the country needed.

▲ Boys gather round a radio in 1929. Radio brought news, sports, and entertainment to millions of Americans.

Those who couldn't get to Yankee Stadium could still enjoy the game. The first radio station, KDKA in Pittsburgh, began broadcasting in October 1920. Four years later there were 576 licensed stations and 5 million radio sets in use. People in Kansas could hear the Yankees play baseball. Radio announcers went to the ball games and described what was happening, play by play. At home, families clustered around their wood-covered radio sets, and, if the static wasn't too bad, listened for the swat of Babe Ruth's bat.

He was trying to beat his own home-run record. But when a reporter asked, "Which one was that, Babe?" the slugger was cool. "I'll hit 'em, you count 'em," he said.

In 1927, the Babe hit 60 home runs. That record stood for 34 years, until 1961, when Roger Maris hit 61. (There were 154 games in the 1927 season and 162 games in 1961.) It took 13 more years for someone to top his career home-run total—714 of them. (Atlanta Brave Hank Aaron did that.)

Babe did everything in a big way—including eating and drinking. So, when he got sick, with a fever and stomach cramps, reporters said it was because he ate 12 hot dogs and drank eight bottles of soda pop. That wasn't true. He ate like that regularly. But this time he was really sick. It was called "the bellyache heard round the world."

In 1935 Ruth was fat from eating too much. He was 40 years old. Still, there was no stopping him. He was now playing for the Boston Braves, and, in his last professional game, hit three home runs! His final home run was said to be the longest ever hit in Forbes Field.

The Other Babe

When Mildred Didrikson was growing up in Beaumont, Texas, she played baseball with the neighborhood boys. When she began hitting homers the boys couldn't catch, they gave her a nickname. What do you think it was? Why, Babe, of course. When it came to athletics, Babe Didrikson seemed to do it all. She was an all-American basketball player. She was a softball star and pitched in baseball exhibition games against major-league teams. She competed in swimming and diving events and played competitive tennis. She did some boxing. She became a national heroine when she earned three medals in track and field at the 1932 Olympic Games at Los Angeles, California. But she is best known as one of America's outstanding women golfers. Once she won 17 golf tournaments in a row. Babe became Babe Didrikson Zaharias (zuh-HAIR-ee-us) in 1938 when she married wrestler George Zaharias. She has been called the outstanding woman athlete of the first half of the 20th century. No American woman before or since has been a champion in so many sports.

▲ "Is there anything you don't play?" a reporter asked Babe. "Yes," she said. "Dolls."

Only the Ball Was White

Some people said that Josh Gibson once hit a ball over the roof at Yankee Stadium—which was farther than the Babe ever did. As for the unbelievable Satchel Paige, his pitching was so accurate they say he could have stayed in the strike zone pitching to Tom Thumb. Did he have a fast ball? Why, Satchel practically invented the fast ball. Someone who batted against him said that you never saw his pitched balls—just heard the thump in the catcher's mitt and knew they'd gone by. And Cool Papa Bell? Well, Paige himself swore that Bell ran so fast he could turn off the light switch and make it to bed before the light went out.

That lights-out story got repeated as a tall tale and a joke, although it happened to be true. Bell explained that he bet Paige he could do it one night when he learned a light switch was faulty.

He won the bet. But usually he didn't need trickery. Cool Papa Bell was fast as Mercury (maybe faster), and Paige and everyone else knew it. Paige and Bell and Gibson were stars of the Negro Leagues. These were Jim Crow times, when, in much of the United States, schools and ball teams and other things for blacks and whites were separate and unequal. Baseball didn't start that way. The brothers Fleet and Welday Walker had played in the old American Association. But when the association died in 1892, Cap Anson (who was a big hitter and a big bigot) made sure that the new leagues fielded whites-only teams. So men of color formed their own leagues.

The Negro Leagues were filled with talented players who played hard and seemed to have a whole lot of fun, too. Not that it was an easy life. Money was usually short, the equipment shabby, the travel brutal, and, in segregated times, blacks almost always had trouble finding hotel rooms or restaurants to eat

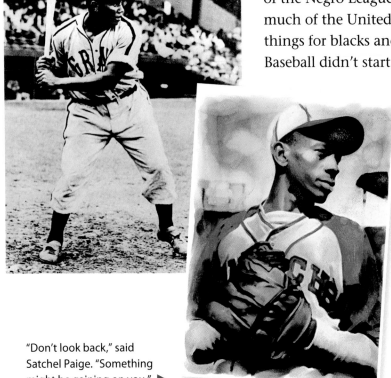

Josh Gibson "can do everything. He hits the ball a mile…. Throws like a rifle," said pitching whiz Walter Johnson. ▼

"Don't look back," said Satchel Paige. "Something might be gaining on you." ▶

◀ At this 1937 game between the Philadelphia Stars and the Homestead Grays at Griffith Stadium in Washington, D.C., "Cool Papa" Bell rounds third base as Buck Leonard is thrown out at first.

in. Sometimes they played 200 or 300 games in a six-month season. (Figure the math on that one.) Since they had no ballparks of their own, they had to rent, and the managers wanted to get their money's worth—so, when lights got put in ballfields, they'd often play a doubleheader, and then a night game, too.

What they did best, besides the regular league games, was barnstorm around the country bringing entertainment and fancy ballplaying to blacks (and some whites) in a whole lot of American towns. They were to baseball what the Harlem Globetrotters later became to basketball: wizards. Sometimes they played in formal attire, sometimes in clown costumes, sometimes in uniforms. They did comic routines, they juggled, they did ball tricks. It was fun, and it was skilled

ball, too. You had to love baseball to keep up the pace. Josh Gibson and Ted Page remembered playing a twilight game in Pittsburgh, driving to St. Louis for a day game, and then on to scorching Kansas City for a doubleheader. That evening the two of them made it to a hotel porch, where they sat, dog-tired, until they heard some kids playing sandlot ball. Naturally, they couldn't resist that, so they joined the game.

▲ Martin Dihigo

Two Cuban teams, the Cuban Stars and the New York Cubans, added a cosmopolitan touch to the Negro Leagues. Martin Dihigo, who played with the Cubans and with the Vera Cruz (Mexico) Eagles, ended up in baseball halls of fame in Cuba, Mexico, and the United States. In a league where everyone seemed versatile, he still managed to be outstanding. As one player said, "I seen them all for the past fifty years and I still think Dihigo was in a class by himself. He'd pitch one day, play center field the next, and the next day he'd be at first base. Sometimes he even played two or three positions in a single game."

World Beater

Sometimes the Toledo Crawfords would feature a guest appearance by their part-owner, Jesse Owens. Owens, a well-known track star, helped draw the crowds. Owens had won four gold medals at the 1936 Olympics in Berlin, Germany (no one had ever won four at once before). That displeased the German leader, Adolf Hitler, who believed in Aryan (white northern European) supremacy and thought Negroes were inferior. Owens would race anyone who wanted to run against him (fans got a 10-yard lead). Owens even raced a horse—and won!

Jesse Owens won four gold medals in the 1936 Olympics in Berlin. ▶

Except for the traveling, most of the ballplayers had a good time, although a few hated having to clown around. They just wanted to play ball. But, being black, or dark-skinned Cuban, or Mexican, they couldn't join the major leagues. It was crazy. One excuse was that blacks and whites wouldn't play together. But that wasn't so. White all-star teams often barnstormed with the blacks, playing exhibition games. (Black teams won more than they lost.) Everyone knew that players like Oscar Charleston, Smokey Joe Williams, and Buck Leonard were major talents.

"I have played against a Negro all-star team that was so good we didn't think we had even a chance," admitted white Dizzy Dean, who pitched for the St. Louis Cardinals and the Chicago Cubs. "There is no room in baseball for discrimination," said Lou Gehrig (one of the best first basemen ever). White catcher Gabby Hartnett (whose three sisters barnstormed in a women's league) said, "If managers were given permission there'd be a mad rush to sign up Negroes." Which is what finally happened.

Striking Out the Babe

It was 1931, and the Yankees were playing an exhibition game against the Chattanooga (Tennessee) Look-outs. The Look-outs had just signed a new pitcher, 17-year-old Jackie Mitchell.

The great Babe came to the plate—and struck out. The Babe threw his bat, stalked off, and the crowd roared. The next batter was big-hitter Lou Gehrig. Jackie threw three times. Gehrig swung three times. And that was that.

Surprise: Jackie Mitchell was a she. Some said that Ruth and Gehrig were just being polite to a woman, but no one who was there believed it. Baseball's commissioner didn't care. He was a misogynist (miss-SODGE-ih-nist—someone who dislikes women). He said Mitchell's contract was void, and baseball lost out.

Space Pioneers

We perceive the universe through our senses, especially our eyes and ears. From our small planet in our minor solar system in the Milky Way, it might seem that our galaxy makes up the whole universe—in other words, that the Milky Way, cosmically, is all there is.

> A *galaxy* is a huge collection of stars, planets, and stardust moving around (orbiting) a common center. Our sun and its planets (including Earth) are part of the Milky Way galaxy.

In the early 20th century, that's what reputable astronomers thought. But Edwin Hubble, sitting at what was the world's largest telescope, on top of chilly Mount Wilson in southern California, would overturn that idea. And that would lead to our modern understanding of the universe.

Hubble was a super athlete and very smart—he won a Rhodes scholarship, which took him to Oxford University in England. He made a promise to his dying father to study law—which he did. But he longed to be an astronomer.

He got a graduate degree in science. Then World War I erupted and, being cut out for heroic things, he joined the army, fought in France, and came home a major. Finally, in 1919, he was ready to accept an offer he'd received from the Mount Wilson Observatory.

For the next few years he painstakingly analyzed photographs and other data from the giant telescope on the peak of Mount Wilson. Today astronomers study data on computer screens. But Edwin Hubble cranked and turned the huge device until it pointed where he wanted it, put his eye to the eyepiece, and saw stars that had never been seen before.

Margaret Bourke-White, a famous photographer, took this picture of Edwin Hubble studying the skies. ▶

▲ Edwin Hubble's ideas helped increase our understanding of the universe. Hubble figured out that the galaxies (including the Andromeda Galaxy, pictured here) are moving away from each other.

Nebula comes from a Latin root that means "cloud." Today scientists use the word to describe clouds of dust and gas in space that are birthplaces of stars. They are not galaxies.

When he pointed the powerful scope at a fuzzy area in the heavens, then called the Andromeda nebula, he saw a swirling collection of stars. Hubble realized he was seeing a separate galaxy with a spiral shape much like our own Milky Way. He soon understood that the universe is much, much bigger than anyone had imagined and that it is strewn with galaxies. But it was when he figured out that the galaxies are all moving—moving away from each other at an astonishing speed—that he changed almost everything we had believed about the heavens.

Over in Switzerland, Albert Einstein had come up with a theory of relativity that showed mathematically that the universe is expanding. But no one could believe it. Not even Einstein. He thought he had made a mistake. Most people believed the universe was exactly as it had been at the creation. Others thought the universe had always existed as it is; they said it had no beginning and no end. Then Edwin Hubble looked through his telescope, saw galaxies racing away from each other, and confirmed Einstein's equations. They showed that the universe isn't static; it has changed over time, which means it has a story to tell. It has a history.

A piece of the handwritten manuscript dating from 1912 in which Einstein explained the Theory of Relativity for the first time ▼

$$E = \frac{m c^2}{\sqrt{1 - \frac{q^2}{c^2}}}$$

Einstein was surprised and elated when he heard of Hubble's conclusions. In 1931 he traveled to Mount Wilson and thanked the great astronomer.

Stars in Women's Eyes

The director of the Harvard College Observatory needed help classifying stars. It was an important but tedious job. He couldn't find many men to do it. Then he realized he could hire educated women at one-third the salary he paid men with the same abilities. That's how some unusual women became astronomers. They not only did tiresome work willingly, they used their brains (which women were not expected to do) and made outstanding contributions to the field.

Henrietta Swan Leavitt (1868–1921) noticed that some stars (called Cepheid stars) vary in brightness at a consistent rate. In 1912 she figured out how to use that information to measure distances between stars. That made Edwin Hubble's discoveries possible.

Annie Jump Cannon (1863–1941) was a graduate of a new woman's college with an excellent physics lab: Wellesley College. She went to work at Harvard classifying stars; no one was able to do the job as well as she. Cannon cataloged more than half a million stars. Doing that, she discovered hundreds of variable stars and novae. Her work served as a foundation for 20th-century astronomy. Despite her renown, Harvard waited until 1938 to officially appoint her an astronomer at the university; she was then 75 years old.

▲ Harvard Astronomer Annie J. Cannon at work

Science is a dual thing: it takes ideas and proofs. Einstein's theories and Hubble's proofs would set a direction for astrophysics in the 20th century. They would provide important knowledge needed to make a trip to the moon. So would the work of a shy professor who dreamed of space and interplanetary travel.

On a cold March day in 1926, Robert Hutchings Goddard stood in an open field in Auburn, Massachusetts. With him were his wife, Esther Kisk Goddard, and two assistants. All were concentrating on a tall structure built of metal pipes. Actually, there was nothing special about the structure. What was attached to it was special. It was a small rocket.

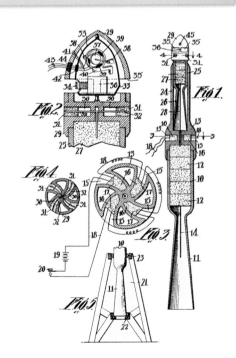

Robert Goddard drew these plans for a patent application on a "rocket apparatus" in 1914. ▶

▲ Physicist Robert Goddard stands beside a launching platform minutes prior to the world's first successful launch of a liquid-fueled rocket.

The rocket had a two-foot-long motor. Pipes ran from the base of the motor to two attached tanks: one tank held gasoline, the other oxygen. Goddard touched a blowtorch to an opening at the top of the rocket. The rocket let out a roar. Slowly it lifted off the launch pad—that is what the metal-pipe structure was—and rose into the air, speeding upward at 60 miles an hour. Then it crashed into the snowy field. The flight lasted three seconds. The space age had begun.

Robert Goddard and his assistants went back to their laboratory. They knew that what they had done that day was as important as what had been done by two brothers from Dayton, Ohio, at Kitty Hawk, North Carolina, in December of 1903. But almost no one else knew that. In 1926, most people would have laughed at a scientist who took the idea of space travel seriously. It would be a long time before the world understood about rockets and rocket travel.

Robert Goddard had dreamed of space travel from the time he was a boy. It all began with two books—*The War of the Worlds*, written by an Englishman, H. G. Wells, and *From the Earth to the Moon,* written by a Frenchman, Jules Verne. Those books are two of the earliest, and best, of the modern science fiction novels. Goddard read them, reread them, and then read them again. They made him believe that space travel was possible. His later studies led him to decide that rockets were the way space would be conquered.

Rockets were nothing new. The Chinese had designed rockets way back in the 11th century. The Chinese rockets were powered by explosive powders. You lit the powder and, *whammo*, the rocket lifted off and the fuel was all used up. Chinese rockets were mostly used for fireworks.

Goddard realized that if a rocket was to soar out of Earth's atmosphere and beyond, it would need a fuel that provided steady power, a fuel that wouldn't burn up all at once. A liquid seemed the answer, but liquid fuels demand oxygen in order to burn. There is no oxygen in space. Now, it doesn't sound terribly complicated to figure all that out and build a rocket that carries its own fuel and oxygen tanks. It doesn't seem difficult because we now know it can be done. The first person to come up with an idea isn't sure it can be done. Or how to do it. It took Robert Goddard 10 years of experimenting to build the little rocket that climbed into the sky on that icy-cold March day in 1926.

A few other scientists—in Germany and Russia—were working on the same problem. They worked with theories. Theories are ideas. Goddard was different. He started with theories, but then he tested them. That is the true scientific way.

When he was 38 (six years before the 1926 test flight), Goddard wrote a paper for the Smithsonian Institution in which he theorized that a rocket of 10 tons might be made powerful enough to reach the moon. He spent much of the rest of his life working to make that possible.

New England isn't a good place to test rockets: too many trees and people. Goddard decided to do his testing in New Mexico, over the desert. Soon his rockets were traveling at 700 miles an hour; some were rising as much as a mile and a half high. He worked out ways to guide and control rockets. He developed the idea of a series of rockets as a means of reaching the moon. He devised parachutes to allow rockets to return to earth smoothly. He patented more than 200 of his ideas.

Robert Goddard died in 1945, 24 years before Apollo 11 landed on the moon. But his spirit must have been riding with the astronauts on that voyage.

Goddard's pioneering experiments in rocketry helped make the Apollo 11 launch possible. ▼

The Lone Eagle

Robert Goddard might never have gone farther than that field in Auburn, Massachusetts, if a young man hadn't come to visit him. The young man was Charles A. Lindbergh, Jr. Newspapers called him the most famous man on the planet.

Lindbergh was wise enough not to be too impressed with himself. He was also wise enough to know the importance of Goddard's work. Lindbergh talked to a philanthropist (fil-AN-thro-pist) named Daniel Guggenheim. (A philanthropist is a person who gives money to good causes.) The Guggenheim Foundation gave Goddard money to build a laboratory in New Mexico.

Why was Lindbergh so famous? Well, back in 1919, a wealthy hotel man offered a prize of $25,000 to anyone who could fly from New York to Paris (or Paris to New York). Several pilots tried for the prize. None made it. Then, in 1927, the competition got fierce. Besides the money, everyone knew there would be much glory for the pilot who first crossed the Atlantic.

In April, Richard E. Byrd took off, crashed, and broke his wrist. That same April, two pilots set out from Virginia, crashed, and were killed. In early May, two French aces (top pilots) left Paris, headed out over the Atlantic, and were never heard of again.

Byrd at the Poles

Richard Evelyn Byrd was the most renowned American explorer of his generation. In May 1926, he and co-pilot Floyd Bennett flew over the North Pole. (Much later, scientists discovered his calculations were off and he had missed the North Pole—but not by much.) Naturally, one pole led to the other. In 1928, he headed an Antarctic expedition, set up a scientific base there named Little America, and, in 1929, flew over the South Pole. Byrd wrote books, made lecture tours, and opened Antarctica to scientific research.

A U.S. Coast Guard cutter plows through icy waters in Antarctica during an expedition led by Admiral Richard E. Byrd. ▶

▲ Lindbergh's
Spirit of St. Louis

◀ Charles Lindbergh in 1927

In mid-May, three planes were being made ready. Newspapers on both sides of the Atlantic were full of their stories. Most of the newspaper attention focused on Byrd, who was famous and eager to try again. His plane had three engines and a well-trained crew. The second plane, with two engines, was to be flown by two experienced pilots.

The third plane, a small single-engine craft, could hold only one person. It was called the *Spirit of St. Louis*, because a group of St. Louis businessmen had helped pay for it. The pilot, Charles Lindbergh, was little known. He'd been a barnstormer, a pilot who went around doing trick flying: circles and loops and daredevil things. In those days, people didn't use airplanes for transportation. Trains were used to get places. Airplanes? No one was quite sure about the future of aviation. But if planes could fly across the ocean safely, they might have an important future.

Lindbergh was a good pilot. He was the first man to fly the U.S. mail from St. Louis to Chicago. There was a bold, daring side to him, and another side that was careful and methodical. It was a rare combination. In a crisis he would not panic.

It was 8 a.m. on May 20 when he took off. The weather wasn't good, but he was anxious to beat the others, and he was used to flying the mail in all kinds of weather.

May 21, 1927—a large crowd awaits Charles Lindbergh as he completes the first solo nonstop transatlantic flight in history. Lindbergh flew 3,610 miles (5,810 kilometers) between Roosevelt Field on Long Island, New York, and Paris, France, in 33 hours, 30 minutes.

His little plane carried so much gasoline that some people thought it would never get into the air. But Lindbergh had planned carefully. There wasn't an extra ounce on the plane. He sat in a light wicker chair and carried little besides the fuel, a quart of water, a paper sack full of sandwiches, and a rubber raft. There was no parachute—it would be of no use over the ocean—and there was no radio. He would be on his own once he left the East Coast.

He headed out to sea, and people around the world learned of it on their radios. And then there was nothing to hear.

Lindbergh had to stay awake or crash. After eight or 10 hours of sitting in one place he began to doze. The night before the flight he had been so excited, and had had so much to do, that he had not slept at all. So he was tired before he got into the air. He got more tired, much more tired.

Luckily the plane was frail. It banged about in the wind, and each time he started to nod it went careening down toward the water. That woke him. Then, miraculously, the fatigue ended, he looked down, and there was Ireland. He was exactly where the charts he had drawn said he should be. Lindbergh, like Columbus, was a superb navigator.

He didn't know that his plane was spotted over Ireland and the news radioed to America and France. People cheered and wept with relief. He was seen over London, and then over the English Channel.

Charles Lindbergh, seated on the back of an open car, is honored with a traditional "ticker tape" parade in New York City. ▶

Thirty-three and a half hours after he left the United States, he circled the Eiffel Tower in Paris. It had taken less time than he expected, so he was worried that no one would be at the airport to meet him. Since he didn't speak French, he wondered how he would find his way from the airport into Paris. Then he looked down and saw a mob of people. They were waving and screaming.

The young flyer, who had brought nothing with him but the paper bag (which still had some sandwiches), was carried about on shoulders and hugged and kissed and cheered. He was rescued from the crowd only after his helmet was put on another American and the mob thought he was Lindbergh. Then the real Charles Lindbergh was taken to the American ambassador's house, where a butler ran his bath and put him to bed. Soon he was meeting kings and princes and more crowds of admirers. He wanted to stay in Europe and see the sights, but President Calvin Coolidge sent a naval cruiser to Europe just to carry him and the *Spirit of St. Louis* back to America. He was a world hero.

People lost their heads over Charles Lindbergh. All over America there were parades and dinners and celebrations for the man they called the "Lone Eagle." It was wild. Nothing quite like it had ever happened before. Why did people go so crazy over Lindbergh?

What he did was daring and brave. But others did daring things. What he did was important. But if he hadn't flown the ocean, someone else would have soon enough. There was more to it than that. The frantic, roaring world of the '20s needed a hero. Lindbergh turned out to be just what was wanted.

You see, he was decent. He didn't drink and he didn't smoke. He was modest. He had good manners. He was offered a great deal of money to pretend to smoke for an advertisement. He wouldn't do it.

▲ In 1922, Bessie Coleman became America's first licensed black pilot. Because of prejudice, she had to learn to fly in France.

In 1939, 12 years after Lucky Lindy's flight (that became Lindbergh's nickname), 22 passengers leave New York on the first commercial transatlantic flight. Their Pan American Airways Clipper has passenger compartments, sleeping berths, a dining room, and a bridal suite. The passengers each pay $375, and, with stops in the Azores and Portugal, it takes them 42 hours and 22 minutes to get to their destination: Marseilles, France.

He wouldn't do anything he didn't believe in. (Lindbergh was a genuine hero as long as he stuck to his specialty—flying. Later, when he got involved with politics, he was out of his league.)

A publisher offered to hire a ghost writer to help him write a book about his flight. He said he'd write it himself. And he did. He turned down many money-making opportunities. He had values and standards, and he didn't lose them.

In the Roaring Twenties, when many people thought only of having fun, or making money, or showing off, Lindbergh reminded people that courage, determination, and modesty were perhaps more satisfying. The American people had found a pretty good hero.

Amelia Earhart

Amelia Earhart was working at a settlement house in Boston in 1928 when she got a chance to be the first woman to cross the Atlantic in an airplane. She was just a passenger, but it made her a celebrity. In 1932 she flew the Atlantic herself, as Lindbergh had done. It was a big moment for women and for aviation. Then she decided to fly around the world. She wrote her husband, "I am quite aware of the hazards. I want to do it because I want to do it. Women must try to do things as men have tried." It was her last flight; she disappeared over the Pacific Ocean.

▲ Amelia Earhart

The Prosperity Balloon Bursts

Nineteen twenty-eight was an election year. Two good men were running for president. One was Herbert Hoover, an engineer and businessman, who had a reputation for accomplishing things. As a young college graduate, Hoover had managed a gold mine in the Australian desert and then gone to China as a mining expert. After that he got involved (successfully) with Burmese tin and Russian oil. He became known as a very capable man. When Woodrow Wilson needed someone to help feed Europe's starving people (during and after the First World War), he chose Herbert Hoover. He couldn't have found a better man for that job.

The other presidential candidate was the governor of New York. His name was Al Smith, and he was called the "Happy Warrior." Smith was colorful, full of fun, and honest and efficient, too. The governor introduced progressive reforms into New York State, appointed women and minorities to state jobs, and was fiscally responsible. (That means he did a good job with New York's budget.) The Happy Warrior was Catholic, Irish, and a New York City boy.

One of the reasons for reading history is to learn from past mistakes. Hoover's campaign was a mistake. Hoover didn't do bad things, but some of his supporters did.

◀ Herbert Hoover campaigned for the presidency in 1928, and he won—but, as he would soon find out, it was an unlucky year to win.

▲ One of Hoover's campaign slogans was "Continued Prosperity." The opposite turned out to be true.

They ran an anti-Catholic hate campaign. It was anti-city and anti-immigrant, too. The miserable Ku Klux Klan was still a powerful force in parts of America. Those are the people who put sheets over their heads and minds. They, and other hate groups, said that the only real Americans were those whose backgrounds were Protestant, English, and white. They said that Catholics, Jews, Asians, Arabs, Germans, Irish, Italians, blacks, and American Indians—of all people—were not real Americans. And then, on top of that, they said they didn't like city people. They said that if Al Smith got elected, the Catholic pope would be ruling America from Rome. Would you believe that nonsense?

Well, sadly, a whole lot of people did.

Hoover was elected by an enormous majority. Perhaps Americans would have chosen him anyway, but the mean-spiritedness of that election should not have happened.

Poor President Hoover. He didn't deserve the bad luck he had. He worked hard, yet his presidency was a disaster. But anyone elected in 1928 would have been in trouble.

No one understood that then. In 1928 most Americans were rejoicing. America seemed to have acquired King Midas's golden touch. (Although hardly anyone thought to remember what happened to Midas in the end.)

By 1928 the balloon of prosperity had been pumped so full of hot air that no one had ever seen anything quite like it. Many people were saying that something new had been found: an economic balloon that would just keep expanding. A few others were saying: "Stand back, cover your ears, and watch out."

In 1927, '28, and '29 it was easy to get rich. All you had to do was put a little money in the stock market. Then you could watch it turn into a whole lot of money. Here is how it worked.

Imagine that you are the owner of a large company: the ABC Automobile Company. You manufacture cars—good cars—and now you want to expand. You want to add new models. You need to build a new plant and buy a lot of equipment. You need money. So you decide to look for investors. You *go public*. You sell *shares* in your company. You sell 10,000 shares at $100 each. The shares are called "stock." Anyone who buys that stock becomes a part owner of the ABC Auto Company.

The new automobile models are a big success. The company earns a great deal of money. The stockholders get a percentage of the profits. The money they get is called a "dividend." The future of your company looks very good; many people want to buy stock in the ABC Company. Here is where a rule of economics, called *the law of supply and demand*, comes in. There are only 10,000 shares available. (That may sound like a lot, but it really isn't.) There is a big demand for ABC stock. People will pay $110 a share for it. Then they will pay $120 a share. Before long, ABC stock is selling for $200.

One stockholder, Mr. Jones, bought 10 shares at $100 each. (How much money did he spend?) Now he will sell them at $200 each. How much money will he have now? What is his profit?

Easy to make money that way, isn't it? In the '20s it was even easier. People bought stocks on *margin*. (That means they borrowed most of the money. Today, laws restrict margin buying.) Margin means you don't have to pay $100 for $100 worth of stock. In 1927, you could pay $10, and borrow the other $90 from the stockbroker. (The person who buys and sells stock for you is called a *stockbroker*.)

Now, if Mr. Jones puts $100 into ABC stock and buys on margin at 10 percent, he can have 10 shares instead of one. For $1,000, he will get 100 shares. If he sells the shares for $200 each, how much money will he have? He has to pay back the money he borrowed—$90 per share—but he still makes a whole lot of money. See if you can figure out how much. The good idea that many people soon had was to buy a lot of stock for very little money and get rich quickly.

The business of buying and selling stocks is called the "stock market." The place where stocks are bought and sold is called a "stock exchange." The most important stock exchange is in New York City, on Wall Street. Brokers from all over the world call Wall Street with orders to buy and sell.

The number of stockholders of American Telephone and Telegraph (AT&T) increased from 139,000 in 1920 to 567,000 in 1930. (That's *stockholders*, not shares of stock.)

Some companies issue millions of shares of stock. In 1997, IBM had 982,261,000 shares outstanding; Coca-Cola, 2,480,344,000. (Yes, that is more than 2 billion!)

▲ Traders check prices at the New York Stock Exchange. In 1928, a newspaper columnist wrote, "If buying and selling stocks is wrong, the government should close the Stock Exchange. If not, [it] should mind its own business."

The stock market usually reflects the business world. If things are going well, stocks go up. If business is poor, stocks go down. Brokers have a nickname for an "up" market. They call it a "bull" market. A down market is a "bear" market. The '20s were a prosperous time. Around 1924, the stock market started rising. At first it was a slow, moderate rise. Then the bulls got frisky.

In 1927, the market began to rise like fury. Almost overnight, stocks doubled and sometimes tripled in value. Everyone was talking about it. Newspapers wrote about it. Many politicians and business leaders were smiling and saying that the boom would just go on and on. Professors from the nation's great universities were saying the same thing.

Now, suppose you are living in 1927. All your friends are getting rich and you aren't. You feel like a dummy, don't you? Why don't you take all your savings and buy as many stocks as you can? Buy them on margin so you can get lots of shares for your money. That's the smart thing to do, say many business experts.

So that is just what you do—in July 1929. And some of your friends do it, too. The stock boom is phenomenal before July. That summer it is fantastic. Some people are buying stock in anything. It doesn't matter if the company has any real worth or not. No one seems to care. Just give me stock and more stock, I want to get rich. The stock balloon grows bigger and bigger and bigger.

And then guess what happens?

Picture a balloon being pumped up. Now watch that pin. You thought the balloon went up fast? Well, *whoosh,* it will come down much faster.

It happens in October of 1929. It is called the "panic." People go wild trying to sell. But now almost no one wants to buy.

▲ Crowds gather outside the New York Stock Exchange on the stock market's day of reckoning— October 24, 1929—known as "Black Thursday."

Remember that $100 stock you bought on margin for $10? Well, when the price drops, your broker sells it. Too bad—you lose your $10. No. It's worse than that.

You see, you owe $90 on that stock. Deduct from the $90 the price your broker gets when he sells the stock. You owe the rest. But you bought 100 shares of stock—or was it 1,000, or 10,000? You put all your savings into the stock market. The experts said that was the smart thing to do.

Sorry, you owe the money. You don't have any money? You can sell your house, or your car, or both.

You just lost your job, too? You worked at the ABC Auto Company. Oh, that's too bad. Most people have stopped buying cars. Now the company is losing money. It has to sell that beautiful new plant. Why doesn't it sell stock to try to raise money? Are you kidding? No one is buying stock now.

And you know about the banks, don't you? The banks are all in trouble, too. You see, the banks lent money to the brokers and all those people who were buying stocks. Now they have no money. They are closing their doors.

What is happening in America?

We're having a *depression*, that's what. It will go on for 10 years. People will be out of work. The country will be in terrible shape.

Years later, economic historians will look at the wild stock-market boom and the awful depression and say that they didn't have to happen. If there had been good leadership and sensible regulations, they could have been prevented. That's where greed gets you, they'll say. That's where out-of-date thinking gets you, they'll say.

But where were those economists when they were needed?

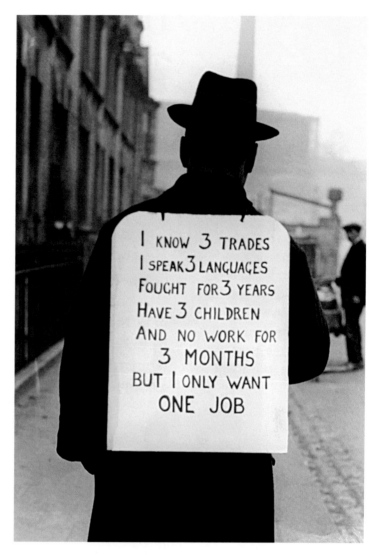

▲ After the stock market crash, many Americans were out of work.

The Securities and Exchange Commission (SEC), an independent government agency, was formed in 1934 to regulate securities (stocks and bonds) markets and investment businesses in the United States. Joseph P. Kennedy was its first chairman. Kennedy had a 17-year-old son, John Fitzgerald, with a big job in his future.

Down and Out

By 1932, at least 12 million people were out of work. That was one in four of all those who normally would work.

America had had depressions before. They were supposed to be a kind of self-regulating part of capitalism. All the early depressions had something in common: it was the poorest workers who were hurt. They lost their jobs. They went hungry. The wealthy and the middle class suffered only slightly.

The Great Depression (which is what it came to be called) was different. It hurt more people—rich and poor—than any previous depression. And it went on, and on, and on.

To begin, the census of 1920 had shown that for the first time more than half the nation was urban. (Cities in the 1920s were small by today's measures; still, they were a big change for people used to farm life.) This was the first major *urban* depression. City people have a terrible time without jobs or income.

A depression is a time of decline in business activity accompanied by falling prices and high unemployment. The Great Depression was a time of severe decline in business activity. Today, the government tries to regulate such drastic ups and downs.

During the Great Depression, unemployed workers wait in line outside a soup kitchen. ▶

Farmers don't have an easy time of it either, but at least they can usually feed themselves. America's farmers, as you remember, had not done well during the '20s. They didn't prosper with the rest of the nation. Crop prices stayed low. So the farmer's income was low, too. In 1929, most farms still didn't have electricity or indoor toilets. During the '30s, things got worse. The price of wheat and other grains dropped so low that it was sometimes below what it cost to grow it. Dairy farmers dumped thousands of gallons of milk onto the land to protest the low price of milk. Other farmers destroyed their own crops. All this waste was happening at a time when city children were hungry. Clearly, something was terribly wrong with our economic system.

Many bankers, brokers, and investors had been wild and irresponsible in the '20s. That irresponsibility caused great hardship in the decade that followed. The American farmer had been irresponsible for generations. Mostly, he hadn't known better, although he should have: European farmers had been practicing crop rotation for over a century.

But, beginning in Jamestown, American farmers had abused land. Farmers used up the fertile land and moved on. They cut down trees and

To *abuse* means to hurt or to treat carelessly.

U.S. Unemployment, 1929–1933

Unemployment rate (y-axis): 0%, 5%, 10%, 15%, 20%, 25%
Year (x-axis): 1929, 1930, 1931, 1932, 1933

Dust Bowl Days

The Dust Bowl is the name given to the region that was devastated by drought during the Depression years. It went from western Arkansas to the Oklahoma and Texas panhandles to New Mexico, Kansas, and Colorado and into Missouri. That area has little rainfall, light soil, and high winds. During World War I (when grain prices were high), farmers had plowed up thousands of acres of natural grassland to plant wheat. When drought struck (from 1934 to 1937), the soil lacked a grassy root system to hold it. Winds picked up the topsoil and turned it into black blizzards. Cattle choked and people fled. The government formed the Soil Conservation Service (in 1935) to teach farmers to terrace the land (to hold rainwater) and to plant trees and grass (to anchor the soil). Artists and writers such as Dorothea Lange, John Steinbeck, and Woody Guthrie photographed, wrote, and sang of the tragedy.

▲ A dust storm swirls around a farmer and his sons as they try to make their way to shelter.

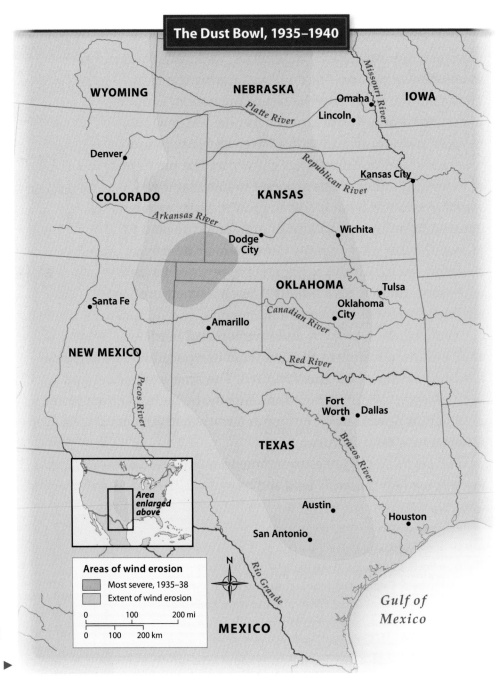

The Dust Bowl, 1935–1940

WYOMING

NEBRASKA

IOWA

Omaha

Lincoln

Platte River

Missouri River

Denver

Republican River

Kansas City

COLORADO

KANSAS

Arkansas River

Dodge City

Wichita

Santa Fe

OKLAHOMA

Tulsa

Oklahoma City

Canadian River

Amarillo

NEW MEXICO

Red River

Pecos River

Fort Worth

Dallas

Brazos River

TEXAS

Area enlarged above

Austin

Houston

San Antonio

Areas of wind erosion

Most severe, 1935–38

Extent of wind erosion

0   100   200 mi

0   100   200 km

N

Rio Grande

MEXICO

Gulf of Mexico

Erosion damaged or destroyed much of the farmland of the Great Plains during the 1930s. ▶

cut up the sod. It didn't have to happen. With careful farming, land can be preserved and enriched. For generations, however, there had seemed to be so much land that few people in America worried. They weren't prepared for nature's tricks: for the droughts and wind storms that came, dried up the land, and turned it to desert. Soil—good, rich topsoil— became dust. Much of the Great Plains just blew away. It was so bad that sailors at sea, 20 miles off the Atlantic coast, swept Oklahoma dust from

▲ In William Gropper's *Migration*, a desperate farm family heads west, carrying their few belongings. More than 3 million people left the Great Plains during the 1930s.

This Hooverville in Seattle was home to thousands of "forgotten" men, women, and children. ▶

the decks of their ships. For drought-stricken farmers, there was nothing to do but leave the land, head for a city, and hope to find a job.

But there were no jobs to be found in the cities. City people were moving in with relatives on family farms.

But many people had no relatives able to take them in and no place to go. Some built shacks out of old boxes and boards on some land near a garbage dump. Hundreds were soon camped in such unhealthy places all over the nation. People call these shanty towns "Hoovervilles," after the president, who says he is trying hard to solve the problem of the homeless and hungry. But nothing he does seems to help. By 1933, a million people in America are living in Hoovervilles.

▲ Photographer Dorothea Lange took this picture in Oklahoma in 1936. It was originally captioned, "People living in miserable poverty."

The Depression was a terrible spiral. Many people were so poor that they stopped buying goods altogether. If people didn't buy goods, manufacturers couldn't make them. So workers couldn't get work, and they, too, couldn't buy anything. So more and more people became poorer and poorer.

Economic Disaster

In 1930, Herbert Hoover made this optimistic claim: "We have now passed the worst and with continued unity of effort shall rapidly recover."

In 1932, he said, "We shall soon with the help of God be within sight of the day when poverty will be banished from the nation." President Hoover seems to have believed the Depression was over. He said the economy was "fundamentally sound." And he said no one was starving in America.

Well, he was wrong about all those things. All he had to do was look out the windows of the White House and he would have seen hungry people. Thousands of veterans of the First World War were camped in the center of Washington, D.C. They were without jobs.

Congress had voted them a bonus for their war service. The bonus was not due to be paid until 1945, but these were difficult times. The men needed the bonus now.

So they marched to Washington to see the president. Some brought their families. They built a Hooverville in Washington, D.C. They had no jobs or money, so they slept in tents, in empty buildings, in shacks on public grass. There were said to be 20,000 of them. They were called the "Bonus Army." Most carried American flags. Some were Medal of Honor winners; some had lost arms or legs in the services. Hoover wouldn't see any of them.

The police asked them to leave. They wouldn't go. So President Hoover sent the army. When the former soldiers first saw the army patrols and tanks and cavalry, they cheered. They thought the troops were parading for them. That was a mistake. The troops came with tear gas, guns, and

The Bonus Army—made up of unemployed World War I veterans seeking early payment of a bonus awarded them in 1924 —camps out on the U.S. Capitol lawn in July 1932. ▼

◀ The Bonus Army's shantytown burns down within sight of the Capitol. Millions watched it on movie newsreels.

bayonets. Their leader, General Douglas MacArthur, went farther than the president wished. His troops tore down the shacks; they used tear gas and billy clubs. People were hurt; a baby died. When it was over, Hoover said he saved the country from mob action. But many Americans hung their heads in shame.

Hoover never understood. Each night he and Mrs. Hoover dressed formally for dinner—in tuxedo and long gown—and were served seven-course dinners by a large staff. Soldiers stood at attention around the table. Hoover thought about cutting down on White House expenditures, he said, but then decided that it would not be good for the people's morale. (Do you think the people agreed?)

Hoover didn't understand the needs of ordinary people. In 1930, when many Americans were going to bed hungry, he said, "The lesson should be constantly enforced that though the people support the government, the government should not support the people." He also said, "I do not believe that the power and duty of the general government ought to be extended to the relief of individual suffering."

This cartoon depicts a well-fed President Hoover watching the march of the Bonus Army. ▼

▲ Adolf Hitler,
Chancellor of Germany

What Hoover meant was that no government money should be spent on relief programs. He thought people could help themselves. If government money was spent it should go to business. That would strengthen the economy, he said, and business money would "trickle down" to the people. Many economists believed as he did.

Hoover believed in *voluntarism*; he thought individuals should help each other. It was a good idea, and there was a lot of neighborliness during the Depression, but it wasn't enough. More needed to be done, much more, or there might be a revolution.

Hoover was scared, and so were many other leaders. Democracy and capitalism seemed to be failing. Some people—who were considered to be sound thinkers—were saying that our system was finished. A new day was dawning, they said, and American democracy was out of date. All over the world the disruptions of war and depression were making people turn to dictators. Mussolini had taken control in Italy; Adolf Hitler was gaining power in Germany; and Joseph Stalin was in control in Soviet Russia. Some people in the United States thought those leaders were great men. We now know that they were terrible, bloodthirsty tyrants, but we are historians. We have the advantage of hindsight. We know how things came out. People in 1932 didn't know that.

Charles Lindbergh went to Germany and reported that Hitler was a fine leader. Wisconsin's governor, Philip LaFollette, was an admirer of Mussolini. Many intellectuals were fascinated with communism. They weren't the only ones. Senator Theodore Bilbo of Mississippi said, "I'm getting a little pink [communist] myself." The nation's favorite humorist, Will Rogers, said, "Those rascals in Russia...have got mighty good ideas...just think of everybody in a country going to work."

Mussolini said, "Democracy is sand driven by the wind." Were the democratic ideals of George Washington, Thomas Jefferson, and Abraham Lincoln truly out of date?

Benito Mussolini
of Italy ▶

◀ Soviet Russia's
Joseph Stalin

APPENDIX:
SOME PRIMARY
SOURCES

Chief Joseph (Hin-mah-too-yah-lat-kekht), "I Will Fight No More Forever": Speech to the U.S. Army (1877)

In 1877, the U.S. government ordered the Nez Perce Indians, then living in eastern Oregon's Wallowa valley, to move to a reservation in Idaho. Several bands, including one led by Chief Joseph, refused to move. Meanwhile, several Nez Perce youth, angered by broken treaty promises, attacked and killed 18 Idaho settlers. For three months in the summer and fall of 1877, the U.S. cavalry and infantry pursued Chief Joseph and 800 of his followers, who were headed toward Canada—and safety. They eluded and outfought 2,000 Army soldiers in 13 battles before finally surrendering in a Montana snowstorm, just 40 miles from the Canadian border. Only 418 men, women, and children survived.

On October 5, Chief Joseph, leader of the Nez Perce, rode up to the American soldiers who had chased his people across 1,200 miles of rugged lands in Idaho, Montana, and Wyoming. He surrendered to them with the stirring words, "From where the sun now stands I will fight no more forever."

> Tell General Howard I know his heart. What he told me before, I have it in my heart. I am tired of fighting. Our chiefs are killed. Looking Glass is dead. Toohoolhoolzote is dead. The old men are all dead. It is the young men who say, "Yes" or "No." He who led the young men is dead. It is cold, and we have no blankets. The little children are freezing to death. My people, some of them, have run away to the hills, and have no blankets, no food. No one knows where they are—perhaps freezing to death. I want to have time to look for my children, and see how many of them I can find. Maybe I shall find them among the dead. Hear me, my chiefs! I am tired. My heart is sick and sad. From where the sun now stands I will fight no more forever.

The Pledge of Allegiance

(1892, revised 1923 and 1954)

The Pledge of Allegiance first appeared in 1892 in *The Youth's Companion*, a popular children's magazine. It was written to commemorate the 400th anniversary of Columbus's discovery of the New World and to unite Americans during a time of massive immigration. We are not sure whether the pledge was written by James B. Upsham (the magazine's editor), Francis Bellamy (an ordained minister), or a combination of the two men. Upsham said that he was inspired to write the pledge after reading a newspaper editorial criticizing flag-raising ceremonies. The editor said that the ceremonies were no more than "worship of a textile fabric." He was convinced that the pledge children said at the time—"I give my hand and heart to my country, one nation, one language, one flag"—was not stirring enough and that the country needed a more impressive pledge.

The pledge has been changed twice over the years. In 1923, the words "the flag of the United States of America" was substituted for "my flag," and Congress added the phrase "under God" in 1954. There has also been a change in the salute to the flag. Originally, people saluted the flag by raising their right arms upward. But to distinguish their show of respect to the flag from the Nazi salute, Americans began to place their right hands over their hearts.

defer: to hold back for a time

> I pledge allegiance
> To the flag of the United States of America
> And to the republic for which it stands,
> One nation under God,
> Indivisible, with liberty and justice for all.

From Booker T. Washington, Address at the Atlanta Exposition (1895)

In a 10-minute speech delivered on a hot September afternoon at the Cotton States Exposition in Atlanta, Booker T. Washington urged African Americans to accept social segregation as the price for acquiring education and economic security. He argued that northern industrialists should be urged to invest in the South and that African Americans should share in the economic growth that northern investment would bring. In return, African Americans should abandon, at least temporarily, the quest for full political and civil rights. "In all things purely social," he explained, "we can be as separate as the fingers, yet as the hand in all things essential to mutual progress." In his speech, Washington opposed labor unions and foreign immigration. He argued that these were not in the interests of African Americans.

W. E. B. DuBois, the nation's first black to earn a doctoral degree, condemned Washington for failing to speak out publicly for racial equality. But in secret, Washington fought lynching and financed court tests of laws that upheld segregation and bars to black voting.

Mr. President and Gentlemen of the Board of Directors and Citizens:

One-third of the population of the South is of the Negro race. No enterprise seeking the material, civil, or moral welfare of this section can disregard this element of our population and reach the highest success. I but convey to you, Mr. President and directors, the sentiment of the masses of my race when I say that in no way have the value and manhood of the American Negro been more fittingly and generously recognized than by the managers of this magnificent exposition at every stage of its progress. It is a recognition that will do more to cement the friendship of the two races than any occurrence since the dawn of our freedom.

Not only this, but the opportunity here afforded will awaken among us a new era of industrial progress. Ignorant and inexperienced, it is not strange that in the first years of our new life we began at the top instead of at the bottom; that a seat in Congress or the state legislature was more sought than real estate or industrial skill; that the political convention or stump speaking had more attractions than starting a dairy farm or truck garden.

enterprise: undertaking

convey: express

sentiment: feeling

stump speaking: traveling around and giving speeches

truck garden: garden for growing vegetables that are put on trucks and sold in the city

A ship lost at sea for many days suddenly sighted a friendly vessel. From the mast of the unfortunate vessel was seen a signal, "Water, water; we die of thirst!" The answer from the friendly vessel at once came back, "Cast down your bucket where you are." And a third and fourth signal for water was answered, "Cast down your bucket where you are." The captain of the distressed vessel, at last heeding the injunction, cast down his bucket, and it came up full of fresh, sparkling water from the mouth of the Amazon River. To those of my race who depend on bettering their condition in a foreign land or who underestimate the importance of cultivating friendly relations with the Southern white man, who is their next-door neighbor, I would say: "Cast down your bucket where you are"—cast it down in making friends in every manly way of the people of all races by whom we are surrounded.

Cast it down in agriculture, mechanics, in commerce, in domestic service, and in the professions. And in this connection it is well to bear in mind that whatever other sins the South may be called to bear, when it comes to business, pure and simple, it is in the South that the Negro is given a man's chance in the commercial world, and in nothing is this exposition more eloquent than in emphasizing this chance. Our greatest danger is that in the great leap from slavery to freedom we may overlook the fact that the masses of us are to live by the productions of our hands, and fail to keep in mind that we shall prosper in proportion as we learn to dignify and glorify common labor and put brains and skill into the common occupations of life; shall prosper in proportion as we learn to draw the line between the superficial and the substantial, the ornamental gew-gaws of life and the useful. No race can prosper till it learns that there is as much dignity in tilling a field as in writing a poem. It is at the bottom of life we must begin, and not at the top. Nor should we permit our grievances to overshadow our opportunities.

To those of the white race who look to the incoming of those of foreign birth and strange tongue and habits for the

superficial: unimportant

substantial: important

gew-gaws: worthless things

prosperity of the South, were I permitted I would repeat what I say to my own race, "Cast down your bucket where you are." Cast it down among the eight millions of Negroes whose habits you know, whose fidelity and love you have tested in days when to have proved treacherous meant the ruin of your firesides. Cast down your bucket among these people who have, without strikes and labor wars, tilled your fields, cleared your forests, built your railroads and cities, and brought forth treasures from the bowels of the earth, and helped make possible this magnificent representation of the progress of the South. Casting down your bucket among my people, helping and encouraging them as you are doing on these grounds, and to education of head, hand, and heart, you will find that they will buy your surplus land, make blossom the waste places in your fields, and run your factories. While doing this, you can be sure in the future, as in the past, that you and your families will be surrounded by the most patient, faithful, law-abiding, and unresentful people that the world has seen. As we have proved our loyalty to you in the past, in nursing your children, watching by the sick-bed of your mothers and fathers, and often following them with tear-dimmed eyes to their graves, so in the future, in our humble way, we shall stand by you with a devotion that no foreigner can approach, ready to lay down our lives, if need be, in defense of yours, interlacing our industrial, commercial, civil, and religious life with yours in a way that shall make the interests of both races one. In all things that are purely social we can be as separate as the fingers, yet one as the hand in all things essential to mutual progress.

There is no defense or security for any of us except in the highest intelligence and development of all. If anywhere there are efforts tending to curtail the fullest growth of the Negro, let these efforts be turned into stimulating, encouraging, and making him the most useful and intelligent citizen. Effort or means so invested will pay a thousand percent interest. These efforts will be twice blessed—""blessing him that gives and him that takes." …

fidelity: faith

treacherous: unreliable, deceitful

bowels: depths

surplus: extra, unneeded

The wisest among my race understand that the agitation of questions of social equality is the extreme folly, and that progress in the enjoyment of all the privileges that will come to us must be the result of severe and constant struggle rather than of artificial forcing. No race that has anything to contribute to the markets of the world is long in any degree ostracized. It is important and right that all privileges of the law be ours, but it is vastly more important that we be prepared for the exercises of these privileges. The opportunity to earn a dollar in a factory just now is worth infinitely more that the opportunity to spend a dollar in an opera house.

In conclusion, may I repeat that nothing in thirty years has given us more hope and encouragement, and drawn us so near to you of the white race, as this opportunity offered by the exposition; and here bending, as it were, over the altar that represents the results of the struggles of your race and mine, both starting practically empty-handed three decades ago, I pledge that in your effort to work out the great and intricate problem which God has laid at the doors of the South, you shall have at all times the patient, sympathetic help of my race; only let this be constantly in mind, that, while from representations in these buildings of the product of the field, of forest, of mine, of factory, letters, and art, much good will come, yet far above and beyond material benefits will be that higher good, that, let us pray God, will come, in a blotting out of sectional differences and racial animosities and suspicions, in a determination to administer absolute justice, in a willing obedience among all classes to the mandates of the law. This, this, coupled with our material prosperity, will bring into our beloved South a new heaven and a new earth.

ostracized: left out

intricate: complicated

material: touchable, real

animosities: discord, hostilities

From John Marshall Harlan, dissenting opinion in *Plessy v. Ferguson* (1896)

In 1896, the Supreme Court declared that racial segregation was acceptable under the Constitution. In *Plessy v. Ferguson* the court upheld a Louisiana law that required railroads operating within the state to provide "separate but equal" accommodations for blacks and whites. The law also required people to ride in railroad cars assigned to them by race. The case involved Homer Plessy, who was one-eighth Negro and who had sat in a whites-only railroad car. He was arrested and the U.S. Supreme Court eventually upheld Louisiana's law by a 7-to-1 vote. The majority ruled that the the 13th Amendment, which abolished all vestiges of slavery, and the 14th Amendment, which guarantees "equal protection of the laws," did not prohibit "distinction based on color." This decision provided the legal basis for segregation for nearly six decades, until the Supreme Court rejected the "separate but equal" doctrine in 1954 in the case of *Brown v. Board of Education*.

ineffectual: unable to perform well

The dissenting vote was cast by John Marshall Harlan, the son of a Kentucky slaveholder. "There is in this country no superior, dominant, ruling class of citizens," he wrote in an angry dissent. "Our Constitution is color-blind...." His grandson and namesake, John Marshall Harlan II, was one of the justices who overturned the Plessy decision and ruled that attempts to segregate public schools were unconstitutional.

> I deny that any legislative body or judicial tribunal may have regard to the race of citizens when the civil rights of those citizens are involved. Indeed, such legislation as that here in question is inconsistent not only with that equality of rights which pertains to citizenship, national and state, but with the personal liberty enjoyed by every one within the United States.
>
> The thirteenth amendment does not permit the withholding or the deprivation of any right necessarily inhering in freedom. It not only struck down the institution of slavery as previously existing in the United States, but it prevents the imposition of any burdens or disabilities that constitute badges of slavery or servitude. It decreed universal civil freedom in this country. This court has so adjudged. But, that amendment having been found inadequate to the protection of the rights of those who had been in slavery, it was followed by the fourteenth amendment, which added greatly to the dignity and glory of American citizenship,

imposition: unfair requirements

decreed: declared

and to the security of personal liberty, by declaring that "all persons born or naturalized in the United States, and subject to the jurisdiction thereof, are citizens of the United States and of the state wherein they reside," and that "no state shall make or enforce any law which shall abridge the privileges or immunities of citizens of the United States; nor shall any state deprive any person of life, liberty or property without due process of law, nor deny to any person within its jurisdiction the equal protection of the laws." These two amendments, if enforced according to their true intent and meaning, will protect all the civil rights that pertain to freedom and citizenship. Finally, and to the end that no citizen should be denied, on account of his race, the privilege of participating in the political control of his country, it was declared in the fifteenth amendment that "the rights of citizens of the United States to vote shall not be denied or abridged by the United States or by any state on account of race, color or previous condition of service."

> *jurisdiction:* area over which an authority has power

These notable additions to the fundamental law were welcomed by friends of liberty throughout the world. They removed the race line from our governmental systems. They had, as this court has said, a common purpose, namely, to secure "to a race recently emancipated, a race that through many generations have been held in slavery, all the civil rights that the superior race enjoy." They declared, in legal effect, this court has further said, "that the law in the states shall be the same for the black as for the white; that all persons, whether colored or white, shall stand equal before the laws of the states; and in regard to the colored race, for whose protection the amendment was primarily designed, that no discrimination shall be made against them by law because of their color."…

It was said that the statute of Louisiana does not discriminate against either race, but prescribes a rule applicable alike to white and colored citizens. But this argument does not meet the difficulty. Every one knows that the statute in question had its origin in the purpose, not so much to

> *prescribes:* establishes
>
> *applicable:* relevant, appropriate
>
> *statute:* law

exclude white persons from railroad cars occupied by blacks, as to exclude colored people from coaches occupied by or assigned to white persons. Railroad corporations of Louisiana did not make discrimination among whites in the matter of commodation for travelers. The thing to accomplish was, under the guise of giving equal accommodation for whites and blacks, to compel the latter to keep to themselves while traveling in railroad passenger coaches. If a white man and a black man choose to occupy the same public conveyance on a public highway, it is their right to do so; and no government, proceeding alone on grounds of race, can prevent it without infringing the personal liberty of each.

It is one thing for railroad carriers to furnish, or to be required by law to furnish, equal accommodations for all whom they are under a legal duty to carry. It is quite another thing for government to forbid citizens of the white and black races from traveling in the same public conveyance, and to punish officers of railroad companies for permitting persons of the two races to occupy the same passenger coach. If a state can prescribe…that whites and blacks shall not travel as passengers in the same railroad coach, why may it not so regulate the use of the streets of its cities and towns as to compel white citizens to keep on one side of a street, and black citizens to keep on the other? Why may it not…punish whites and blacks who ride together in street cars or in open vehicles on a public road or street? Why may it not require sheriffs to assign whites to one side of a court room, and blacks to the other? And why may it not also prohibit the commingling of the two races in the galleries of legislative halls or in public assemblages convened for the consideration of the political questions of the day? Further…why may not the state require the separation in railroad coaches of native and naturalized citizens of the United States, or of Protestants and Roman Catholics?…

The white race deems itself to be the dominant race in this country. And so it is, in prestige, in achievements, in education, in wealth, and in power. So, I doubt not, it will continue to be for all time, if it remains true to its great heritage, and holds

coaches: railroad cars

guise: disguise, deceptive appearance

compel: force

conveyance: vehicle

assemblages: gatherings

fast to the principles of constitutional liberty. But in view of the constitution, in the eye of the law, there is in this country no superior, dominant, ruling class of citizens. In respect of civil rights, all citizens are equal before the law. The humblest is the peer of the most powerful. The law regards man as man, and takes no account of his surroundings or of his color when his civil rights as guarantied by the supreme law of the land are involved. It is therefore to be regretted that this high tribunal… has reached the conclusion that it is competent for a state to regulate the enjoyment of citizens of their civil rights solely upon the basis of race.

tribunal: court

In my opinion, the judgment this day rendered will, in time, prove to be quite as pernicious as the decision made by this tribunal in the Dred Scott case…. The present decision… will not only stimulate aggressions, more or less brutal and irritating, upon the admitted rights of colored citizens, but will encourage the belief that it is possible, by means of state enactments, to defeat the beneficent purposes which the people of the United States had in view when they adopted the recent amendments of the constitution, by one of which the blacks of this country were made citizens of the United States and of the states in which they respectively reside…. Sixty millions of whites are in no danger from the presence here of eight millions of blacks. The destinies of the two races, in this country, are indissolubly linked together, and the interests of both require that the common government of all shall not permit the seeds of race hate to be planted under the sanction of law. What can more certainly arouse race hate, what more certainly create and perpetuate a feeling of distrust between these races, than state enactments which, in fact, proceed on the ground that colored citizens are so inferior and degraded that they cannot be allowed to sit in public coaches occupied by white citizens? That, as all will admit, is the real meaning of such legislation as was enacted in Louisiana.

pernicious: harmful in its effects

beneficent: well intended

indissolubly: unable to break apart

enactments: laws

The sure guaranty of the peace and security of each race is the clear, distinct, unconditional recognition by our governments…of every right that inheres in civil freedom,

inheres: exists naturally

and of the equality before the law of all citizens of the United States, without regard to race. State enactments regulating the enjoyment of civil rights upon the basis of race, and cunningly devised to defeat legitimate results of the [Civil War], under the pretense of recognizing equality of rights, can have no other result than to render permanent peace impossible, and to keep alive a conflict of races, the continuance of which must do harm to all concerned....

arbitrary: random, without reason

The arbitrary separation of citizens, on the basis of race, while they are on a public highway, is a badge of servitude wholly inconsistent with the civil freedom and the equality before the law established by the constitution. It cannot be justified on any legal grounds.... We boast of the freedom enjoyed by our people above all other peoples. But it is difficult to reconcile that boast with a state of the law which, practically, puts the brand of servitude and degradation upon a large class of our fellow citizens,—our equals before the law. The thin disguise of "equal" accommodations for passengers in railroad coaches will not mislead any one, not atone for the wrong this day done....

atone: make up for

I am of opinion that the state of Louisiana is inconsistent with the personal liberty of citizens, white and black, in that state, and hostile to the spirit and letter of the constitution of the United States. If laws of like character should be enacted in the several states of the Union, the effect would be in the highest degree mischievous. Slavery, as an institution tolerated by law, would, it is true, have disappeared from our country; but there would remain a power in the states, by sinister legislation, to interfere with the full enjoyment of the blessings of freedom, to regulate civil rights, common to all citizens, upon the basis of race, and to place in a condition of legal inferiority a large body of American citizens, now constituting a part of the political community, called the "People of the United States," for whom, and by whom through representatives, our government is administered....

sinister: having harmful intentions

Woodrow Wilson, "The Fourteen Points": Address to Congress (1918)

The Fourteen Points were a set of principles proposed by President Woodrow Wilson in 1918 as the basis for ending World War I and for preserving world peace. Convinced that a harsh peace treaty would be the basis of future wars, Wilson opposed stripping Germany of territory or imposing reparations (huge financial penalties) on the losers. To ensure future economic prosperity, he called for free trade and freedom on the seas. He also recognized the growth of nationalism by calling for the right of all people to national self-determination, the freedom to determine their own form of government. Finally, to preserve peace, President Wilson called for open diplomacy, arms reduction, and an international organization to solve disputes between nations.

Peace forces within Germany agreed to surrender on the basis of the Fourteen Points. In 1918, a brief revolution in Germany forced the kaiser to step down. Yet despite promises of a just peace, Wilson was unable to win support for his Fourteen Points. The treaty ending World War I imposed a harsh settlement. It required Germany to pay $34 billion in reparations, far more than it could afford. In addition, Germany was stripped of territories where many ethnic Germans lived and had to accept blame for causing the war.

Gentlemen of the Congress:

...It will be our wish and purpose that the processes of peace, when they are begun, shall be absolutely open and that they shall involve and permit henceforth no secret understandings of any kind. The day of conquest and aggrandizement is gone by; so is also the day of secret covenants entered into in the interest of particular governments and likely at some unlooked-for moment to upset the peace of the world. It is this happy fact, now clear to the view of every public man whose thoughts do not still linger in an age that is dead and gone, which makes it possible for every nation whose purposes are consistent with justice and the peace of the world to avow now or at any other time the objects it has in view.

henceforth: from now on

conquest: military victory

aggrandizement: growing more powerful by exploiting others

covenants: agreements

We entered this war because violations of right had occurred which touched us to the quick and made the life of our own people impossible unless they were corrected and the world secured once for all against their recurrence. What we demand in this war, therefore, is nothing peculiar to ourselves. It is that the world be made fit and safe to live in; and particularly that it be made safe for every peace-loving nation which, like our own, wishes to live its own life, determine its own institutions, be assured of justice and fair dealing by the other peoples of the world as against force and selfish aggression. All the peoples of the world are in effect partners in this interest, and for our own part we see very clearly that unless justice be done to others it will not be done to us. The program of the world's peace, therefore, is our program; and that program, the only possible program, as we see it, is this:

I. Open covenants of peace, openly arrived at, after which there shall be no private international understandings of any kind but diplomacy shall proceed always frankly and in the public view.

II. Absolute freedom of navigation upon the seas, outside territorial waters, alike in peace and in war, except as the seas may be closed in whole or in part by international action for the enforcement of international covenants.

III. The removal, so far as possible, of all economic barriers and the establishment of an equality of trade conditions among all the nations consenting to the peace and associating themselves for its maintenance.

IV. Adequate guarantees given and taken that national armaments will be reduced to the lowest point consistent with domestic safety.

V. A free, open-minded, and absolutely impartial adjustment of all colonial claims, based upon a strict observance of the principle that in determining all such questions of sovereignty the interests of the

frankly: honestly

territorial waters: the first few miles of the ocean, closest to the shore, that belong to a country

economic barriers: ways that governments control the flow of goods in and out of their borders

national armaments: weapons held by a country

impartial: fair

colonial: involving people or a territory ruled by another, stronger power

populations concerned must have equal weight with the equitable claims of the government whose title is to be determined.

VI. The evacuation of all Russian territory and such a settlement of all questions affecting Russia as will secure the best and freest cooperation of the other nations of the world in obtaining for her an unhampered and unembarrassed opportunity for the independent determination of her own political development and national policy and assure her of a sincere welcome into the society of free nations under institutions of her own choosing; and, more than a welcome, assistance also of every kind that she may need and may herself desire. The treatment accorded Russia by her sister nations in the months to come will be the acid test of their good will, of their comprehension of her needs as distinguished from their own interests, and of their intelligent and unselfish sympathy.

evacuation: removal of an occupying force

unhampered: free

acid test: a test that absolutely proves something, beyond doubt

VII. Belgium, the whole world will agree, must be evacuated and restored, without any attempt to limit the sovereignty which she enjoys in common with all other free nations. No other single act will serve as this will serve to restore confidence among the nations in the laws which they have themselves set and determined for the government of their relations with one another. Without this healing act the whole structure and validity of international law is forever impaired.

sovereignty: rule

validity: truth

VIII. All French territory should be freed and the invaded portions restored, and the wrong done to France by Prussia in 1871 in the matter of Alsace-Lorraine, which has unsettled the peace of the world for nearly fifty years, should be righted, in order that peace may once more be made secure in the interest of all.

IX. A readjustment of the frontiers of Italy should be effected along clearly recognizable lines of nationality.

nationality: national origin

automomous: independent

counsel: advice, diplomacy

integrity: wholeness

unmolested: unbothered

free passage: a waterway through which ships can travel without having to present documents or pay taxes

erected: built

indisputably: unarguably

mutual: affecting both sides equally

rectifications: rightings

Imperialists: governments trying to establish empires

X. The peoples of Austria-Hungary, whose place among the nations we wish to see safeguarded and assured, should be accorded the freest opportunity of autonomous development.

XI. Rumania, Serbia, and Montenegro should be evacuated; occupied territories restored; Serbia accorded free and secure access to the sea; and the relations of the several Balkan states to one another determined by friendly counsel along historically established lines of allegiance and nationality; and international guarantees of the political and economic independence and territorial integrity of the several Balkan states should be entered into.

XII. The Turkish portions of the present Ottoman Empire should be assured a secure sovereignty, but the other nationalities which are now under Turkish rule should be assured an undoubted security of life and an absolutely unmolested opportunity of autonomous development, and the Dardanelles should be permanently opened as a free passage to the ships and commerce of all nations under inter national guarantees.

XIII. An independent Polish state should be erected which should include the territories inhabited by indisputably Polish populations, which should be assured a free and secure access to the sea, and whose political and economic independence and territorial integrity should be guaranteed by international covenant.

XIV. A general association of nations must be formed under specific covenants for the purpose of affording mutual guarantees of political independence and territorial integrity to great and small states alike.

In regard to these essential rectifications of wrong and assertions of right we feel ourselves to be intimate partners of all the governments and peoples associated together against the Imperialists. We cannot be separated in interest or divided in purpose. We stand together until the end.

For such arrangements and covenants we are willing to fight and to continue to fight until they are achieved; but only because we wish the right to prevail and desire a just and stable peace such as can be secured only by removing the chief provocations to war, which this program does not remove. We have no jealousy of German greatness, and there is nothing in this program that impairs it. We grudge her no achievement or distinction of learning or of pacific enterprise such as have made her record very bright and very enviable. We do not wish to injure her or to block in any way her legitimate influence or power. We do not wish to fight her either with arms or with hostile arrangements of trade if she is willing to associate herself with us and the other peace-loving nations of the world in covenants of justice and law and fair dealing. We wish her only to accept a place of equality among the peoples of the world—the new world in which we now live—instead of a place of mastery.

prevail: win

provocations: reasons

impairs: harms

distinction of learning: feat of scholarship

pacific: peaceful

enviable: admirable

hostile: unfriendly

Neither do we presume to suggest to her any alteration or modification of her institutions. But it is necessary, we must frankly say, and necessary as a preliminary to any intelligent dealings with her on our part, that we should know whom her spokesmen speak for when they speak to us, whether for the Reichstag majority or for the military party and the men whose creed is imperial domination.

presume: try

modification: change

We have spoken now, surely, in terms too concrete to admit of any further doubt or question. An evident principle runs through the whole program I have outlined. It is the principle of justice to all peoples and nationalities, and their right to live on equal terms of liberty and safety with one another, whether they be strong or weak. Unless this principle be made its foundation no part of the structure of international justice can stand. The people of the United States could act upon no other principle; and to the vindication of this principle they are ready to devote their lives, their honor, and everything that they possess. The moral climax of this the culminating and final war for human liberty has come, and they are ready to put their own strength, their own highest purpose, their own integrity and devotion to the test.

Reichstag: German parliament from 1867 to 1945

creed: set of beliefs

vindication: proving the moral correctness

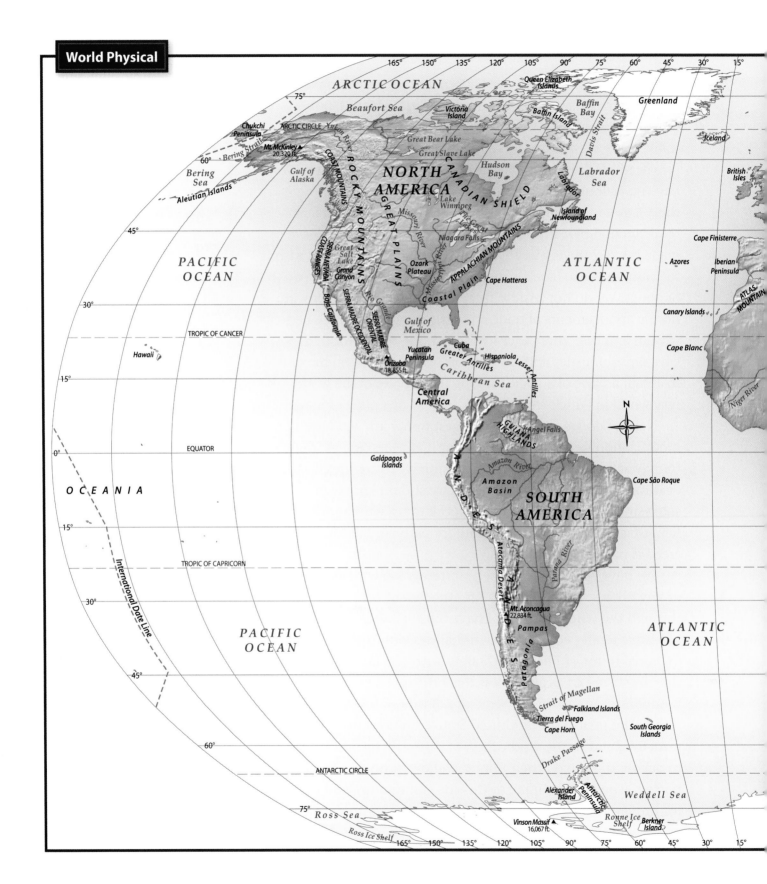

ARCTIC OCEAN

Beaufort Sea

Queen Elizabeth Islands

Greenland

Victoria Island

Baffin Island

Baffin Bay

Chukchi Peninsula

ARCTIC CIRCLE

Great Bear Lake

Great Slave Lake

Davis Strait

Iceland

Bering Strait

Mt. McKinley 20,320 ft.

Bering Sea

Gulf of Alaska

COAST MOUNTAINS

ROCKY MOUNTAINS

NORTH AMERICA

CANADIAN SHIELD

Hudson Bay

Labrador Sea

Labrador

British Isles

Aleutian Islands

Lake Winnipeg

Island of Newfoundland

PACIFIC OCEAN

GREAT PLAINS

Missouri River

Great Salt Lake

Grand Canyon

SIERRA NEVADA

COAST RANGES

Ozark Plateau

Mississippi River

Niagara Falls

APPALACHIAN MOUNTAINS

Cape Hatteras

ATLANTIC OCEAN

Cape Finisterre

Azores

Iberian Peninsula

ATLAS MOUNTAINS

TROPIC OF CANCER

SIERRA MADRE OCCIDENTAL

Rio Grande

SIERRA MADRE ORIENTAL

Baja California

Gulf of Mexico

Coastal Plain

Canary Islands

Cape Blanc

Hawaii

Yucatan Peninsula

Orizaba 18,855 ft.

Cuba

Greater Antilles

Hispaniola

Lesser Antilles

Caribbean Sea

Central America

Niger River

EQUATOR

Galápagos Islands

GUIANA HIGHLANDS

Angel Falls

Amazon River

Cape São Roque

N

OCEANIA

Amazon Basin

SOUTH AMERICA

ANDES

TROPIC OF CAPRICORN

Atacama Desert

Parana River

International Date Line

Mt. Aconcagua 22,834 ft.

Pampas

ATLANTIC OCEAN

PACIFIC OCEAN

Patagonia

Strait of Magellan

Falkland Islands

Tierra del Fuego

Cape Horn

South Georgia Islands

ANTARCTIC CIRCLE

Drake Passage

Alexander Island

Antarctic Peninsula

Weddell Sea

Ross Sea

Vinson Massif 16,067 ft.

Ronne Ice Shelf

Berkner Island

Ross Ice Shelf

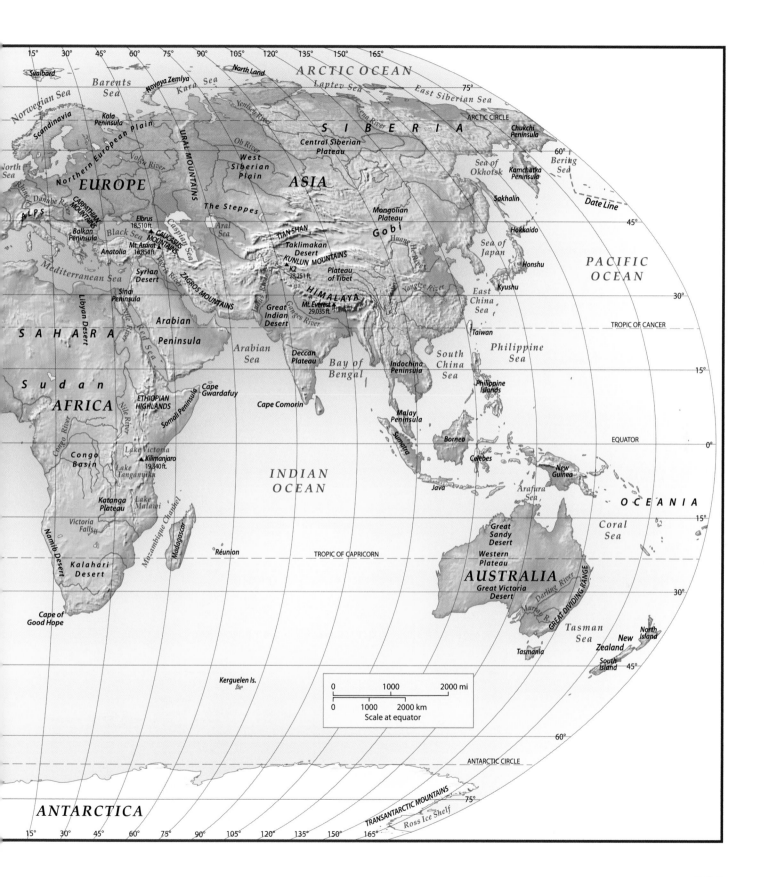

ARCTIC OCEAN

Svalbard
Barents Sea
Novaya Zemlya
Kara Sea
North Land
Laptev Sea
East Siberian Sea
75°
Norwegian Sea
Scandinavia
Kola Peninsula
Northern European Plain
Yenisei River
S I B E R I A
ARCTIC CIRCLE
Chukchi Peninsula
North Sea
Ob River
Central Siberian Plateau
60°
Bering Sea
EUROPE
URAL MOUNTAINS
West Siberian Plain
A S I A
Sea of Okhotsk
Kamchatka Peninsula
Lena River
Danube R.
The Steppes
Mongolian Plateau
Sakhalin
Date Line
ALPS
CARPATHIAN MOUNTAINS
Volga River
Aral Sea
45°
Elbrus 18,510 ft.
Balkan Peninsula
Black Sea
CAUCASUS MOUNTAINS
TIAN SHAN
Gobi
Hokkaido
Anatolia
Mt. Ararat 16,854 ft.
Caspian Sea
Taklimakan Desert
KUNLUN MOUNTAINS
Huang He
Sea of Japan
Honshu
PACIFIC OCEAN
Mediterranean Sea
Syrian Desert
ZAGROS MOUNTAINS
K2 28,251 ft.
Plateau of Tibet
Yangtze River
East China Sea
Kyushu
30°
Sinai Peninsula
HIMALAYA
Mt. Everest 29,035 ft.
TROPIC OF CANCER
Libyan Desert
Red Sea
Arabian Peninsula
Great Indian Desert
Ganges River
Taiwan
S A H A R A
Nile River
Arabian Sea
Deccan Plateau
Bay of Bengal
Indochina Peninsula
South China Sea
Philippine Sea
15°
S u d a n
Cape Gwardafuy
Cape Comorin
Philippine Islands
AFRICA
ETHIOPIAN HIGHLANDS
Somali Peninsula
Malay Peninsula
Congo River
Sumatra
Borneo
EQUATOR
0°
Congo Basin
Lake Victoria
Kilimanjaro 19,340 ft.
Celebes
Lake Tanganyika
INDIAN OCEAN
Java
New Guinea
O C E A N I A
Katanga Plateau
Lake Malawi
Arafura Sea
15°
Namib Desert
Victoria Falls
Mozambique Channel
Madagascar
Great Sandy Desert
Coral Sea
Kalahari Desert
Western Plateau
AUSTRALIA
Murray R.
Darling River
GREAT DIVIDING RANGE
30°
Cape of Good Hope
Réunion
TROPIC OF CAPRICORN
Great Victoria Desert
Tasman Sea
New Zealand
North Island

Kerguelen Is.

| 0 | 1000 | 2000 mi |
| 0 | 1000 | 2000 km |

Scale at equator

Tasmania
South Island
45°

60°

ANTARCTIC CIRCLE

ANTARCTICA
TRANSANTARCTIC MOUNTAINS
Ross Ice Shelf
75°

15° 30° 45° 60° 75° 90° 105° 120° 135° 150° 165°

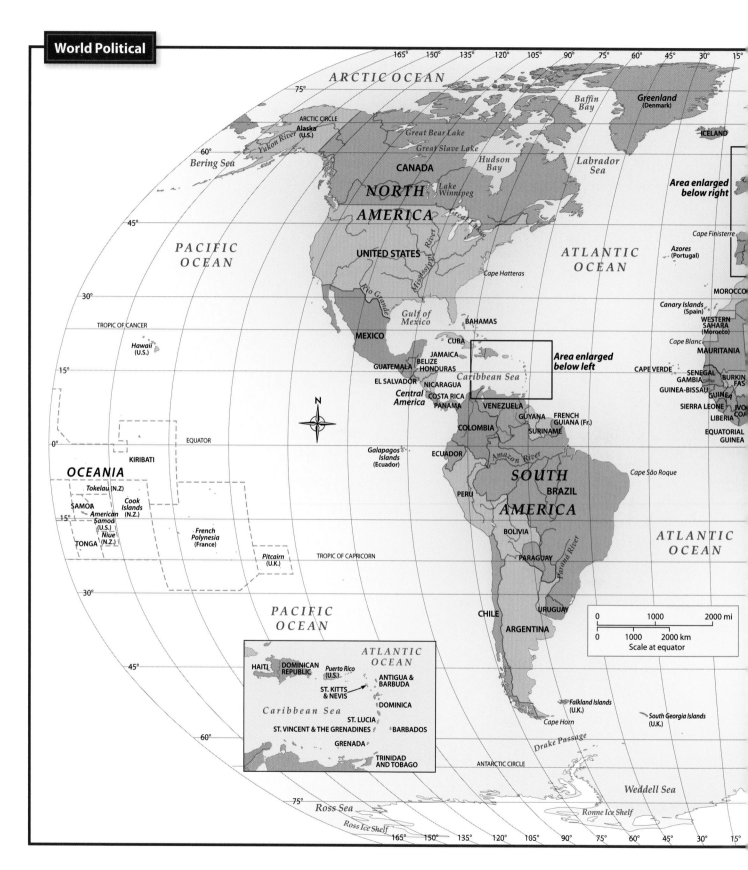

ARCTIC OCEAN

75°

ARCTIC CIRCLE

Alaska
(U.S.)

Yukon River

Great Bear Lake

Great Slave Lake

Baffin Bay

Greenland
(Denmark)

ICELAND

60°

Bering Sea

CANADA

Hudson Bay

Labrador Sea

NORTH
AMERICA

Lake Winnipeg

Area enlarged
below right

45°

PACIFIC
OCEAN

UNITED STATES

Mississippi River

Great Lakes

ATLANTIC
OCEAN

Cape Finisterre

Azores
(Portugal)

30°

Rio Grande

Cape Hatteras

MOROCCO

TROPIC OF CANCER

Gulf of Mexico

BAHAMAS

Canary Islands
(Spain)

WESTERN
SAHARA
(Morocco)

Hawaii
(U.S.)

MEXICO

CUBA

JAMAICA

Area enlarged
below left

Cape Blanc

MAURITANIA

15°

GUATEMALA

BELIZE
HONDURAS

Caribbean Sea

CAPE VERDE

SENEGAL

BURKINA
FASO

EL SALVADOR

NICARAGUA

GAMBIA

Central
America

COSTA RICA
PANAMA

VENEZUELA

GUYANA

FRENCH
GUIANA (Fr.)

GUINEA-BISSAU

GUINEA

IVORY
COAST

COLOMBIA

SURINAME

SIERRA LEONE

LIBERIA

0°

EQUATOR

Galapagos Islands
(Ecuador)

ECUADOR

Amazon River

EQUATORIAL
GUINEA

OCEANIA

KIRIBATI

Cape São Roque

Tokelau (N.Z.)

SAMOA

Cook Islands
(N.Z.)

PERU

SOUTH
AMERICA

BRAZIL

15°

American Samoa
(U.S.)

Niue (N.Z.)

French Polynesia
(France)

BOLIVIA

ATLANTIC
OCEAN

TONGA

Pitcairn
(U.K.)

TROPIC OF CAPRICORN

PARAGUAY

Paraná River

30°

PACIFIC
OCEAN

CHILE

URUGUAY

0   1000   2000 mi

0   1000   2000 km

Scale at equator

ARGENTINA

Falkland Islands
(U.K.)

South Georgia Islands
(U.K.)

45°

HAITI

DOMINICAN
REPUBLIC

Puerto Rico
(U.S.)

ATLANTIC
OCEAN

ANTIGUA &
BARBUDA

ST. KITTS
& NEVIS

DOMINICA

Cape Horn

Caribbean Sea

ST. LUCIA

60°

ST. VINCENT & THE GRENADINES

BARBADOS

GRENADA

Drake Passage

TRINIDAD
AND TOBAGO

ANTARCTIC CIRCLE

Weddell Sea

75°

Ross Sea

Ross Ice Shelf

Ronne Ice Shelf

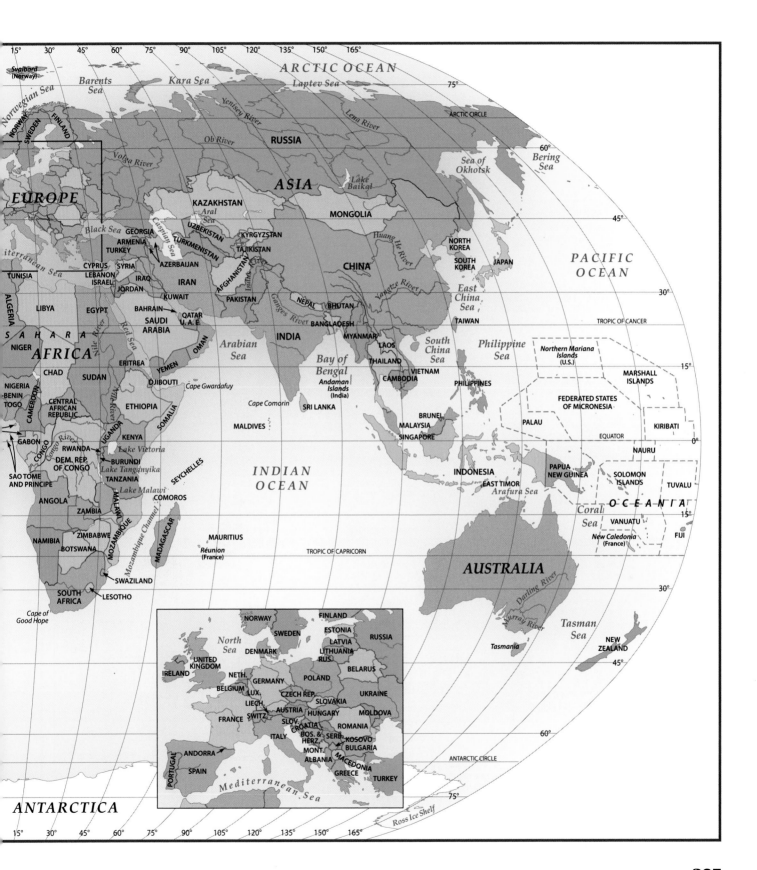

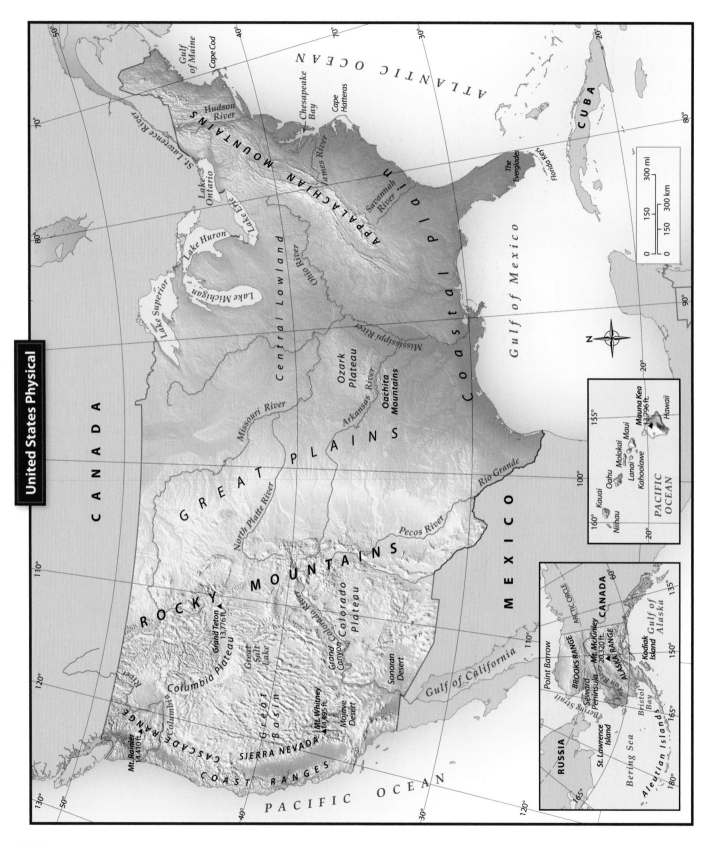

United States Physical

CANADA

ATLANTIC OCEAN

Gulf of Maine
Cape Cod
Hudson River
St. Lawrence River
Lake Ontario
Lake Erie
Chesapeake Bay
Cape Hatteras
James River
APPALACHIAN MOUNTAINS
Savannah River
Lake Huron
Lake Michigan
Lake Superior
Coastal Plain
The Everglades
Florida Keys
CUBA

Central Lowland
Ohio River
Mississippi River
Gulf of Mexico

Missouri River
Ozark Plateau
Arkansas River
Ouachita Mountains

GREAT PLAINS

North Platte River
Rio Grande
Pecos River

MEXICO

Gulf of California

ROCKY MOUNTAINS

Grand Teton 13,776 ft.
Great Salt Lake
Columbia Plateau
Columbia River
Colorado River
Grand Canyon
Colorado Plateau
Sonoran Desert

Great Basin
Mt. Whitney 14,495 ft.
Mojave Desert

CASCADE RANGE
Mt. Rainier 14,410 ft.
SIERRA NEVADA
COAST RANGES

PACIFIC OCEAN

Mauna Kea 13,796 ft.
Hawaii
Oahu
Molokai Maui
Lanai Kahoolawe
Kauai
Niihau
PACIFIC OCEAN

RUSSIA
Point Barrow
ARCTIC CIRCLE
BROOKS RANGE
CANADA
Mt. McKinley 20,320 ft.
ALASKA RANGE
Seward Peninsula
Yukon River
Bering Strait
Bristol Bay
St. Lawrence Island
Bering Sea
Aleutian Islands
Kodiak Island
Gulf of Alaska

300 mi
150
0
0 150 300 km

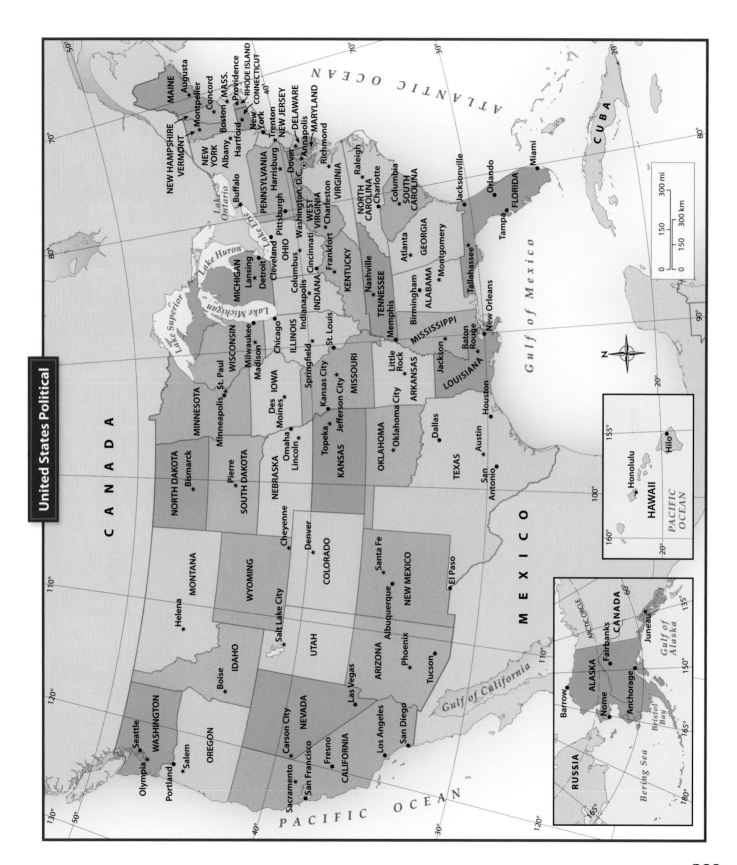

ATLANTIC OCEAN

CANADA

MAINE
Augusta★
NEW HAMPSHIRE
VERMONT
Montpelier★ Concord★ MASS.
Boston★ RHODE ISLAND
Providence★
Hartford★ CONNECTICUT
NEW YORK
Albany★ New York
Buffalo●
PENNSYLVANIA
Harrisburg★ Trenton★ **NEW JERSEY**
Pittsburgh● Dover★ **DELAWARE**
Washington, D.C.✪ Annapolis★ **MARYLAND**
WEST VIRGINIA
Charleston★ Richmond★ **VIRGINIA**
Raleigh★ **NORTH CAROLINA**
Charlotte●
Columbia★ **SOUTH CAROLINA**

Lake Ontario
Lake Erie
Lake Huron
Lake Superior
Lake Michigan

MICHIGAN
Lansing★ Detroit●
OHIO
Cleveland● Columbus★
Cincinnati● Frankfort★ **KENTUCKY**
INDIANA
Indianapolis★
Nashville★ **TENNESSEE**
ILLINOIS
Springfield★ St. Louis●
Memphis●
WISCONSIN
Milwaukee●
Madison★
Chicago●

MINNESOTA
Minneapolis● St. Paul★
Des Moines★ **IOWA**

GEORGIA
Atlanta★
ALABAMA
Birmingham● Montgomery★
MISSISSIPPI
Jackson★
LOUISIANA
Baton Rouge★ New Orleans●
Tallahassee★ **FLORIDA**
Jacksonville●
Orlando●
Tampa●
Miami●

Jacksonville

ARKANSAS
Little Rock★

Gulf of Mexico

CUBA

300 mi
300 km
0 150 300
0 150 300

N

NORTH DAKOTA
Bismarck★
SOUTH DAKOTA
Pierre★

NEBRASKA
Lincoln★
Omaha●

KANSAS
Topeka★ Kansas City●
MISSOURI
Jefferson City★

OKLAHOMA
Oklahoma City★
Dallas●

TEXAS
Austin★
Houston●
San Antonio●

Cheyenne★
WYOMING
Denver★
COLORADO

Santa Fe★
NEW MEXICO
Albuquerque●
El Paso●

MONTANA
Helena★

IDAHO
Boise★

Salt Lake City★
UTAH

NEVADA
Carson City★
Las Vegas●

ARIZONA
Phoenix★
Tucson●

WASHINGTON
Seattle●
Olympia★
Portland●
Salem★
OREGON

CALIFORNIA
Sacramento★
San Francisco●
Fresno●
Los Angeles●
San Diego●

MEXICO

Gulf of California

PACIFIC OCEAN

HAWAII
Honolulu●
Hilo●
PACIFIC OCEAN
155° 160° 20°

ALASKA
Barrow●
Nome●
Fairbanks●
Anchorage●
Juneau★
Bering Sea
RUSSIA
CANADA
Gulf of Alaska
Bristol Bay
ARCTIC CIRCLE
135° 150° 165° 180° 60°

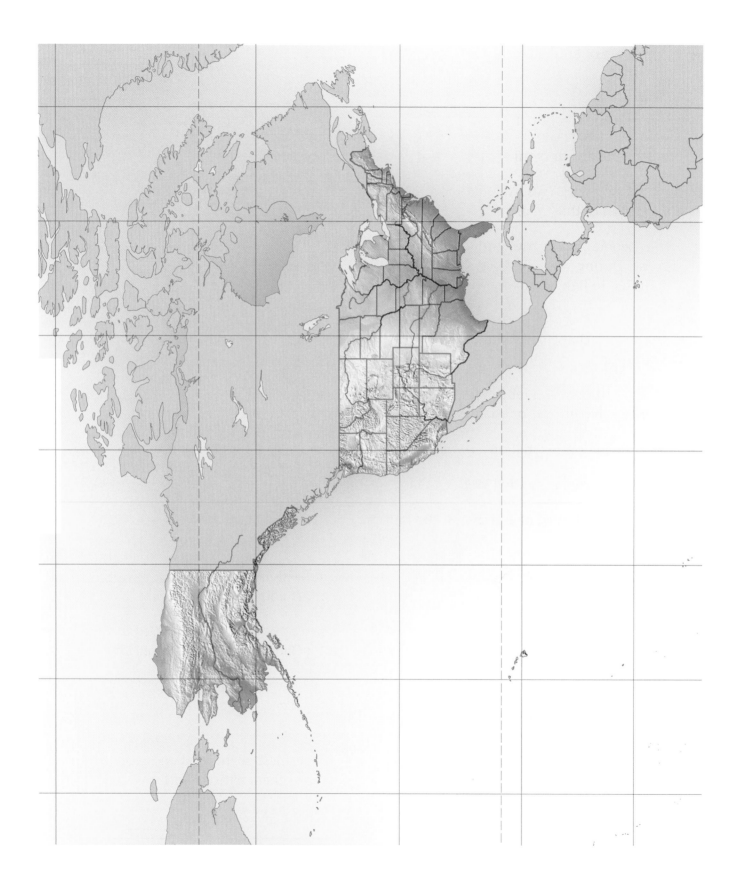

Glossary

abolitionist   person who believed slavery was wrong and tried to stop it

agrarian   related to farming

alien   person who lives in a country but is not a citizen of that country

allies   people or countries united for a specific purpose. During World War II, the countries that united to fight Germany were called the Allies

amendment   change or addition to the U.S. Constitution

anarchist   person who rebels against any authority, government, or established power

annex   to add on to a nation's territory

antebellum   before the Civil War

anti-Semitism   hatred of and prejudice against Jews

appeal   request for a higher court to review a case

armistice   temporary peace agreement

assembly line   row of factory workers and machines along which work is passed

bigotry   intolerance, prejudice

Bill of Rights   first ten amendments to the Constitution

black codes   laws passed by Southern states after the Civil War to limit the rights of former slaves

bootlegger   person who illegally made, transported, or sold liquor during Prohibition

boycott   to refuse to deal with a nation, company, or organization in order to show disapproval or force a change

canal   waterway built for transportation

candidate   someone running for political office

capital   money for funding a business or other venture

carpetbaggers   derogatory name used by Southerners to label people from the North who went to the South during Reconstruction

centennial   hundredth anniversary

citizen   someone with all the rights, protections, and responsibilities guaranteed under a nation's government

civil rights   rights guaranteed to all citizens by the Constitution and acts of Congress

collective   bargaining negotiation between organized workers and an employer

communism   government where the state owns most of the land and property and shares them with the citizens

congress   group of representatives who come together for discussion, voting, and action

constituents   people who are represented by an elected official

Constitution   the document that outlines the plan of government in the United States

consumers   people who buy goods and services for personal needs

corporation   business owned by stockholders who hold shares in it

currency   paper bills and coins in circulation within an economy

democracy   government of the people

deport   force to leave a country

depression   time of severe economic decline, including high unemployment and falling prices

dictator   ruler with complete authority and no accountability; an autocrat

discrimination   showing favor toward or prejudice against people because they belong to a particular group

economy   management and flow of resources and money in a community

emigrant   person who leaves one country to settle in another

exile   to banish someone from his or her home or country

exposition   exhibition, often a large, public one

flappers   young women of the 1920s who dressed in a bold new style

forty-niners   people who moved to California during the gold rush of 1849

Fourteen Points   President Woodrow Wilson's plan for world peace after World War I

franchise   the right to vote

free enterprise   economic system allowing private industry to operate with little government control

free trade   business between nations that is carried out without major restrictions

Freedmen's Bureau   organization set up by Congress to help ex-slaves

Gilded Age   period between 1870 and 1900, characterized by rapid economic growth, political corruption, and lavish displays of wealth

greenback   paper money established during the Civil War, named for its color

Homestead Act   law passed in 1862 that offered settlers 160 acres of land in return for living and farming there for at least five years

Hoovervilles   settlements of makeshift houses built by homeless people during the Great Depression

immigrants   people who move to a new country or region

impeach   to charge a public official with crimes or misconduct

imperialism expanding a nation by taking other lands

industrialization process of going from an agricultural system to one based on factories and machines

inflation steady rise in the price of goods and services increase

isolationism belief that one nation should not interfere in the affairs of another nation

Jim Crow system of laws beginning in the late 1800s that segregated blacks and forced them to use separate and inferior facilities

jury group chosen to make a judgment, especially in a court of law

Ku Klux Klan organization formed in the South in 1866 that used lynching and violence to intimidate and control blacks and others

labor unions associations of workers formed to promote and protect the rights of members

League of Nations organization proposed by President Woodrow Wilson after World War I to unite nations in working for peace and security

lynching kidnapping and execution of a person by a mob

Manifest Destiny belief held by many Americans in the 19th and 20th centuries that it was God's will that the United States expand its borders

market economy system in which people earn wages and provide for their needs by buying goods and services

merchant person who buys and sells goods

migration movement of a group from one country or region to another

missionary member of a religious group who tries to persuade others to adopt his or her religion

monarchy government headed by a single ruler, especially a king or queen

monopoly complete control of an industry, product, or service by a single company

muckraker journalist who wrote articles exposing injustice and corruption

nativism practice of favoring native-born citizens over immigrants

naturalization process that grants citizenship to immigrants

Northwest Ordinance law passed in 1787 that set out rules for how new territories should govern themselves and how they could eventually become states

orator effective public speaker

ordinance law or regulation

pension retirement pay or old-age insurance

philanthropist person who works to help others, often by giving money to charitable causes

pogrom   organized massacre of helpless people, particularly of Jews in Eastern Europe

political machine   unofficial city organization designed to keep a particular party or group in power

prejudice   dislike of another ethnic group, gender, race, or religion based on stereotypes and ignorance

progressive   person who thinks that life can be improved by government reforms

progressivism   political and social reform movement of the late 1800s and early 1900s that included socialism, the labor movement, municipal reform, prohibition, and other movements

Prohibition   Constitutional amendment in force between 1920 and 1933 that outlawed the manufacture, transportation, sale, and possession of alcoholic beverages

propaganda   spreading ideas or rumors to influence public opinion

pueblos   Indian villages built of sun-dried clay mud

range   series of adjacent mountains; also, open land for grazing cattle

ratify   to formally approve a suggested action

Reconstruction   period from 1865 to 1877 when the federal government controlled the former Confederate states

reds   nickname for communists or people thought to be communists

reformer   someone who wants to make the world better by improving social conditions

reservation   public land set aside for special use, especially land set aside for Indian peoples after European Americans took over Indian land

scab   slang for a person hired to replace a striking worker

Scopes trial   Tennessee trial in 1925 that challenged a law against teaching evolution in schools

segregation   the practice of separating one racial, ethnic, or religious group from another, especially in public places

self-determination   the right of citizens to choose the form of government under which they will live

settlement house   institution offering social and educational services to immigrants and poor people

share   a piece of ownership of a corporation

socialism   government ownership of factories and services with wages determined by workers' needs

speakeasy   illegal saloon that flourished during Prohibition

stock exchange   trading center where shares of stock are bought and sold

stock market   stock exchange and associated businesses for the buying and selling stocks

strike   work stoppage to protest low wages or bad working conditions

strikebreaker   in a labor disagreement, someone who interferes with workers' protest against management

subsidy   grant of money, land, or something else of value

suffrage   right to vote

sweatshop   factory where employees work long hours in poor conditions for low wages

tariff   tax on imports or exports

tax   money that citizens and businesses are required to contribute to pay for the cost of government and the services it provides

temperance   movement campaign against consumption of alcoholic beverages

tenement   run-down, overcrowded, low-rent apartment

totalitarian   form of dictatorship that has total control over all aspects of life and that suppresses all political or cultural opposition

Trail of Tears   forced march of 15,000 Cherokees from the Southeast to reservations in the West from 1837 to 1838

transcontinental railroad   railroad completed in 1869 that spanned North America

treaty   formal agreement between nations

trust   form of monopoly where many different companies in one industry are all owned and run by the same people

tyranny   absolute power, especially when it is unjustly or cruelly used

U-boats   German submarines

urban   of a city

veteran   person who has served in the military, especially one who has fought in a war

Wall Street   main financial center of the United States, in New York City

yellow journalism   sensational but generally untrue stories published in newspapers to attract readers

Illustrations Credits

Key: t=top; b=bottom; c=center; l=left; r=right

Front cover: © Corbis

Back cover: (l) W. Langdon Kihn/ National Geographic Stock; (cl and cr) © Corbis; (r) Dirk Anschutz/Getty Images

iii © Corbis

v © 2011 Sara Tyson c/o theispot.com

Part 1: 1 (l) © Yuliya Kryzhevska/ iStockphoto; (r) © Mateusz Koc/ iStockphoto. **2** Peter Newark American Pictures/The Bridgeman Art Library. **3** (l) © Bettmann/Corbis; (r) Fotosearch/ Getty Images. **4** © North Wind/North Wind Picture Archives. **6** © Wolfgang Kaehler/SuperStock. **7** (t) © North Wind Picture Archives/Alamy; (b) The Granger Collection, New York. **8** © North Wind Picture Archives/Alamy. **9** (t) Peter Newark American Pictures/The Bridgeman Art Library; (b) The Granger Collection, New York. **10** © Mary Evans Picture Library/ Alamy. **11** The Art Archive/Bill Manns. **12** (t) © Bettmann/Corbis; (b) The Art Archive/Bill Manns. **14** The Granger Collection, New York. **15** (t) MPI/Getty Images; (b) Peter Newark American Pictures/The Bridgeman Art Library. **16** Autry National Center; 2002.3.1. **17** A.J. Russell/Getty Images. **19** The Granger Collection, New York. **20** (l) Library of Congress, Prints and Photographs Division, rbpe 13401300; (r) Nebraska State Historical Society, 1nbhips.0755. **21–22** The Granger Collection, New York. **23** © World History/Topham/The Image Works. **24** © SuperStock; (frame) © Jupiterimages. **25** © Bettmann/Corbis. **26** (l) © Gary Holscher/AGE Fotostock; (c) © Bettmann/Corbis; (r) © Everett Collection/ Alamy. **27–29** Dover Publications. **30** © World History Archive/Alamy. **31** The Granger Collection, New York. **32** © Everett Collection/SuperStock. **33** (l) John N. Choate/MPI/Getty Images; (r) John N. Choate/MPI/Getty Images. **34–35** The Granger Collection, New York. **36** Stock Montage/Getty Images. **37** MPI/Getty Images. **38** Peter Newark

American Pictures/The Bridgeman Art Library. **39** The Granger Collection, New York. **40** © Bettmann/Corbis. **41** U.S. Army Signal Corps/Time & Life Pictures/ Getty Images; (frame) © Jupiterimages. **42** © Keystone Archives/HIP/The Image Works. **44** The Granger Collection, New York. **45** The Granger Collection, New York. **46** (l) © PoodlesRock/Corbis; (r) The Granger Collection, New York. **47** The Granger Collection, New York. **48** Everett Collection. **49** The Granger Collection, New York. **50** © North Wind/ North Wind Picture Archives. **51** The Granger Collection, New York; (frame) ElementalImaging/iStockphoto. **52** The Granger Collection, New York. **53** Picture History. **54** The Granger Collection, New York. **55** The Granger Collection, New York. **56** © Museum of the City of New York/Corbis. **57** (l) The Granger Collection, New York; (r) The Granger Collection, New York. **58** The Granger Collection, New York. **59** The Granger Collection, New York. **60** The Granger Collection, New York. **61** © North Wind/ North Wind Picture Archives. **62** (t) Picture History; (b) © akg-images/The Image Works. **63** The Granger Collection, New York. **64** Everett Collection. **66** The Granger Collection, New York. **68** © Emily Riddell/photolibrary.com. **69** The Granger Collection, New York. **70** Everett Collection. **71** (t) Everett Collection; (b) © Artville. **72** (t) © Dennis MacDonald/AGE Fotostock; (b) The Granger Collection, New York. **73** (t) The Stapleton Collection/ Art Resource, NY; (b) Art Resource, NY. **74** The Granger Collection, New York. **76** © Everett Collection/Alamy. **77** (t) The Granger Collection, New York; (frame) © Jupiterimages; (c) AP Photo; (frame) © Jupiterimages; (b) © Bettmann/Corbis. **78–79** Free Library of Philadelphia. **80** Art Resource, NY. **81** The Granger Collection, New York. **82** (t) The Granger Collection, New York; (b) The Art Archive/ Museum of the City of New York/Byron Company Collection. **83** © PoodlesRock/ Corbis. **84** Library of Congress, Prints and Photographs Division, LC-USZ62-33505.

85 (t) bpk, Berlin/Art Resource, NY; (c) © Schenectady Museum; Hall of Electrical History Foundation/Corbis; (b) © Visuals Unlimited/Corbis. **86** dpa/Landov. **87–88** © Bettmann/Corbis. **89** (t) © Michael Maslan Historic Photographs/Corbis; (b) The Granger Collection, New York. **90** © VisualField/iStockphoto. **91** Peter Newark American Pictures/The Bridgeman Art Library. **92** © Terry Smith Images/ Alamy. **94** © Corbis. **96** Schomberg Center/Art Resource, NY; (frame) © bubaone/iStockphoto. **98** (t) © Corbis; (b) Schomberg Center/Art Resource, NY. **99** Eon Images; (frame) ElementalImaging/ iStockphoto. **100** Library of Congress, Prints and Photographs Division, LC-USZ62-65197. **101** (t) Library of Congress, Prints and Photographs Division, LC-USZ62-2248; (b) Photodisc; (c) Hulton Archive/Getty Images. **102** (l) Buyenlarge/Getty Images; (r) Library of Congress, Prints and Photographs Division, LC-USZ62-133985. **103** © E.A. Kennedy, III/The Image Works. **104** Schomburg Center/Art Resource, NY. **105** The Granger Collection, New York. **106** (t) Kean Collection/Getty Images; (b) Library of Congress, Prints and Photographs Division, LC-DIG-ppmsca-05523.

Part 2: 107 (l) © Yuliya Kryzhevska/ iStockphoto; (r) © Mateusz Koc/ iStockphoto. **108** (t) The Granger Collection, New York; (b) The Granger Collection, New York. **109** Buyenlarge/ Getty Images. **110** (t) Dover Publications; (b) The Granger Collection, New York. **111** The Granger Collection, New York; (frame) © Jupiterimages. **112** Library of Congress, Prints and Photographs Division, LC-DIG-ppmsca-05523. **113** (t) © Corbis; (b) © Hulton-Deutsch Collection/Corbis. **115** The Granger Collection, New York. **116** (t) The Granger Collection, New York; (frame) ElementalImaging/iStockphoto; (b) © Bettmann/Corbis. **117** Hulton Archive/ Getty Images. **118** MPI/Getty Images. **119** Denver Public Library, Western History Collection/The Bridgeman Art Library. **120** (t) The Granger Collection, New

York; (frame) louoates/BigStock; (b) © Corbis. **121** (t) The Granger Collection, New York; (b) The Granger Collection, New York. **123** The Art Archive. **125** © Everett Collection/SuperStock. **126** © Museum of the City of New York/ Corbis. **127** The Granger Collection, New York. **128** © Vosts Images/Alamy. **129** (t) © Corbis; (b) © Bettmann/Corbis. **130** © Museum of the City of New York/ Corbis. **131** Library of Congress, Prints and Photographs Division, LC-B8184- 10690. **132** (t) Library of Congress, Prints and Photographs Division, LC-USZ62-13018; (b) Cornelia Adèle Strong Fassett/U.S. Senate Collection. **133** (t) Library of Congress Prints and Photographs Division, LC-USZ62-48559; (b) The Granger Collection, New York. **134** © Science Faction/SuperStock. **135** The Granger Collection, New York. **136** The Granger Collection, New York. **137** The Granger Collection, New York; (frame) © Jupiterimages. **138** The Granger Collection, New York. **140** The Granger Collection, New York. **141** The Granger Collection, New York. **142** MPI/Getty Images. **143** © Everett Collection/Alamy. **145** © Culver Pictures, Inc./SuperStock. **146** © Corbis. **147** (t) © Bettmann/Corbis; (b) © Bettmann/Corbis. **148** © Photos 12/Alamy. **149** The Granger Collection, New York. **150** Coin's Financial School, 1894. **151** Library of Congress, Prints and Photographs Division, LC-USZC2-6259; (frame) © bubaone/iStockphoto. **152** The Granger Collection, New York. **153** The Granger Collection, New York. **154** Kean Collection/Getty Images. **155** © Library of Congress - digital ve/Science Faction/Corbis. **156** © Bettmann/Corbis. **158** (l) Snark/Art Resource, NY; (r) The Granger Collection, New York. **159–160** The Granger Collection, New York. **161** © Brown Brothers. **162** (l) Library of Congress Prints and Photographs Division, LC-USZ62-23757; (r) © Lewis W. Hine/ George Eastman House/Getty Images. **163** FPG/Hulton Archive/Getty Images. **164** Kean Collection/Getty Images. **165** Stock Montage/Getty Images. **167** (l) The New York Public Library/Art Resource, NY; (r) Erich Lessing/Art Resource, NY. **168** Library of Congress, Prints and Photographs Division, LC-USZ62-19867.

169 (t) The Granger Collection, New York; (b) CSU Archives/Everett Collection. **170** © Underwood & Underwood/ Corbis. **171** The Granger Collection, New York. **172** (l) Everett Collection; (r) The Granger Collection, New York. **173** (t) © Bettmann/Corbis; (b) Library of Congress, Prints and Photographs Division, LC-DIG-nclc-02119. **174** Library of Congress, Prints and Photographs Division, LC-DIG-nclc-04783. **175** Library of Congress, Prints and Photographs Division, LC-DIG-ppmsca-06591. **176** The Granger Collection, New York. **177** © Everett Collection/Alamy. **178–180** The Granger Collection, New York. **181** (t) © Underwood & Underwood/Corbis; (b) The Granger Collection, New York. **182** © Bettmann/Corbis. **183** (t) © Brown Brothers; (frame) © Jupiterimages; (b) © Culver Pictures, Inc. **184** (t) akg-images; (b) Harmon T. Swearingen/FPG/Hulton Archive/Getty Images. **185** © Momatiuk - Eastcott/Corbis. **186** The Granger Collection, New York. **187** © Bettmann/ Corbis. **188** © Library of Congress - digital ve/Science Faction/Corbis. **189** The Granger Collection, New York. **190** © Corbis. **191** Everett Collection. **192** Erich Lessing/Art Resource, NY . **193** (t) The Art Archive/Culver Pictures; (b) Lewis W. Hine/George Eastman House/Getty Images. **194** The Granger Collection, New York; (frame) © Jupiterimages. **195** Chicago Daily News/Chicago History Museum, DN_0076596. **196** The Granger Collection, New York. **197** (t) © Bettmann/Corbis; (b) © Francis G. Mayer/ Corbis. **198** The Granger Collection, New York.

Part 3: 199 (l) © Mateusz Koc/ iStockphoto; (r) © Mateusz Koc/ iStockphoto. **200** 520.11-005, Theodore Roosevelt Collection, Houghton Library, Harvard University; (frame) louoates/ BigStock. **201** R500.P69a-011, Theodore Roosevelt Collection, Houghton Library, Harvard University; (frame) ElementalImaging/iStockphoto. **202** Carr Clifton/Minden Pictures/National Geographic Stock. **203** Underwood And Underwood/Time & Life Pictures/Getty Images. **204** (l) Library of Congress, Prints and Photographs Division,

LC-USZC4-4698; (r) © Francis G. Mayer/ Corbis. **205** Snark/Art Resource, NY; (frame) © Jupiterimages. **206** (l) © David J. & Janice L. Frent Collection/Corbis; (r) © Bettmann/Corbis. **207** © Bettmann/ Corbis. **208** Snark/Art Resource, NY. **210** The Granger Collection, New York. **211** Hulton Archive/Getty Images. **212** © Charles O'Rear/Corbis. **213** The Granger Collection, New York. **214** The Bridgeman Art Library. **215** SSPL/National Media Museum/Art Resource, NY. **216** Legacy Archive/Photolibrary. **217** The Granger Collection, New York; (frame) © bubaone/ iStockphoto. **218** (l) © Brown Brothers; (frame) © bubaone/iStockphoto; (r) Victoria & Albert Museum, London/Art Resource, NY. **219** The Granger Collection, New York. **220** Hulton Archive/Getty Images. **221** The Art Archive/Domenica del Corriere/Gianni Dagli Orti. **222** © Bettmann/Corbis. **223** Hulton Archive/ Getty Images. **224** (t) Hulton Archive/ Getty Images; (b) © Science and Society/ SuperStock. **225** © SuperStock. **226** © tci/ AGE Fotostock. **227** Mary Evans Picture Library. **228** © SuperStock. **229** (t) The White House Historical Association (White House Collection); (frame) ElementalImaging/iStockphoto; (b) Library of Congress, Prints and Photographs Division, LC-DIG-ggbain-11216. **230** New Hampshire Political Library. **231** David Chasey/Photodisc/Getty Images. **232** Library of Congress, Prints and Photographs Division, LC-DIG-pga-02580 DLC. **234** Everett Collection; (frame) © Jupiterimages. **235** (t) National Portrait Gallery, Smithsonian Institution/Art Resource, NY; (b) National Geographic Stock. **236** The Art Archive/Domenica del Corriere/Gianni Dagli Orti. **237** © Scherl/SV-Bilderdienst/The Image Works. **238** (l) © Mary Evans/ILN/The Image Works; (r) © Scherl/SV-Bilderdienst/The Image Works. **239** akg-images. **240** Erich Lessing/Art Resource, NY. **241** (t) Dover Publications; (b) © Bettmann/Corbis. **243** "Over There," by George M. Cohan, 1917. (Music #1170). Image courtesy of the Rare Book, Manuscript, and Special Collections Library, Duke University, Durham, North Carolina. **244** © Topham/The Image Works. **245** Library of Congress, Prints and Photographs Division,

LC-USZ62-19271. **246** Hulton Archive/ Getty Images. **248** Time & Life Pictures/ Getty Images. **249** Hulton Archive/Getty Images. **250–251** © Corbis. **252** (NCP 001603) Courtesy of the National Museum of Health and Medicine, Washington, D.C. **253** The Granger Collection, New York. **254** © Bettmann/Corbis. **255** ullstein bild/ The Granger Collection, New York. **256** The Granger Collection, New York. **257** (t) © Everett Collection/SuperStock; (b) The Art Archive/Granger Collection. **258** © A.H.C./Age Fotostock. **259** © Brown Brothers. **260** ullstein bild/The Granger Collection, New York. **261** (t) Library of Congress, Prints and Photographs Division, LC-USZ62-111092; (b) Rue des Archives/The Granger Collection, New York. **263** Library of Congress, Prints and Photographs Division, LC-USZ62-130973. **264** The Granger Collection, New York. **265** CSU Archives/Everett Collection; (frame) © Jupiterimages. **266** © Bettmann/Corbis. **267–268** The Granger Collection, New York. **269** © Bettmann/Corbis. **270** (l) Mary Evans/ WALT DISNEY PICTURES/Ronald Grant/ Everett Collection (10399592); (r) ©

Culver Pictures, Inc./SuperStock. **271** (t) © Everett Collection/Alamy; (b) The Granger Collection, New York. **272** (l) Peter Newark American Pictures/The Bridgeman Art Library; (r) © Bettmann/ Corbis. **273** The Art Archive/Culver Pictures. **274** © Francis G. Mayer/Corbis. **275** The Granger Collection, New York. **276** (t) Dover Publications; (b) Georgia O'Keeffe American, 1887–1986, Blue and Green Music, 1919/21, Oil on canvas, 58.4 cm x 48.3 cm (23 in. x 18 in.), Alfred Stieglitz Collection, gift of Georgia O'Keeffe, 1969.835, The Art Institute of Chicago. **277** Dover Publications. **278** The Granger Collection, New York. **279** AP Photo. **280** © Underwood & Underwood/Corbis. **281** © Bettmann/ Corbis. **282** (l) National Baseball Hall of Fame Library, Cooperstown, New York; (r) Michael Hogue KRT/Newscom. **283** (t) The Granger Collection, New York; (b) Transcendental Graphics/Getty Images). **284** Mary Evans Picture Library. **285** Margaret Bourke-White/Time & Life Pictures/Getty Images. **286** (t) © Matthew Russell/Visuals Unlimited/Corbis; (b) akg-images. **287** (t) © Bettmann/Corbis;

(b) The Granger Collection, New York. **288** © Bettmann/Corbis. **289** NASA. **290** © Hulton-Deutsch Collection/Corbis. **291** (l) © Bettmann/Corbis; (r) Eric Long, National Air and Space Museum, Smithsonian Institution. **292** (t) © Bettmann/Corbis; (b) © Bettmann/Corbis. **293** National Air and Space Museum, Smithsonian Institution. **294** © Hulton-Deutsch Collection/Corbis. **295** © Corbis. **296** The Art Archive/Granger Collection. **297** © H. Armstrong Roberts/Robertstock. **298** Peter Newark American Pictures/The Bridgeman Art Library International. **299** © Hulton-Deutsch Collection/Corbis. **300** PhotoQuest/Getty Images. **301** Arthur Rothstein/Library of Congress/Time Life Pictures/Getty Images. **303** (t) Collection of Arizona State University Art Museum; (c) AP Photo; (b) Library of Congress, Prints and Photographs Division, LC-USF34-009694-E. **304** © Bettmann/ Corbis. **305** (t) © Bettmann/Corbis; (b) The Granger Collection, New York. **306** (t) The Granger Collection, New York; (c) © Culver Pictures, Inc./SuperStock; (b) ullstein bild/The Granger Collection, New York.

Index

Page references in bold refer to maps.

White House, 131, 133, 197, 200, 209, 218–219, 240, 244, 256–257, 264, 304–305
white supremacy, 60, 157
Wichita, Kansas, **12**, 13
Williams, Smokey Joe, 284
Wilson, Woodrow, 189, 230, 233, 234–235, 263 *see also* Fourteen Points
  integrity of, 245
  isolationism of, 239, 251
  selection of Hoover, 295
  women's rights and, 236, 257–258
  World War I, 237–238, 240–241, 244–245, 247–251
Wisconsin, 2, **17**, 22, **30**, 67, 160, 172, 186, 276, 306
Wobblies *see* Industrial Workers of the World
women, 53, 78–79, 96, 110, 124, 126, 169–171, 176–177, 196–197, 214, 217, 227–228, 236, 253–254, 264, 272, 294–295, 303 *see also* women's rights
  astronomers, 287
  athletes, 263, 281, 284
  flappers, 266–267
  homesteaders, 20
  journalists, 93–98, 179, 181, 263
  lawyers, 74
  in the military, 244
  penitentiary for, 263
  suffrage, 68–70, 72, 74–77, 256–259
  in West, 13
  Women's Christian Temperance Union, 73
Women's Christian Temperance Union, 73
women's rights, 72, 75, 110, 170–171, 176, 217, 236, 257–259, 263–264
Wood, Grant, 270, 277
Workingmen's Party, 60, 62
World War I, 176, 179, 213, 236–242, **242**, 243–248, 250, 252–254, 260–262, 285, 295, 301, 304
Wounded Knee massacre, 32–33, 38
Wright, Frank Lloyd, 127–128
Wright, Orville, 225–228
Wright, Wilbur, 225–228
writers and writing, 34, 43, 48–49, 57, 69, 77, 84, 93, 96, 98, 103, 111–112, 114, 168, 175, 179, 181–183, 187, 191, 196, 204–205, 215, 218–219, 226, 233–234, 254, 270–271, 273, 276, 294, 301 *see also* journalists and journalism
Wyoming, 7, **17**, 19, 30, 68–70, 72, 154, 189, 264

Y

Ybor, Don Vincente Martinez, 171
Ybor City, Florida, 171, 205
yellow fever, 95, 172, 220 *see also* disease
yellow journalism, 205 *see also* journalists and journalism
Yellowstone National Park, 189
Yick, Lee, 64–67
Yick Wo v. Hopkins, Sheriff, etc., 65–66
Yoncalla, Oregon, 259
Yosemite National Park, 188–189, 204
Yosemite Valley, 187, 189

Z

Zaharias, George, 281
Zimmermann, Arthur von, 240
Zimmermann Telegram, 240